Mennonites and Media: Mentioned in It, Maligned by It, and Makers of It

Mennonites and Media: Mentioned in It, Maligned by It, and Makers of It

How Mennonites Have Been Portrayed in Media and How They Have Shaped Media for Identity and Outreach

Steven P. Carpenter

Foreword by
Donald B. Kraybill

WIPF & STOCK · Eugene, Oregon

MENNONITES AND MEDIA: MENTIONED IN IT, MALIGNED BY IT, AND MAKERS OF IT
How Mennonites Have Been Portrayed in Media and How They Have Shaped Media for Identity and Outreach

Copyright © 2015 Steven P. Carpenter All rights reserved. Except for brief quotations in critical publications or reviews, no part of this book may be reproduced in any manner without prior written permission from the publisher. Write: Permissions, Wipf and Stock Publishers, 199 W. 8th Ave., Suite 3, Eugene, OR 97401.

Wipf & Stock
An Imprint of Wipf and Stock Publishers
199 W. 8th Ave., Suite 3
Eugene, OR 97401

www.wipfandstock.com

ISBN 13: 978-1-62564-525-8

Manufactured in the U.S.A.   12/31/2014

Dedicated to the women in my life: my nonagenarian mother
Elsie who still thinks of me, the youngest of her four sons, as her baby;
my wife Chris, who is the love of my life and my editor-in-chief; and
my daughter Janelle, who is carrying our first grandchild.

Dedicated also to the memory of my daughter,
Michelle Renee Carpenter (January 1, 1984—September 25, 1995),
whom I still miss every day.

" . . . from Issachar, men who understood the times . . ."
1 CHR 12:32

"'For in him we live and move and have our being.' As some of your own poets have said, 'We are his offspring.'"
ACTS 17:28

Contents

Illustrations | viii
Foreword | xi
Acknowledgments | xiii
Introduction | xv

PART I – How Mennonites Have Been Portrayed in Media

1. Aural Media | 3
2. Print Media | 11
3. Visual Media | 40
4. The Ngram and a Summary of Part I | 69

PART II – How Mennonites Have Used Media to Shape Identity and for Outreach

Introduction | 77

5. Toward a Mennonite Theology of Media | 81
6. Tracts, *Martyrs Mirror*, Signs, and Bookracks | 89
7. Music and Radio | 100
8. Art, Performance, and Television | 107
9. Film | 116
10. Books | 126
11. The Internet | 145
12. Beyond Anecdotal Evidence to Hard Data | 158
13. Conclusions | 158

Bibliography | 158
Index | 173

Illustrations

1. *Barney & Clyde* comic strip | 32
2. *The Mennonite Minister*, Painting by Rembrandt | 46
3. Ngram query "Catholic" and "Jew" | 70
4. Table 1 – Summary of Positive Mennonite Depictions in Media | 72
5. Table 2 – Summary of Negative Mennonite Depictions in Media | 73
6. Table 3 – Summary of Neutral Mennonite Depictions in Media | 73
7. Image of Dirk Willems from *Martyrs Mirror* | 92
8. Photo of the Landis family by Dale Gehman | 95
9. Photo of a scripture sign by the author | 97
10. Photo of Warren Rohrer's block print of Menno Simons by the author | 108
11. Photo of Esther Augsburger's *Love Essence* sculpture by the artist | 110
12. Photo of Esther Augsburger's *Guns to Plowshares* sculpture by the artist | 111
13. Chart of Website traffic October 2010 from *The Mennonite* by Anna Groff | 146

Illustrations

14. Table of Third Way's on-line subscriptions | 152
15. Ngram query "Anabaptist" | 152
16. Ngram query "Mennonite" | 153
17. Ngram query "Catholic" and "Jew" | 154
18. Ngram query "Jew, Methodist, Mormon, Mennonite" | 154
19. Ngram query "Mormon, Mennonite" | 155
20. Ngram query "Amish, Mennonite" | 155
21. Ngram query "Plymouth Brethren, Mennonite" | 156

Foreword

WHAT MIGHT JAMES MICHENER'S novel *Centennial* and the Mexican film *Silent Light* share? In this book they align as representations of Mennonites' life in public media. The first section of *Mennonites and Media* traces a wide assortment of Anabaptist and Mennonite representations in the media since 1525. The second part of the project explores a multitude of ways in which Mennonites have used media—from gospel tracts to the contemporary music of groups like Steel Wheels—to tell their story in popular culture.

The arch of Steven Carpenter's remarkable study covers a host of media forms from audio, print, and visual to performance, television, and the Internet. *Mennonites and Media* does not claim to be exhaustive but it does provide a groundbreaking contribution by gathering dozens of "appearances" of Mennonite representations together in a single volume.

In popular parlance the word media often points to advertising, journalism, and entertainment. In its broader sense however, media depicts any vehicle that conveys meaning via comic books to sculpture, via billboards to old-fashioned print books like the one you are reading. Carpenter has assembled an interesting sample of Mennonite representations in various realms of media over several centuries.

One of the ironies of the late twentieth and early twenty-first centuries is that the separatist, publicity averse Amish have been catapulted into the media spotlight despite their protests of their new stardom. They first drew heavy journalistic scrutiny for their boycott of public high school in the 1960s and 1970s; an act that led to imprisonment and eventually a US Supreme Court decision in 1972 that granted them a waiver from attending high school. More recently, an avalanche of Amish-themed television programs and bonnet novels have spewed beards, bonnets, and buggies into

Foreword

popular culture. Meanwhile Mennonites, who were assimilating into public life more rapidly than the Amish, rarely found themselves covered by print and television media.

In this first-of-a-kind study, Carpenter delves into the historic ore and extracts a remarkable number of Mennonite appearances in various types of media. Apart from the study's value of identifying individual snippets of Mennonites lurking in the media, it is helpful to have all of these appearances clustered together in one collection. Carpenter covers not only Mennonites as subjects but also demonstrates how Mennonites have shaped their public persona in ways that tell their story and also offers a witness to the larger society. The narrative does not chart Mennonite contributions in scholarly publications but rather focuses on how the Mennonite brand is constructed and its associated meanings in public life.

One of the unique aspects of this study is the use of data generated by Ngram, a web-based tool, with the capacity to track the frequency of occurrences of words such as "Anabaptist" and "Mennonite" in print from a database of 500 billion words in some 5.2 million books. This technique traces the peaks and dips of these words over several centuries. It also provides a comparative perspective by charting the frequency of Mennonite appearances alongside those of other religious communities such as Catholic, Mormon, Methodist, and Jewish.

With such a variety of fascinating examples of Mennonite appearances in disparate forms of media *Mennonites and Media* is an easy and interesting read. The compilation of these appearances in a single volume contributes to our knowledge of the significant role that media played and continues to play in shaping Mennonite identity in the public square.

Donald B. Kraybill

Acknowledgments

MANY PEOPLE ASSISTED IN my research, with advice, and by reviewing drafts of this book. However, I would like to give special recognition to three people. My thanks go to Professor Nate Yoder who served as my academic and thesis advisor while I pursued a Master of Arts in Religion from Eastern Mennonite Seminary. I also greatly appreciated the several classes on faith and media which I took with Professor Jerry Holsopple, who also served as a reader and critic in the defense of my thesis.

Finally, my deepest thanks go to my wife Chris who tirelessly reviews and edits all of my writings, including this book. I draw strength from her patience, encouragement, and love. Thank you Nate, Jerry, and Chris.

Introduction

MEDIA IS POWERFUL! It reflects the culture from which it emerges. It conveys information and shapes perceptions. Media is also ubiquitous. North Americans' lives are saturated by the Internet, television, film, books, billboards, and radio. New forms of media, such as blogging, Twitter, and Facebook, further inundate modern life. Even two thousand years ago, when Jesus and his disciples walked this earth, media was present and shaped perceptions. The Apostle Paul knew this and engaged Greek culture to promote the gospel. When he addressed the people of Athens he referenced the statute to "an unknown god" crafted by one of their artists. He also quoted a Greek poet (Acts 17:16–34).

Some Christians shy away from media and the culture it reflects. In the 1920s and 1930s, Fundamentalist Christians rejected popular culture, seeking rather to be separate and maintain the purity of the church. By the mid-twentieth century, partly in reaction to the Fundamentalist movement, men like Billy Graham and others coined a new term, "evangelical" derived from the Greek evangelon meaning "the good news" or "the gospel." Unlike Fundamentalists, mainstream evangelicals sought to engage the culture in order to transform it. The Mennonite Church USA, which is the largest Mennonite denomination in North America, is stylistically evangelical.[1] MC USA has named seven denominational priorities for itself including "Holistic Christian Witness" and "Leadership Development" which calls for the development of "missional leaders."[2] These priorities drive MC USA to become a missional church concerned with reaching neighbors across

1. Falsani, "Evangleical, Fundamentalist, Born Again Aren't the Same," MWR, November, 6.
2. Mennonite Church USA Executive Board, "Priorities."

Introduction

the street, as well as strangers around the world, with a wholistic expression of the gospel of Jesus Christ. Just as the Apostle Paul knew and understood Greek culture, the Mennonite Church must engage the broader culture through media. If the Mennonite church is to thrive in the post-Christian, post-modern, environment of twenty-first century, it must learn to wisely use modern media tools.

The first step in that process is to understand how the broader culture perceives Mennonites. This can be discerned, in part, through an examination of how Mennonites have been *portrayed* in popular media. The second step is to examine those media pieces *produced* by Mennonites which have been successful in reaching a broad North American audience or in reshaping religious thought. If one is aware of both categories of media (portrayed and produced) they provide touchstones into the broader culture and may support the church's priority of bearing witness to those outside its membership. Although a small group, Mennonites have made inroads into popular media resulting in many touchstones for further discussion about matters of faith. This text examines some of the most prominent of these popular media expressions about or by Mennonites.

If one were to approach people on the street in an urban area of North America and ask them "What is an Anabaptist?" chances are few would have a clue. However, if one were to ask them if they were familiar with Voltaire's *Candide* or Joseph Heller's *Catch-22* one would likely receive many more positive responses. Both of these major literary works contain favorable portrayals of Anabaptist characters and provide a point of reference to explain the Anabaptist faith.

Likewise, if one were to ask a U.S. citizen "What is a Mennonite?" one would likely get a blank stare. The respondents might be more knowledgeable in Canada where Mennonites have made significant inroads into Canadian literature as will be illustrated in chapter ten which examines the writings of Rudy Wiebe and Miriam Toews. Ask that same person, "Have you ever seen *Witness* with Harrison Ford and Kelly McGillis, or read James Michener's *Centennial*, or James Lee Burke's *Heaven's Prisoners*?" and they might say "Yes." If one were to bump into a homemaker during one of these hypothetical inquiries and ask "Have you heard of the *Fix-it and Forget-it* or *More-with-Less* cookbooks, chances are they may know about these bestselling staples of many kitchens. Others would likely know of Malcolm Gladwell, the author of several books including *The Tipping Point* and *David and Goliath*. Each of these very popular media expressions was either

Introduction

written by a Mennonite, contains a Mennonite reference, or has a Mennonite character. They provide a point of commonality to speak with someone outside the church about what it means to be Mennonite.

This text examines the relationship between Mennonites and media, both how Mennonites have been portrayed in popular media and how they shaped media for identity and outreach. The focus is primarily on U.S. media but some space is also given to prominent Canadian Mennonite authors. It begins by defining two terms, "media" and "Mennonite," and is patterned after Diane Zimmerman Umble and David L. Weaver-Zercher's two part book, *The Amish & the Media*. In Part I, titled "The Old Order Amish as Media Images," the authors examine depictions of plain people in film, documentaries, poetry, nonfiction, tourism, and television. Part II of their text, "The Old Order Amish as Media Producers and Consumers," deals with Amish informants, internal publications such as *The Budget*, publishing enterprises, and truth telling in relation to media. It concludes with a chapter on the Nickel Mines School shooting.[3]

Similarly, this book is divided into an introduction and two distinct parts. Part I will examine how those outside the faith have portrayed Mennonites in the media from 1525 to the present. There are few references to Mennonites in popular culture; therefore, Part I is a fairly thorough examination of those which do exist. Some of these popular references may seem trivial, yet their very presence is significant, considering Mennonites are a very small and relatively unknown group. Cultural references are organized by media type; aural, print, and visual. Each reference is examined individually in light of historical developments in the Anabaptist movement. The examples and analysis are not exhaustive but are indicative of the various perceptions of Mennonites held by those outside this group. Mennonite faith and media presence will be contrasted with three other distinct religious groups, two larger, Jews, and Mormons, and one smaller, Plymouth Brethren, to demonstrate Mennonites have a media footprint in excess of their size. Particular emphasis will be placed on gaining an understanding of the term "sect" and how the broader culture perceives the "religious other."

In contrast to the scarcity of popular references to Mennonites by people outside the faith, there are many examples of media produced by Mennonite authors and artists. Therefore, Part II, which examines how Mennonites have used media to both shape their identity and to reach out in witness, focuses primarily on books, art, music, and films which have

---

3. Umble and Weaver-Zercher, eds., *Amish and Media*.

Introduction

been directed outward. Only books which have succeeded in reaching a North American audience beyond Mennonite circles *and* exposed them to Mennonite beliefs and practices are included in this research. There are many significant books by Mennonite theologians and scholars which are not included, such as Arthur McPhee's *Friendship Evangelism*, John Drescher's *Seven Things Children Need*,[4] and David Augsburger's *Caring Enough to Confront*.[5] All three of these books were written by Mennonites and reached a broad North American audience, but, they do not tell their readers about Mennonite faith or practices. There are also several prominent authors such as Jim Wallis, editor of *Sojourners* magazine, and Tom Sine, Executive Director of Mustard Seed Associates, who are sympathetic to Mennonites and have been influenced by them but do not self-identify as being Mennonite. Their readers may be exposed to Anabaptist theology through their writings but it is seldom, if ever, identified as integral to Mennonite faith or practice. This research does not deal extensively with internally focused periodicals and publishers such as *The Gospel Herald*, *The Mennonite*, *Mennonite World Review* and Cascadia Publishing House/Pandora Press except to categorize Mennonite attitudes toward media and illustrate Mennonite attempts at outreach using media. Some *Herald Press* books, the Mennonite Church USA denominational imprint, are examined, specifically the *More-with-Less* cookbook, and several other titles. There is not an entire section devoted to Herald Press since the denominational publisher was primarily internally focused, especially during its first fifty years, 1908-1958.[6] There is, however, a section on Good Books, a Mennonite owned publisher which closed in 2013 but which had been successful in reaching a broader audience beyond just Anabaptists.

Part II begins to develop a Mennonite theology of media. It references the trajectory of the Anabaptist movement from a group of firebrands witnessing as they were being burned at the stake, to "the quiet in the land," and back toward reengagement with the broader society. Media examples are sorted into broad categories including: tracts; *Martyrs Mirror*; signs and bookracks; music and radio; art, performance and television; film; books;

---

4. *Seven Things Children Need*, first published in 1976, sold nearly 160,000 copies and was translated into twenty languages. It was twice featured in condensed form in *Reader's Digest*.

5. *Caring Enough to Confront* was a joint publication of Herald Press and Regal Books. As of January 1, 2001 there were 545,000 copies in print from 45 total printings including 13 by Herald Press.

6. Hostetler, *God Uses Ink*, 203.

Introduction

and the Internet. This text concludes with comparative data of denominational references drawn from an online research tool call the Ngram.

The Amish have been studied extensively elsewhere, particularly in Umble and Weaver-Zercher's text *The Amish and the Media*. Therefore, Amish examples are not included, except in works citing both Amish and Mennonites or noting Mennonite scholars who serve as interpreters of Amish culture for the broader society.

Media

In defining "the media," Zimmerman Umble and Weaver-Zercher describe the interaction of three distinct elements:

> (1) mediators of information; (2) the medium by which the mediators transmit their information; and (3) consumers of the mediated information. The first two elements taken together comprise "the media," and the work they accomplish in concert with their consumers is "mediation." *In other words, mediation is the process of creating and recreating meaning to be shared.* The media provide the raw materials—images, stories, and explanations—that media consumers use to make sense of the world in which they live and, in many cases, to make sense of their own lives.[7]

Broadly defined, "media" includes any device which facilitates or mediates one's perception of the world. Many have experienced, or been an eye witnesses to, a fire or traffic accident. Later, when reading about it in the newspaper, one may wonder whether the reporter was writing about the same event. The reporter's description and the physical newsprint both facilitate and alter the readers' knowledge and perception of the event. Eyewitnesses experience the event much differently than someone who only reads about it in the newspaper. The eyewitness' reality is often more visceral, yet narrower, in scope. The eyewitness may not have taken in, or known, all of the facts surrounding the event. For example, in the case of a traffic accident, he or she may not have been aware of the vehicle operators' medical condition, or altered mental state due to drugs or alcohol. The witness may not have known the condition of the brakes and safety systems of the cars involved. Yet, the witness was more aware than the newspaper reader of the sights, sounds, and smells at the scene of the accident observed the

---

7. Umble and Weaver-Zercher, eds., *Amish and Media*, 12. Italics in original.

Introduction

day before. Thus the newspaper mediates events for its readers. All media in some way filter and alter reality.

Marshall McLuhan, Canadian educator, philosopher, and scholar who lived from 1911 to 1980, has been called the guru of media. He is perhaps best known for coining the phrases "the media is the message" and "the global village." His work is considered foundational in the scholarly study of media.[8] In the 1960s, when McLuhan spoke of media he included tools. Some tools, such as an automobile, significantly alter or mediate one's experience of reality. Anyone who has ridden in an automobile and thoughtfully contrasted that experience with the sensation of walking can understand McLuhan's point. Life, as it whizzes by outside the car windows, appears very different than when one is walking. Old Order Mennonites continue to refrain from owning an automobile because of its perceived deleterious impact on their communal life. In this regard, and in others, Mennonites are media shy.

This project traces Mennonites in traditional forms of media: oratory, books, art, newspapers and magazines, radio, film, and television.

Mennonites and Anabaptism

Size

Mennonites are a small, non-conformist religious group, with roots in sixteenth century Anabaptism, who have traditionally separated themselves from the larger society and lived in agrarian settlements or colonies. The Mennonite Church USA is the largest Mennonite body in North America, yet they number only about one-hundred thousand. Including other Mennonite groups, there are just over three-hundred thousand in North America and about 1.7 million worldwide in eighty countries.

In order to understand what a small group the Mennonites are, and to access their media footprint, it is helpful to compare them to the Methodists, a mainline Protestant denomination. Methodists number more than 8 million in the U.S. There are more Methodists in the state of Virginia, three hundred and thirty two thousand, than there are Mennonites in North America. Yet, Methodists are only the third largest Christian denomination

---

8. Wikipedia, "Marshall Mcluhan," online, introduction.

Introduction

behind the thirty four million who identify themselves as Baptists and the fifty one million who call themselves Catholic.[9]

Mennonites can also be compared to other non-mainline religious groups. There are five and one half million Mormons or Latter-Day Saints (LDS) in North America with another million in Mexico and thriteen million worldwide, nearly as large a religious group as Jews who number 13.3 million worldwide. Half of the worldwide Jewish population, or 6.1 million people, live in North America. Like Jews, about half of the worldwide members of the LDS church, or 6.5 million, reside in North America making each group more than twenty times as large a religious body as North American Mennonites but only eight times larger on a worldwide scale. When considering their numbers, Mennonites have drawn media attention far in excess of their relative size, as this text will demonstrate.

The Swiss Brethren

In order to understand how Mennonites have been portrayed by media and how they have used it for identity and outreach, it is important to understand how this denomination got started, what makes them distinct, and wrestle with the question, "Are Mennonites a sect?" This background material allows the reader to better understand why other Christian denominations, and a Communist scholar, perceive Mennonites as they do.

The Anabaptist movement arose in the context of the 1524 Peasant's Revolt in the Black Forest of Germany. The peasants arose against the oppressive economic conditions and unfair practices toward the poor by ruling officials. Many early Anabaptists were poor themselves, or sympathetic with the plight of the poor. Anabaptists strove to return to the pure roots of the New Testament church which practiced "all things in common" as described in Acts 2:44. They practiced mutual aid by helping one another with material needs, but most did not practice a communal form of ownership. The Moravian Hutterites, however, did develop common-purse communities, and some such expressions continue today.[10]

Yet, the Anabaptist movement had neither unity of doctrine nor effective organization. Many of its leaders, martyred at an early age, were never able to solidify the group's theology, nor its polity. The Swiss Anabaptist movement, from which the Mennonites emerged, began with Conrad

---

9. "The Virginia Conference of the United Methodist Church," VCUMC web site.
10. Murray, *The Naked Anabaptist*, 121.

INTRODUCTION

Grebel and Felix Mantz, both supporters of Ulrich Zwingli. Zwingli's break with the Catholic Church led to the formation of the Reformed Church in the Protestant tradition. Although Grebel and Mantz agreed with Zwingli on many issues, they were impatient to implement changes they felt were clear from Scripture. Zwingli insisted on allowing the city council to dictate the pace of reform, thus his style of church reform became known as the Magisterial Reformation. Grebel and Mantz soon broke from Zwingli's ranks in what came to be called the Radical Reformation.[11] This term refers not to radical theology but to the founders' intent to get back to the authentic root (radix). Their critics called them "mad dogs," "fanatics," and much worse. The term Anabaptist is itself a derogatory name meaning "re-baptizers." In January 1525, George Blaurock performed the first adult rebaptisms in the Reformation period.

Soon after the suppression of the Peasants' Revolt, the Radical Reformation entered a new, hostile environment, and many abandoned its principles. Those who stayed became increasingly concerned with separation from the world, for their own safety, and to maintain purity. By January 5, 1527, Felix Mantz was arrested, tried, and drowned in the Limmat River, becoming the first Anabaptist martyred by Protestants. The movement quickly went underground as persecution increased.[12]

The first Anabaptist statement, written by Michael Sattler in February 1527, was more about practice than doctrine. Known as the Schleitheim Articles, this statement was named after the Swiss town bordering southern Germany where Anabaptist leaders gathered in conference just one month after Felix Mantz's martyrdom. These articles continue to define key Anabaptist principles including: refusal to take oaths of allegiance to civil authorities, the practice of church discipline to maintain the purity of the church, refusal to serve in the military, and a high regard for the priesthood of all believers.

Anabaptists were hunted and killed by leaders in both the Catholic and Protestant churches. In 1527, the same year that Felix Mantz was martyred and soon after Michael Sattler crafted the Schleitheim Confession which united the fledgling movement, Sattler had his tongue cut out, was repeatedly tortured with glowing tongs, and was burned at the stake. Shortly thereafter in 1528, Balthasar Hubmaier, who possessed a Doctorate in Theology and developed well thought out Anabaptist positions

---

11. Durnbaugh, *The Believers' Church*, 20.
12. Snyder, *Anabaptist History and Theology*, 60.

Introduction

concerning the Lord's Supper and adult baptism, was burned at the stake by the Hapsburg authorities in Vienna.[13]

These were perilous times. Much of the language of the Schleitheim Articles carries a stark and defiant "over and against" tone. Refusing military service and oaths of allegiance to civil governments, Anabaptists remained a persecuted minority for centuries.

Although Anabaptist factions disagreed on many things, they were unified and adamant in their refusal to baptize infants, thus forming a "Believers' Church" comprised entirely of adults who professed faith and were baptized as a sign of their desire to be Christ's disciples. This Believers' Church model, rooted in New Testament practice, had been lost but was being recovered by the Radical Reformers. This model was very different from the practices of both the Catholic and Lutheran Churches, which baptized infants and existed as "State Churches" where the ruling prince chose the faith tradition of his subjects and baptized them into it. Anabaptists continued to migrate, seeking religious liberty, as persecution increased.

Münster, Menno Simons, and Dutch Anabaptism

Nowhere did Anabaptists' quest for liberty go so far astray, or their persecutors act with such violent force in response, as in the debacle at Münster. On March 30, 1535 a group of violent Anabaptists, under the leadership of Jan van Leyden, attempted to impose a revolutionary kingdom. The Catholic bishop's army retook the town and massacred most of the adult males. Three Anabaptist leaders were placed in cages, which were suspended above the main street, as a public spectacle where the people watched them rot. Those cages still hang from the walls of St. Lamberti Tower in Münster, Westfalen. Menno Simons' own brother Peter Simons was involved with Leyden in this travesty. Menno Simons condemned this violent approach in his first writing, *The Blasphemy of Jan van Leyden*, and promoted a kingdom of Christ which forsook the sword and practiced nonresistance.[14] This was a defining moment for the Anabaptists with regard to both self-identity and how they were perceived by others.

Following Münster, Menno Simons led the Anabaptists in the Netherlands and Northern Germany from 1537, when he broke with the Catholic Church, until his death of natural causes at the age of sixty-six in 1561.

13. Dyck, *Introduction to Mennonite History*, 75.
14. George, *Theology of the Reformers*, 260.

He wrote twenty-five books and tracts as well as numerous letters, hymns and meditations. Thereafter his followers were known as Mennonites, a title they carry to this day.[15]

European Mennonites were not always hunted down and killed as heretics. In the Dutch Netherlands they migrated from rural to urban areas, especially in the northern part of the province of Holland. They achieved considerable prosperity during the "Dutch Golden Age" which followed the emergence of the Protestant Republic of the Seven United Netherlands around 1585.[16] Their wealth came because of their rejection of extravagance, their inter-marriage which kept family fortunes together, and their work ethic. With this newfound affluence Dutch Mennonites participated in the literary and artistic culture where they made significant contributions to seventeenth century Dutch paintings.[17]

The Amish

The Amish share the same theological and historical root as Mennonites. In 1693 in Switzerland, Jacob Amman and his Alsatian Anabaptist followers split with their Swiss-Mennonite brethren, led by Hans Reist, over a dispute concerning the frequency of communion and shunning. Amman's followers became known as Amish. Old Order Mennonites and Old Order Amish have similar beliefs and customs. They resemble each other in dress and the use of horse and buggy to the exclusion of the automobile. For this reason, the public often confuses Old Order Mennonites with the Amish.

Mennonite Migration to Russia

In order to understand how Mennonites got the label "the quiet in the land" and how this affected their relationship to media, it is important to review the history of the Mennonite colonies in Russia. Several political factors influenced the Mennonite migration from Prussia to Russia in the 1780s. In 1762, two decades before German-born Catherine II succeeded her husband Peter III on the throne, she issued an invitation to Germans and other Europeans to come and settle in southern Russia on lands vacated by the

15. Ibid., 262-63.
16. Visser, "Aspects of Social Criticism and Cultural Assimilation," 69.
17. Ibid., 69.

Introduction

Turks. Within a decade nearly one hundred German colonies had begun. The French revolution, which spanned the decade between 1789 and 1799, caused great upheaval in Europe. Monarchs across Europe responded by strengthening their military. Meanwhile, Mennonite landowners, who were living in Prussia on approximately three hundred thousand acres, refused to support military preparations or the state church, both of which were funded through land taxes. This lost revenue resulted in government controls which prevented Mennonites from buying more Prussian land. Eventually Mennonites' refusal to pay taxes, in the face of the government's increasing need for revenue to support military preparations, and the need for additional land to support growing families led to their migration.[18]

In 1786 George Trappe, a special emissary of Catherine II, visited the Prussian Mennonite colonies to explore the possibility of having them resettle in Russia. In 1788, encouraged by a special charter which granted religious freedom and exemption from military service, Mennonites began emigrating to Russia. In accordance with Russian policy at the time, the Mennonites were secluded from the native population. Thus, a large and prosperous Mennonite colony grew up in Russia separate and distinct from the Russian people. Implicit in their charter was an agreement that the Mennonites not proselytize.

In Prussia, Catherine II issued the "Manifesto of 1763, which states . . . foreign colonists settling in Russia were to have the right to exercise their religion freely in accord with their church rules and practices without any molestation, but that "everyone is warned that none of the Christian believers residing in Russia should under any pretext be persuaded or misled to accept or join the faith and the church" of the foreign colonists." [19] Although, Mennonites did not come to Russia until 1788, these provisions would still have been in effect even though they were not specifically included in the agreement made between the Mennonites settling in Danzig and the government officials.[20]

Additionally, since only German was spoken in the Mennonite colony, they had little spiritual impact on their Russian-speaking neighbors. Records indicate that by 1845 the Prussian Mennonites had translated only one religious book from German into Russian. The Prussian Mennonites' proclivity to marry others exclusively from their group led to a unique self

---

18. Dyck, *Introduction to Mennonite History*, 164.
19. Global Anabaptist Mennonite Encyclopedia Online, "Russia," 2.1.
20. Ibid.

INTRODUCTION

and group consciousness. This progressed to the point where to be Mennonite was no longer a religious label but an ethnic one.[21] This tendency, toward seclusion with limited interaction with neighbors outside of ethnic Mennonite colonies, has led some to call Mennonites "the quiet in the land," a characterization which has persisted among many Mennonite and Anabaptist groups into the twenty-first century.

Early American Mennonites

The first permanent settlement of Mennonites in America migrated from Krefeld, Germany to Germantown, Pennsylvania in 1683. Another wave of Mennonite immigrants settled in Lancaster, Pennsylvania, some fifty miles further west in 1710. Around 1736, Amish settlers began moving into close proximity with Mennonites in Lancaster and Berks Counties in Pennsylvania. By the time of the American Revolution, Mennonites had moved further south into the Shenandoah and Cumberland Valleys of Virginia and Maryland.[22]

At the beginning of the nineteenth century most American Mennonites were isolated from the rest of the world in eastern Pennsylvania where they spoke a dialect of Palatinate German known in America as "Pennsylvania Dutch." The barriers of language, their refusal to bear arms in military service, and non-participation in civic affairs such as voting, further isolated these American Mennonites. At the same time, they were rubbing shoulders with other German speaking church people. Mennonites would have been comfortable with some Pietist groups, many of whom had pacifist leanings although they did not officially embrace pacifism the way the Amish and Mennonites did.[23] Pennsylvanian Mennonites were greatly influenced by German Pietism. For them, "Humility reinforced by Pietism became one more reason to be "the quiet in the land.""[24] The term "Stillen im Lande" or "quiet in the land" has been applied to Pietist groups as well as Mennonites.[25] This humility and reluctance to engage the broader society greatly contributed to the tendency, common among Mennonites, to be media shy.

21. Dyck, *Introduction to Mennonite History*, 175.
22. Schlabach, *Peace, Faith, Nation*, 20-21.
23. Ibid., 88.
24. Ibid., 105.
25. Ibid., 22.

Introduction

Religious Identity

How one becomes Mennonite contrasts with how Jews and Mormons approach membership. It is difficult for most people to distinguish the dress worn by conservative Mennonites and Amish people from the dress of Orthodox Jews, but in this regard they are different—Anabaptist children do not inherit their parents' faith. In the Jewish faith children born of a Jewish mother are considered Jewish.[26] In Judaism it is difficult to distinguish faith from heritage or blood, as demonstrated in the nation of Israel which, since 1948, has practiced a national Jewish religion. In Judaism, children are born Jewish. It is difficult for male Gentiles (non-Jews) to convert in part because of the requirement to be circumcised, a painful procedure for an adult, and the necessity that all initiates learn Hebrew, a difficult ancient language. The Jewish people do not proselytize.[27]

In contrast, in the LDS church children are baptized at the age of eight and are heavily indoctrinated. "During the school year all high school youth in grades nine through twelve attend daily "seminary" classes to study church history, scriptures, doctrine and theology."[28] After high school young people are expected to give two years to missionary service. Mormon missionaries in turn practice a persistent form of proselytizing. As a result "The LDS church is the fifth largest church in America, with 6 million members... [It] is the fastest-growing religion in America, growing by about 19 percent from 1990 through 2000."[29] In the LDS faith, it is difficult to leave and easy to join.

Although many Mennonite and other Anabaptist communities are close-knit, they are deliberate in allowing their young people to make a choice to either embrace or reject the faith. As pacifists, Mennonites practice non-coercion as a tenant of faith. Most parents are reluctant to pressure their own children into accepting their faith. Those young people who choose to become Mennonite are baptized and join the church. Others frequently leave the church and community. Although there are some who claim a Mennonite ethnicity from their parents, in the Believers' Church tradition of which Mennonites are a part, one must make a profession of faith and be baptized to become Mennonite. There are no blood-line Mennonites.

---

26. Rich, "Judaism 101."
27. Ibid.
28. Hanks and Williams, *Mormon Faith in America*, 23.
29. Ibid., 12.

Introduction

World class cyclist Floyd Landis was raised Mennonite in Lancaster County, Pennsylvania. He left his community, turned his back on his parents' Mennonite faith, and moved to Southern California to train in his sport. In July 2006, on the Sunday prior to the start of the world renowned Tour de France bike race, a major article about Landis ran in *The Washington Post*. Much of it focused on his Mennonite upbringing.[30] When Paul Schrag, editor of the internally influential *Mennonite Weekly Review*, learned about Landis and *The Washington Post* article he refused to write about it saying, "This is not the *former* Mennonite Weekly Review."[31] When, surprisingly, Landis won the Tour de France, Schrag relented and ran a feature article on the front page of the next edition. However, the article focused on the cyclist's parents, Paul and Arlene Landis, who are members of the Martindale Mennonite Church, which is part of Lancaster Mennonite Conference, a member conference of Mennonite Church USA.[32]

There was another story in the *Mennonite Weekly Review* which also addressed the issue of Mennonite identity. When Republican Jerry Moran won election as a senator from Kansas the front page of the Nov. 15, 2010 edition of the *MWR* carried the headline, "Kansas M.B. [Mennonite Brethren] Elected to U.S. Senate" even though Moran's web page lists his religious affiliation as Methodist.[33] It became clear in the ensuing letters to the editor that some Mennonites think Moran does not embrace Anabaptist theology and is therefore not really Mennonite. However, Schrag noted, since 1996 Moran has been a member of North Oak Community Church, an MB congregation in Hays, Kansas and is therefore technically Mennonite.[34] Religious identity is often not easy to define.

In summary, although no one is born Mennonite, it has been difficult, until very recently, for those not raised Mennonite to embrace the Mennonite faith. Barriers of culture, race, dress, and practice have limited the number of non-ethnic Mennonites, those not born to Mennonite parents, from becoming Mennonite. Welcoming outsiders continues to be an issue for many Mennonite groups. However, in 1995 the General Conference Mennonite Church (GC) and the Mennonite Church (MC), in preparation for their eventual merger as Mennonite Church USA, issued a new

30. Kaufman, "Break Away," D1.
31. Schrag, telephone conversation, July 3, 2006.
32. Rhodes, "Landis' Mother Sees God's Purpose in Victory," 1.
33. *MWR* Staff, "Kansas M.B. Elected to U.S. Senate," 1.
34. Schrag, "Kansan Leads Race for Senate," 1.

INTRODUCTION

joint *Confession of Faith in a Mennonite Perspective*, which dropped many cultural barriers such as requiring women to wear a prayer covering and men to have short hair. The new denomination, MC USA, formed in 2002, adopted a missional identity which openly welcomes others to join their distinct religious expression of radical discipleship which presses on to follow Christ, even in his pacifism. Still, for many, it is easy to leave the Mennonite faith and difficult to join it. This Mennonite cultural norm contrasts sharply with some other faiths where it is easy to join but difficult to leave. As a result, Mennonites remain a small group. Yet, despite their size they have a significant presence in the media of North American culture.

Sects

Although it is the editorial policy of most newspapers not to report a subject's religious affiliation unless it is pertinent to the story, sometimes magazines, newspapers, and other media forms report on "Mennonite" businesses. When Bovine Spongiform Encephalopathy (BSE), more commonly known as Mad Cow Disease, was emerging, at least one newspaper referred to the presence of Mad Cow Disease on a "Mennonite farm." Libertarian blogger Phil Leggiere's post proclaims "PA. State Troopers Raid Mennonite Farm for Raw Milk."[35] Others advertise "Mennonite Sausage" made in Ontario, Canada in the same way "Amish Furniture" or "Amish Craftsmanship" is touted in Lancaster County, Pennsylvania. This raises the question, "What is a 'Mennonite' business?" Why not an Episcopalian farm or Methodist sausage? Perhaps a more accurate term would be a "Mennonite family farm" or "Mennonite-made sausage." In any regard, most would not refer to businesses run by persons from other religious faiths in this way, with the possible exception of Jews. This gives rise to a discussion of the concept of sects, a label often applied to both Mormons and Mennonites.

An exploration of the term "sect" is necessary to gain a deeper understanding of why Mennonites, and other distinct religious groups, are popular media subjects. German sociologist Max Weber worked with the concept of sect in his 1922 book *The Sociology of Religion*. Writing an introduction to a later edition Talcott Parsons says, "the case Weber has in mind in his concept of religious community is that of a collectivity with a distinctive religious character, which is not a society, but rather a religiously

---

35. Leggiere, "Pa. State Troopers Raid Mennonite Farm from Raw Milk Sales."

specialized subgroup with a society, a "sect" ... in Western terms, a community which is both "church" and "state" at the same time."[36]

Weber places Mennonites within this sectarian expression noting the close connection between ethical religion and rational economic development achieved by this group and others including Quakers, Zwinglians, Reformed Baptists, and Methodists.[37] In another of Weber's texts he notes, "the connection of a religious way of life with the most intensive development of business acumen among those sects whose otherworldliness is as proverbial as their wealth, especially the Quakers and the Mennonites."[38] Weber used the term "sect" descriptively in a sociological sense and not pejoratively. Others use the term differently.

The influential American Protestant theologian H. Richard Niebuhr, in his classic text *Christ and Culture*, outlines five ways Christians have related to the surrounding society; Christ against culture, the Christ of culture, Christ above culture, Christ and culture in paradox, and Christ transforming culture. Niebuhr states those holding to the "Christ against culture" model uncompromisingly affirm Christ as the Christian's sole authority and reject any claim the culture may place on the Christians' loyalty.[39] This fierce loyalty to Christ and the Christian community results in the rejection of society's culture. Niebuhr labels this approach "Protestant sectarianism—to use that label in its narrow, sociological meaning"[40] and holds Mennonites up as the quintessential model of a Christian denomination embracing the "Christ against culture" model saying, "The Mennonites have come to represent the attitude most purely, since they not only renounce all participation in politics and refuse to be drawn into military service, but follow their own distinctive customs and regulations in economics and education."[41]

Niebuhr claims those who embrace the "Christ against culture" model withdraw from society and relinquish all responsibility for the world. Although Niebuhr's text is written in an objective voice, it is clear from a careful reading that he was dismissive of this approach and of sects. Mennonite theologian John Howard Yoder responded to Niebuhr's thesis and

36. Weber, *The Sociology of Religion*, xxxvii.
37. Ibid., 93.
38. Weber, *The Protestant Ethic and the Spirit of Capitalism*, 44.
39. Niebuhr, *Christ and Culture*, 45.
40. Ibid., 56.
41. Ibid., 56.

Introduction

challenged his assumptions in a draft manuscript, written in 1976 which remained unpublished until 1999, titled *The Problem in How H. Richard Niebuhr Reasoned*. Yoder claims Niebuhr's assertion with regard to Mennonites "is both unfair and unlogical[sic]. Unfair because it misrepresents the intention and practice of most Mennonite groups, . . . inconsistent because the criticism directed toward this minority group is precisely that it has a culture of its own 'economics and education.'"[42] Yet Mennonites continue to be categorized as sectarian.

The label "Mennonite" carries distinct connotations. Mennonites are often the subject of media because of their distinct beliefs and practices, yet Mennonites are not prone to judge another's faith and would *not* claim "salvation is only found in the Mennonite Church," as some sects do. Rather, it is Mennonites' distinct practices, dress, and theology which make them interesting subjects in art and film.

Most religious communities acknowledge persons of other faiths are different while deeming them worthy of respect and mutual dialogue. However, the term "sect" describes groups which are outside the boundaries of mainstream religious expressions. In common usage today, this label allows persons to dismiss others and paint them negatively. Sects often live communally apart from the broader society.

Philip D. Kenneson distinguishes three aspects of sectarian identity: sociological, ecclesiological, and theological. These three facets of sectarian identity help explain why Mennonites are interesting media subjects. Kenneson's three part definition provides a framework to categorize various media portrayals of Mennonites as positive, negative, and neutral. In a sociological setting, sect means "a group of people whose beliefs and practices are substantially distinct from those of the host society."[43] Kenneson goes on to define a sect in ecclesiological terms as any group which, through its beliefs and practices, threatens the unity of the church. He points to Augustine's criticism of the Donatists because they divided the church and insisted they were the only true Christians. This refrain has been picked up by other religious groups which insist there is no salvation outside of their church.[44] A third context for the term is theological. In the New Testament the word "hairesis" is often translated as "sect." This is the term used to

---

42. J. H. Yoder, "The Problem in How H. Richard Niebuhr Reasoned," 11. This essay was published in 1996 in *Authentic Transformation*, ed. Stassen.

43. Kenneson, *Beyond Sectarianism*, 8.

44. Ibid., 15.

describe three Jewish groups: the Pharisees, the Sadducees, and the Nazarenes. The Apostle Paul was a Pharisee, while John the Baptist, and the Old Testament prophet Samuel, were Nazarenes.

Kenneson explains, "On the contemporary scene, these three senses sometimes coincide. . . . Some would argue, for example, that the Boston Church of Christ is sectarian in all three senses. It would be a mistake, however, to assume either that these three senses of sectarianism have always coincided historically, or that they need to do so logically. . . . For example, many Franciscans and Mennonites could be regarded as sectarian in the sociological and theological senses even though they have not been sectarians in the ecclesiological sense."[45]

In the summary of Part I, contained in chapter four, Kesseson's threefold definition of sect will be used as a framework to examine and categorize each media reference examined herein.

45. Ibid., 19.

PART I

How Mennonites Have Been Portrayed in the Media

CHAPTER 1

Aural Media

Leaders' Proclamations

Leaders of the Catholic, Lutheran, and Reformed Churches, the three established state churches of sixteenth century Europe, condemned the Anabaptist faith as heretical. Anabaptists were considered to be a cancer within the European societies, controlled by Church and State, which must be forcibly removed. The penalty for heresy was death. The State Churches went so far as to outlaw Anabaptism in the Peace of Augsburg (1555) and later in the Peace of Westphalia (1648). Against this backdrop of official condemnation, other voices defended the Anabaptists including President Abraham Lincoln and General Stonewall Jackson.

Although these condemnations are found in published church confessions and doctrinal statements, they have been included in this section under "aural media" because the people in the congregation would have heard them spoken by the priest or pastor. Likewise, the comments of U.S. political and military leaders Abraham Lincoln and Stonewall Jackson were originally proclamations, spoken in the presence of others, and are thus included in this section on aural media.

Catholics

Catholic interrogators made clear their condemnation of Anabaptists despite the integrity of the prisoners' moral lives. Franz Agricola, a sixteenth century Roman Catholic and staunch opponent of Anabaptists, was both appalled by what he perceived as their heresies and confused by their godly lifestyle. He expressed his contradictory conclusions in the 1582 document *Against the Terrible Errors of the Anabaptists*, "As concerns their outward public life they are irreproachable. No lying, deception, swearing, strife, harsh language, no intemperate eating and drinking, no outward personal display, is found among them, but humility, patience, uprightness, neatness, honesty, temperance, straightforwardness in such measure that one would suppose that they had the Holy Spirit of God!"[1]

Of course, Agricola could not accept that these people, who preached against the Pope and certain practices in the Roman Catholic Church, could actually have the Holy Spirit of God. To him they were nothing but heretics and as such they deserved death.

Lutherans

The former Catholic priest Martin Luther also detested Anabaptists. He called them "schwarmar," a German word which means "fanatics" and refers to an unruly and uncontrollable swarm of dangerous bees. Lutheranism characterized Anabaptists as "non-conforming fanatics, enthusiasts, and rebels."[2] Some Lutheran confessions of faith condemn Anabaptists for not practicing infant baptism. The 1530 Augsburger Confession contains at least seven condemnations of Anabaptists. Article IX, on Baptism, states, "In our Churches no Anabaptists have arisen, because the people have been fortified by God's Word against the wicked and seditious faction of these robbers. And as we condemn quite a number of other errors of the Anabaptists, we condemn this also, that they dispute that the baptism of little children is unprofitable."[3]

The Lutheran Church's 1530 Augsburg Confession continues railing against the Anabaptists. In *Article XVII: Of Christ's Return to Judgment* it makes several statements concerning Christ's return, while condemning Anabaptist who think differently. The point of this Lutheran condemnation of Anabaptists is a disagreement over eschatological doctrine. Lutherans believed sinners, both human and devils, were condemned to eternal

---

1. Quoted by Murray, *The Naked Anabaptist*, 58.
2. Callen, *Radical Christianity*, 1999), 57.
3. Melanchthon, "The Augsburg Confession of Faith," article 17.2.

damnation, whereas Anabaptists, consistent with their emphasis on reconciliation, believed God's grace would prevail.[4]

These condemnations of Anabaptists within the Augsburg Confession, which is now more than 480 years old but still held up as the most authoritative Lutheran statement of faith, provided the basis for legal action, punishment, and even death. Other Protestant groups also took note of the Anabaptists and warned their followers to avoid them.

Anglicans

The Church of England (Anglican) and American Episcopal Church continued this practice of condemning Anabaptists in their articles of faith. The thirty-eighth article of the *Thirty-Nine Articles of Religion* reads, "The riches and goods of Christians are not [held in] common, as touching the right, title, and possession of the same, as certain Anabaptists do falsely boast."[5] It is interesting to note, there were few Anabaptists in England at the time this article was written and none which would have held property in common. Yet, this historical condemnation remains a part of the *Book of Common Prayer*, the central text uniting Anglicans and Episcopalians around the world, to this day. It is fascinating to see that the Anabaptist movement, small, marginalized, and all but forgotten for centuries, so threatened the Church of England that their doctrines and practices were called out as erroneous in this prominent religious text. To be fair, the Anabaptist movement did attract thousands of followers in the early 1500s, despite, and perhaps because of its widespread persecution. At times the movement saw the conversion and baptism of entire towns.[6]

U.S. Political and Military Leaders

Abraham Lincoln, the sixteenth President of the US, who governed during the American Civil War, had a more positive attitude toward Mennonites and members of other historic Peace Churches. The US Military History Institute, in a 1950 book titled *Conscientious Objection*, reported,

---

4. Ibid.
5. Murray, *The Naked Anabaptist*, 120.
6. Bender, "Waldshut," Gameo. Online.

PART I—How Mennonites Have Been Portrayed

President Lincoln held an understanding attitude toward conscientious objectors. In answer to people who urged him to force Friends [Quakers], Mennonites and Brethren into the Army, he replied substantially as follows: 'No, I will not do that. These people do not believe in war. People who do not believe in war make poor soldiers. Besides, the attitude of these people has always been against slavery. If all our people held the same views about slavery as these people hold there would be no war.

These people are largely a rural people, sturdy and honest. They are excellent farmers. The country needs good farmers fully as much as it needs good soldiers. We will leave them on their farms where they are at home and where they will make contributions better than they would with a gun.[7]

Likewise, Confederate General Stonewall Jackson had this to say about members of the historic Peace Churches, "There live a people in the valley of Virginia, that are not hard to bring to the army. While there they are obedient to their officers. Nor is it difficult to have them take aim, but it is impossible to get them to take correct aim. I, therefore, think it better to leave them at their homes, that they may produce supplies for the army."[8]

Music and Radio

Music, *Amish Paradise*

Amish Paradise, a 1996 single by "Weird Al" Yankovic, which parodies a hip-hop song, *Gangsta's Paradise* by Coolio, calls the Amish "crazy Mennonites." *Amish Paradise* was recorded in Houston, Texas by the Scotti Brothers. It reached number fifty-three in the U.S. Billboard Hot one hundred list and number twenty-two in single sales. In contrast the original reached number one in both categories and earned a Grammy for *Best Rap Solo Performance.*

In the original, Coolio laments his dangerous and expectedly short life as a gangster. In contrast, Weird Al, playing an Amish farmer, praises his simple life in Lancaster County, Pennsylvania. At the very end of the song the Amishman sings, "We're all crazy Mennonites, living in an Amish paradise . . . You'd probably think it bites, living in an Amish paradise."

Yankovic's song and accompanying music video is a double parody. It parodies Coolio's gangster rap while also poking fun at the Amish. They are

7. Quoted by Schrock, "Lincoln and Cos," 8.
8. Quoted in Durnbaugh, *The Believers' Church*, 258.

portrayed, in a humorous way: shunning electrical appliances, telephones, and buttons while being hard working, communal, Bible centered, and nonviolent, e.g., "turning the other cheek." However, in Yankovic's case, the cheek is not on the face but buttocks. Although the song mentions Mennonites, it says nothing about them except to imply they are closely affiliated with the Amish who are peace loving. It is, nonetheless, noteworthy in that it mentions Mennonites.

Radio

A Prairie Home Companion

Garrison Keillor's weekly radio program *A Prairie Home Companion* has aired on National Public Radio since 1974. Approximately four million listeners hear it over more than six-hundred Public Radio stations. The program is popular among Mennonites, perhaps because of its good clean humor, gospel music, and religious content. Keillor weaves gospel hymns and stories of faith throughout his broadcast. He grew up in a strict Plymouth Brethren fundamentalist home, yet the denomination at the center of his antics is not the Plymouth Brethren, but rather the Lutherans. The program originates out of Minneapolis, Minnesota, an area with many Norwegian Lutherans. Keillor's tales are set in Lake Woebegon, a fictitious Midwestern town on the edge of the prairie. In addition to the Lutheran Church, Lake Woebegon is home to a Catholic Church, Our Lady of Perpetual Responsibility. Keillor also occasionally mentions a "local Mennonite church" in his "News from Lake Woebegon" story telling segment. There are several other references to Mennonites on Keillor's show.

Each week the show's staff collects greetings, some of which are read on-air. This greeting was posted on May 26, 2005. It is not clear if it was read on-air. "To: Mennonite Central Committee Bangladesh Alumni. After listening to tapes of PHC in Bangladesh with our Canadian friends years ago, we finally made it to a live broadcast. Here's to great memories of PHC in the tropics!—Sharon and Conrad Swartzentruber."[9]

In Keillor's "Guy Noir-private eye" script, aired on March 4, 2006, Guy is hired by Andrea's husband to find her. She had been missing for a week when Guy Noir finds her at a casino. Andrea and her husband are from North Dakota, and this trip with her husband was her first taste of

---

9. "A Praire Home Companion," Online at www.prairehome.publicradio.org.

PART I—HOW MENNONITES HAVE BEEN PORTRAYED

big city night life. When Guy finds her, she is doing a burlesque dance on top of a piano in the bar. He asks her husband if she is drunk to which he replies, "Andrea is Mennonite, Mr. Noir. She's never had a beer." Keillor is poking fun at simple folks from North Dakota and this naive Mennonite girl who "started to get woozy from the second-hand smoke and suddenly . . . vanished." In this stereotype of Mennonites, they live in North Dakota and neither smoke nor drink.

Keillor presents an annual show dedicated entirely to telling jokes. One joke, which aired on April 17, 2004 and again in a slightly different form on Nov 6, 2004, involved Mennonites. "What does it take to keep an Amish woman happy? Two 'men–a–night.'" Although this is merely a play on words, it reminds us of a link between the Amish and Mennonites, but the nature of the connection is unclear. The joke is funny, for those who understand the beliefs and practices of the Amish and Mennonites, because sexual promiscuity is not typically associated with either of these strict religious groups.

On Wednesday, October 15, 2013 Keillor performed at Goshen College, a Mennonite Church USA affiliated school in Goshen, Indiana. This was not his popular live Saturday night broadcast of the NPR program *A Prairie Home Companion*, but rather a one man, two hour comedy routine. Keillor enjoyed himself and commented about the show on his personal Facebook page the next day. Goshen major Allan Kauffman, himself a Mennonite, read Keillor's blog and reposted it on his Facebook page, calling Keillor's praise "a wonderful tribute!" *The Elkhart Truth* posted Keillor's comments in reporter Dan Spaulding's blog *Truthiness*.

> I think I maybe did the best show of my life Tuesday night and all thanks to the audience, a thousand Mennonites and their neighbors in a small town in Indiana. It was mostly impromptu, fast-paced, jumpy, with a big complicated pontoon-boat story in the middle, and at the beginning and end we sang. They sang beautiful four- and six-part harmony in a fine acoustic hall and I sang a modest bass . . . the sound of this impromptu choir made everyone intensely happy. I steered them directly from one verse of a song to a chorus of another, no pausing, and when I did pause once, trying to figure out where to go next, they did not applaud. Marvelous. Because it was not a show. It was for real. Mennonites are quiet, peace-loving, kind-hearted people, salt of the earth, If I knew a church where people sang like that, I'd be there every Sunday, sitting right smack in the middle. Thank you, Goshen College.[10]

10. Spaulding, "Garrison Keillor Tips His Hat" Online blog.

Since that performance, it has been announced Keillor's *Prairie Home Companion* radio show will be performed and broadcast live from Goshen College's Sauder Concert Hall on Saturday, May 2, 2015. From Keillor's comments and his return visit, it is obvious Keillor knows and appreciates Mennonites, perhaps because he too grew up in a strict and isolated Christian sect. But, it seems, what he appreciates most about Mennonites, apart from their peace position, is their a cappella singing.

Goshen College and the National Anthem

In 2011, Mennonites got a lot of national media attention, particularly online and via radio, over a decision by Goshen College's governing board to stop playing the national anthem. Goshen's decision to stop playing the national anthem reversed a decision, made about a year and a half earlier, when it began playing an instrumental version of the anthem, followed by a prayer, at intercollegiate sporting events. That decision was made in an effort to be more welcoming to the college's non-Mennonite students, who constitute about 50 percent of the student body. Typically, members of the Mennonite church, a historic peace church dedicated to following the Prince of Peace in radical discipleship, avoid oaths and military service. Many also abstain from voting, saying the pledge of allegiance, or singing the national anthem. Goshen's decision to revert back to its traditional practice of not singing the national anthem created a brouhaha in print and on conservative talk radio shows in Goshen Indiana, where the college is located. In making the decision the board of directors asked President James Brenneman to find an alternative.

The *Star Spangled Banner*, written by Francis Scott Key after witnessing the British bombardment of Fort McHenry near Baltimore, Maryland during the War of 1812, became the national anthem of the United States in 1931. Goshen began playing intercollegiate sports in 1957 but did not play the national anthem on campus until an instrumental version was introduced prior to a baseball game held on March 23, 2010. The prayer of Saint Francis of Assisi followed the anthem that day.

Local media outlets picked up on the controversy about the decision to go back to *not* using the national anthem, but were initially refused interviews by college officials. However, after a brief article about this decision appeared in the June 6 issue of the *Chronicle of Higher Education*, the story was launched. It went national on June 7, 2011 when National Public

PART I—HOW MENNONITES HAVE BEEN PORTRAYED

Radio (NPR) broadcast a news segment about it.[11] On June 7, 2011, Todd Stames, of *Fox News Radio*, ran a news item about Goshen's decision.[12] The following week James Brenneman, President of Goshen College, granted an on-air interview to Robin Young, host of NPR's *Here and Now*. That five minute dialogue aired on June 13, 2011.[13]

The story was propelled from radio to television when Mark Schloneger's article, "Why I Don't Sing the National Anthem," was picked up by Cable News Network (CNN) and posted June 26th on their "Belief Blog." Schloneger's TV appearance is explored in a later chapter.

---

11. Peralta, "Goshen College Bans National Anthem at Sporting Events," Online blog.

12. Stames, "National Anthem Banned at Mennonite College's Sporting Events," *Fox News* online.

13. Young, "Indiana's Goshen College Stops Playing the National Anthem," *Here and Now* online.

CHAPTER 2

Print Media

Books

The focus in this section is on books which feature prominent Anabaptist characters or make significant observations about Mennonites, and have gained a wide readership or made a significant scholarly impact. In contrast, certain books such as Jonathan Franzen's *The Corrections*, which won a national Book Award and was a 2002 finalist for a Pulitzer Prize for Fiction, are omitted. Mentioning Mennonites three times on a single page, he writes, "'I had a summer job when I was seventeen,' Don said. 'I worked for an old Mennonite couple that had a big antique store . . . . I had the idea the Mennonites were underpaying me . . . so I started to borrow their pickup at night. I had a girlfriend who needed rides. I crashed the pickup, which was how the Mennonites found out I'd been using it, and my then-stepdad said if I enlisted in the Marines he would deal with the Mennonites and their insurance company.'"[1] And yet, none of Franzen's characters are Mennonite, and, apart from these passing remarks, he makes no further references to Mennonites. Such books are not included here.

The first book to be examined was written by Helen R. Martin and published in 1904. It presents a mixed view of the Mennonite faith.

---

1. Franzen, *The Corrections*, 366.

PART I—HOW MENNONITES HAVE BEEN PORTRAYED

Tillie, A Mennonite Maid by Helen R. Martin, 1904

Tillie: A Mennonite Maid tells the story of a young Pennsylvania Dutch girl who longs for an education but her gruff father, Jacob Getz, stymies her efforts by pulling her out of school at age twelve so she can work full-time on the family farm. However, during her last year in school her village teacher, Miss Margaret, encourages Tillie in her educational pursuits. Later, Walter Fairchilds, a Harvard graduate who replaces Margaret as the local teacher, also encourages Tillie to continue her education.

Tillie dislikes her strict upbringing and environment, which the author characterizes as inhabited by harsh, uneducated men. As the novel ends, Tillie accompanies Walter Fairchild to Millersville, Pennsylvania where she attends Normal School to study and train for the teaching profession. Eventually, Tillie and Walter are married.[2]

The title *Mennonite Maid* refers to the lead character as both a maiden or young girl, and a maid, or servant, of the Lord. The book has been criticized for its portrayal of Mennonites. The story's primary antagonist is Tillie's father, Jacob Getz, who is portrayed very harshly. But the author makes it clear Getz is not Mennonite but Evangelical. The author's depiction of the other men who serve with Getz on the school board is also quite harsh. Martin paints them as outwardly pious but inwardly selfish and power hungry. However, this is not a smear upon Mennonites, but rather a slur upon uneducated, rural Pennsylvania farmers at the beginning of the twentieth century. Martin depicts the rural Pennsylvania Dutch farmers as hard working but ignorant and prejudiced against all outsiders. The term Pennsylvania Dutch refers to German immigrants who came from southwestern Germany and began arriving in the US in the late seventeenth century and continuing for about one-hundred years. At first, they settled in the northwestern section of Philadelphia County but soon spread to the interior of the state. Pennsylvania Dutch is a cultural term, referring to the amalgamation of the many German dialects, spoken by those who immigrated, into one regional language. Those who came to speak Pennsylvania Dutch were primarily Lutherans but also of the Reformed and Anabaptist faiths.[3]

The religious affiliation of the characters in *Tillie* include Amish, Mennonite, Dunkard (Brethren), Evangelical, atheist, and "Truth Seekers" among others, but it is the Mennonites who are spoken of most. Tillie has

---

2. English, "Martin, Helen Reimensnyder."
3. Wikipedia, "Pennsylvania Dutch," online, introduction.

an Aunt Em who is New Mennonite and referred to as "a member of the meeting." Aunt Em is a sympathetic character who runs the local hotel, employs Tillie, and conspires against Tillie's father (Em's brother) to allow the child to educate herself while working and living at the hotel. In chapter X, when Tillie attends a funeral service and is converted to "the ascetic faith of the New Mennonites," the reader learns they are "a sect largely prevailing in southeastern Pennsylvania." Their "plain dress," which Tillie adopts, is described physically but also with the words "their prescribed form of dress was sacred." The author calls New Mennonites "the most puritanical and exclusive of all sects" but tells her readers they are not opposed to education as the Amish are.[4]

Martin is very evenhanded in her portrayal of what the Amish call shunning and what the Mennonites in *Tillie* call "set back" whereby one of their members is disciplined, in this case Tillie for vanity in allowing her curly hair to be exposed outside of her modest head covering. While a member is under discipline, they are not allowed to talk to or eat with any other church member, not even family. Martin accurately describes this seemingly harsh punishment as "a discipline imposed in all love, to bring the recalcitrant member back into the fold."[5] She also describes Mennonites' deep and practical faith, their pacifism, and the practice of excommunication. Although the author is not particularly sympathetic to the Mennonites, she is accurate in her portrayal of their faith and practices.

Although the distinctions between the Amish and Mennonites would be difficult for an outsider to discern in 1904, before automobiles, the funeral practices described in the book closely resemble those of Reformed Mennonites.[6]

Martin published thirty-five books, most set in Lancaster County, Pennsylvania where she was raised. *Tillie* was her most successful undertaking, so much so that it was transformed into a play by Frank Hone in 1926. It may be the first romance novel set among the "Plain People." Yet, Martin was criticized for her harsh portrayal of the Pennsylvania Dutch and for her inauthentic capturing of their dialect.[7]

According to Rosanna M. Y. Hostetler, great-niece of Joseph W. Yoder, Mennonite educator and author of *Rosanna of the Amish*, her great-uncle

---

4. Martin, *Tillie*.
5. Ibid.
6. Ritzel, "A Grievous Tragedy."
7. English, "Martin, Helen Reimensnyder."

considered *Tillie, A Mennonite Maid* to be "a slur on plain people."[8] *Tillie*, in part, provided Yoder with the incentive to write *Rosanna* to more sympathetically portray Anabaptist people and faith. Like *Tillie* before it, *Rosanna* was hugely successful with more than 400,000 copies in print.

Enthusiasm: A Chapter in the History of Religion by Ronald Knox, 1950

Catholic scholar Ronald Knox painted all Mennonites with a broad brush calling them "an eccentric people who immaturely allowed themselves to be swept up in the wild current of mere emotion—a waiting on the spirit somehow gone wrong."[9] Oxford Scholarly Classics reissued a number of great academic works from the archives of Oxford University Press, in a uniform series. Knox's book *Enthusiasm*, a survey of Christian mystical movements from the time of the Corinthians through Father Divine, is one in the series. The emotional characteristic described by Knox was descriptive of some early Anabaptists, particularly those who followed Jan Matthys when he took over Münster, and his even more radical successor Jan ven Leyden, who set himself up as a Davidic king. Referring to Münster Knox writes, "The town fell in 1535; and from that time forward the doctrines of Anabaptists survived only sporadically, while the name itself is shunned even by those who trace their spiritual origins from its influence."[10] There were other Anabaptists during the movement's beginnings, who were so passionate for Christ and his kingdom that they expected his immediate return and waited for the coming of the New Jerusalem. Knox's description, like most stereotypes, applies to some Anabaptists but not to all.

Catch-22 by Joseph Heller, 1961

Joseph Heller's antiwar classic *Catch-22* includes a character identified as an Anabaptist chaplain. At the time of its publication, the *Chicago Sun-Times* called *Catch-22* "an apocalyptic masterpiece." *Washington Post* columnist, humorist and political satirist Art Buckwald called it "a masterpiece . . . one of the greatest war books," while the *New Republic* wrote,

---

8. J. W. Yoder, *Rosanna of the Amish*, 10.
9. Knox, *Enthusiasm*, 136.
10. Ibid., 127.

"explosive, subversive, brilliant . . . one of the most bitterly funny books in the language."[11] The Modern Library ranked *Catch-22* as number seven (by review panel) and as number twelve (by public) on its list of the greatest English language novels of the twentieth century.[12]

Joseph Heller's satirical novel is set in the Mediterranean Sea, on the island of Pianosa, west of Italy, during the closing months of World War II among the fictional 256th Squadron of the U.S. Army Air Forces. While his comrades are being successively killed during combat flight missions, Bombardier John Yossarian, the novel's central character, is determined to stay alive and see the end of the war. The novel's title refers to a "double bind," or illogical circular logic, which prevents anyone from avoiding military flight assignments. Since the novel's publication in 1961 the term "Catch-22" has entered the American lexicon and refers to any no-win situation a person may face.

As the story begins Yossarian has checked himself into the base hospital with vague complaints about his liver. The opening lines read, "It was love at first sight. The first time Yossarian saw the chaplain, he fell madly in love with him."[13] Some 455 pages later, as the book concludes, the chaplain, one of the novel's central characters, is still beside Yossarian. Chaplain Tappman, who repeatedly self-identifies as an Anabaptist, bookends the novel. "It isn't necessary to call me Father,' the chaplain explains. 'I'm an Anabaptist.'"[14] Heller's novel is satirical and not to be taken literally but there is no such thing as an Anabaptist chaplain. Military chaplains are appointed by their denominations. It is theoretically possible to have a Mennonite chaplain, although highly unlikely since Mennonites refuse to take military oaths, but it is not possible to have an Anabaptist chaplain, since the Anabaptist label refers to a larger religious group and not a specific denomination. Perhaps Heller is making a joke when he identifies the chaplain as an Anabaptist. The novel is a powerful antiwar story which has much in common with Anabaptist theology. Perhaps this is why Heller chose to place the novel's chaplain in this theological stream.

Heller's readers do not learn much about Anabaptists, but the chaplain, much like Voltaire's Jacque in *Candide*, is the only decent and sympathetic character in the entire novel. The author may know of the Anabaptist/

---

11. Heller, *Catch-22*, jacket cover.
12. Wikipedia, "Catch-22," online, 11.
13. Heller, *Catch-22*, 1.
14. Ibid., 8.

PART I—HOW MENNONITES HAVE BEEN PORTRAYED

Mennonite proclivity to fight against injustices, as it is the chaplain who goes to bat for Yossarian with the squadron commander, arguing against the arbitrary changes he is making in the number of combat missions the men must fly before their responsibilities are fulfilled.

In two other scenes in the novel, the author points toward a deeper understanding of Anabaptism. He writes, "It was already some time since the chaplain had first begun wondering what everything was all about. Was there a God? How could he be sure? Being an Anabaptist minister in the American Army was difficult enough under the best of circumstances; without dogma it was almost intolerable."[15]

Although Heller never identifies the chaplain as a pacifist, he seems to understand the contradiction of a pacifist Anabaptist being a military chaplain and the conflict between church and state inherent when a minister is also a government employee.

The second scene is reminiscent of the many trials and tribunals faced by the early Anabaptists who were often tortured and martyred for their faith. Here the chaplain is being interrogated by military police at Group Headquarters where they set him down, put a spotlight in his face, and intimidate him with brass knuckles and matches. Characteristic of Heller's dark humor, the dialogue becomes comical.

> "Chaplain," he asked casually, "of what religious persuasion are you?"
>
> "I'm an Anabaptist, sir."
>
> "That's a pretty suspicious religion, isn't it?"
>
> "Suspicious?" inquired the chaplain in a kind of innocent daze. "Why, sir?"
>
> "Well, I don't know a thing about it. You'll have to admit that, won't you? Doesn't that make it pretty suspicious?" . . .
>
> "Chaplain, I once studied Latin. I think it's only fair to warn you before I ask my next question. Doesn't Anabaptist simply mean that you're not a Baptist?"
>
> "Oh, no, sir. There's much more."
>
> "Are you a Baptist?"
>
> "No, sir."

15. Ibid., 266.

"Then you are not a Baptist, aren't you?"

"Sir?"

"I don't see why you're bickering with me on that point. You've already admitted it. Now, Chaplain, to say you are not a Baptist doesn't really tell us anything about what you are does it? You could be anything or anyone." [16]

Heller may understand the "much more" to which Chaplain Tappman alludes but his readers are left clueless.

Film director Mike Nichols and writer-actor Buck Henry, who were coming off their enormously successful project in *The Graduate*, joined forces again to adapt Heller's book for film. Released in 1970, *Catch-22* had an all-star cast including Alan Arkin as Yossarian, Anthony Perkins (of *Psycho* fame) as Chaplain Tappmann, Jon Voight, and Martin Sheen. The film version closely parallels the novel and includes two references to the Chaplain being an Anabaptist. However, the Anabaptist references are quick, and most viewers would not pick up on them. The film did not gain a broad audience, in part because it was overshadowed by Robert Altman's similar anti-war farce, *M.A.S.H.* which was released the same year.

Here an Anabaptist character appears in a prominent piece of popular fiction, logging yet another media footprint as this little known religious group marches toward consciousness in the minds of North Americans.

Communism in Central Europe in the Time of the Reformation by Karl Kautsky, 1966

It is not surprising Communist apologist Karl Kautsky was disappointed by the development of the Anabaptist movement, which sprung up from the Peasants' Revolt and whose members practiced a form of communal life characterized by mutual aid. He wrote, "They have maintained themselves till the present day, but for a long time have formed nothing more than small, well-to-do middle class communities, of no importance, either to the proletarian struggle for emancipation, or to the development of socialist ideas."[17] Kautsky's point about forming well-to-do middle class communities is true. This came about in part because Mennonites withdrew from society, in response to severe persecution, and focused on their work and

---

16. Ibid., 384.
17. Kautsky, *Communism*, 292.

communities. Many became prosperous, particularly in Russia, and in the later part of the twentieth century, in Canada and the U.S. If Kautsky thought, as the above quote implies, that Anabaptism was about politics or communism he was sure to be disappointed. Anabaptists pursue justice, stewardship and community, but as a means to bring about the Kingdom of God, not a political reality on Earth. Anabaptism was, and is, a serious attempt at Christian discipleship, loving both neighbors and enemies.

The writings of James A. Michener

In *Centennial*, published in 1974, American author James A. Michener includes prominent Mennonite characters, namely Jacob Zendt, the butcher, and his sons, Levi and Mahlon. Michener never knew his biological parents which may be one reason he was so fascinated with history. He was raised in Doylestown, Pennsylvania in a Quaker home, by his adoptive mother. Known for his meticulous research, Michener weaves historical facts into sweeping fictional sagas by tracing families through many generations while focusing on a specific location. A Pulitzer Prize winner for *South Pacific*, his forty books have collectively sold more than seventy-five million copies. *Centennial* is one of his popular fictional sagas set in the fictitious Colorado town of the same name. In it Michener tells a tale about the Mennonite Zendt family which begins in the chapter "The Wagon and the Elephant." Michener traces the Zendt family's migration in a Conestoga wagon from Lancaster County, Pennsylvania, west along the Oregon Trail, to the edge of the Rocky Mountains in what would become Colorado.

Michener describes the frugal practices and religious devotion of these hardworking Mennonite farmers. He distinguishes them from their Amish neighbors saying, "In most other parts of the world the Mennonites would have seemed impossibly rigid, but when compared to the Amish they were downright frivolous, for they indulged in minor worldly pleasures, were expert in conducting business and allowed their children other choices than farming. Some Mennonite children even went to school."[18]

Michener tells his readers little about Mennonite theology. In fact, he fails to understand the Mennonite Believers' Church tradition as distinct from the State Churches when he says, "Arriving mostly from [Germany], they brought with them a rigorous Lutheranism, which in its extremes

---

18. Michener, *Centennial*, 247.

manifested itself as the Amish or the Mennonite faith."[19] Michener even omits any mention of Mennonites' pacifism.

NBC made *Centennial* into a popular twelve part television miniseries of the same name which aired from October 1978 through February 1979, providing the non-reading public with another brief glimpse into Mennonite faith.

In 1991 Michener released *The Novel* about a struggling Mennonite writer, Lukas Yoder, from the fictitious rural Pennsylvania town of Dresden. *The Novel* was a departure from Michener's historical fiction style and was not well received by his readers. It tells the story of the publishing industry from four different perspectives: through the eyes of a writer, editor, critic, and reader. There is little religious content to the Mennonite characters in the book although the action revolves around many Amish areas of Pennsylvania. Wayne North, a Mennonite pastor and overseer in Virginia Mennonite Conference of Mennonite Church USA, after reading *The Novel* wrote to Owen Burkholder, then Virginia Mennonite Conference Minister, saying, "I found it to be one of the least satisfying of Michener's works. I think my disappointment came because of his treatment of the Mennonite theme. There was no religious dimension to the characters. The Jewish people as well as the Mennonite/Amish were identified as such but that fact really made no noticeable difference, except for some cultural emphasis."[20]

When *The Novel* was released in 1991, Michener was already eighty-four years old with twenty novels and twenty-three nonfiction works to his credit. He was past his prime and experimenting with a different style to which his readers did not respond favorably. It is significant the book is dedicated "To the Pennsylvania Dutch students who attended school with me."[21] Michener graduated from Doylestown High School in 1925 and undoubtedly became familiar with Mennonite customs and beliefs, but he fails to fully understand the Anabaptist tradition, or in any regard to accurately share glimpses of the Mennonites and Amish with his readers.

Mennonites in James Lee Burke's Writings

American author James Lee Burke, two-time winner of the Edgar Award for "Best Crime Novel of the Year" and named Grand Master by the Mystery

19. Ibid., 247.
20. North, Email, February 23, 2000.
21. Michener, *The Novel*, preface.

PART I—HOW MENNONITES HAVE BEEN PORTRAYED

Writers of America, has written twenty-nine novels and two collections of short stories. At least two of his books, and one of his short stories, contain Mennonite characters.

Two of his novels, *Heaven's Prisoners* and *Two For Texas*, have been made into motion pictures. Burke is best known for his murder mystery series featuring detective Dave Robicheaux. He has been called "America's best novelist" by the *Denver Post*. Burke's experience, growing up working class along the Texas-Louisiana gulf coast, heavily influenced his writing which includes oft repeated themes of ordinary people confronting evil, the contrast of natural beauty with human violence, and sin and redemption. Many of his characters are down and outers: thugs, pimps, prostitutes, alcoholics, and drug addicts. His serial books feature two protagonists who are really the same character in different settings. Dave Robicheaux is an ex-New Orleans police officer and recovering alcoholic, while Billy Bob Holland is a former Texas ranger and now a Texas based lawyer. Both are conflicted between their higher spiritual nature and base carnal instincts.

Heaven's Prisoners (1998) is the second of Burke's murder mystery series centered on Dave Robicheaux's exploits in and around New Orleans. Dave's second wife, Annie Robicheaux, is introduced in the opening pages of Burke's narrative as " . . . my Mennonite Kansas girl with curly gold hair . . . and the most electric blue eyes I'd ever seen . . . . [She was] always awed by cultural differences . . . [although] she came from a background of wheat farmer pacifists that was so pervasively eccentric that she couldn't recognize normality when she saw it." Annie is not a stereotypical Mennonite. She is portrayed as a beautiful thirty-something woman fond of seducing her older husband. The only Mennonite belief on display is her peaceful disposition which contrasts sharply with her husband's violent nature. When Annie disapproves of Dave carrying a revolver to protect his family, he responds, "When you love someone you don't put limits on their protection."[22] He objects to her unwillingness to kill, even in self-defense. This tension, between her desire to live peaceably and honor life, and his violent nature, mixed with a need to protect her even if it means killing someone he deems to be a threat, runs throughout the novel. Burke's description of Annie's mother as a quiet, heavy-set, Mennonite woman unacquainted with air travel is a stereotype of Mennonites, or perhaps a stereotype of Kansas wheat farmers many of whom are Mennonite.

22. Burke, *Heaven's Prisoners*.

Though Robicheaux frequently reverts to violence in his police work, he feels a tremendous sense of remorse after killing a criminal in self-defense. Burke's writing frequently points out the emotional and spiritual costs inflicted on those who perpetuate violence, whether in the Vietnam War, through criminal endeavors, or via police action. He notes violence eats away at the soul of the criminal, soldier, or cop. In the climactic scene of the novel, Robicheaux successfully arrests his wife's killer without resorting to violence. Though Robicheaux has a personal vendetta against this man, the killer will live to face the courts and likely be incarcerated for a long time, unlike the previous criminal, whom Robicheaux killed. The crusty detective feels good about the outcome saying, "It's the Mennonite way of doing things." Although Burke's characters frequently resort to violence coupled with strong language, he clearly admires peaceful Mennonites, enough so that he bookends this particular novel with them.

Heaven's Prisoners was made into a film and released in 1996. Alex Baldwin, of *Thirty Rock* fame, stars as Dave Robicheaux while Teri Hatcher, one of the original *Desperate Housewives*, plays the role of Bubba Rocque's Cajun wife Claudette. It is difficult for movie directors to condense a novel, with its dense character development and complex insights into their thoughts and motivations, into a two hour film without resorting to a narrator's voice over. Mennonites and their pacifist beliefs are not well known in society. Perhaps because of this, all references to Mennonites were removed in the screen play; in contrast to the book, in the film Annie picks up a rifle and fights back. The book's focus on the tension between Dave's violence and Annie's pacifism is dropped entirely. Instead, the movie emphasizes Dave's alcoholic disease and his constant desire to drink.

A Mennonite reference shows up in the first line of the first sentence of another of Burke's fictional novels—*Bitterroot* (2001). One of the book's main characters is a mysterious Vietnam veteran, Doc Voss, whose "folks were farmers of German descent, Mennonite pacifists who ran a few head of Brahman outside of Deaf Smith, Texas."[23] Continuing on in the opening page, Burke describes him saying, "When Doc got his draft notice his senior year in high school, a lot of us thought he might apply for exemption as a conscientious objector. Instead, Doc enlisted in the Navy and became a hospital corpsman attached to the Marines."[24] This complex character is a Mennonite farm boy with high ideals who went to Vietnam as a

23. Burke, *Bitterroot*, 9.
24. Ibid.

PART I—HOW MENNONITES HAVE BEEN PORTRAYED

healer and became a killer, a recovering intravenous addict who publishes poems, a man whose soft voice belies his potential for violence. Burke portrays Mennonites as interesting characters that epitomize an innocent, though naïve, idealism.

Continuing with the opening page of *Bitterroot*, Burke describes Doc coming home from the war and burning his Marine-issue tropical uniform. He then notes, "He joined a fundamentalist church, one even more radical in its views than his family's traditional [Mennonite] faith."[25] From this description, and Burke's earlier characterization of Annie's eccentric wheat farmer pacifist ancestors, he portrays Mennonites as pacifists and radicals, though not as radical as Texas fundamentalists. Since Mennonites sprang from the Radical Reformation, using the term "radical" to describe them isn't surprising, although, as mentioned earlier, the word "radical" in its original context had a different meaning. It referred to "cutting to the root" or restoring Christian faith to the purity of the Early Church model.

At least one other Mennonite character emerges from Burke's writing. It appears in a collection of short stories called *Jesus Out to Sea* (2007) in a brutal story titled "The Village," which is told from the perspective of an American CIA operative who is covertly killing Nicaraguan village resistance fighters and those sympathetic to them. A Mennonite woman is introduced by the narrator. In the end the CIA operative murders her. "I didn't have no grief with the Mennonite broad. I saw her in the city once. I tipped my hat to her. I admired her. She was a homely little Dutch wisp of a thing working in a s—hole most people wouldn't take time to spit on."[26]

As with all of Burke's writings, there is a hint of redemption. Throughout this brief four page tale, the protagonist spouts a litany of excuses for shedding innocent blood, including that of a village priest. However, at the very end, while engaged in the brutal act of killing this troublesome unnamed Mennonite woman, he appears to acknowledge wrongdoing by repeating her final words, "You must change your way."[27]

Many of Burke's characters are unusual people, and most are conflicted. Therefore it is not surprising to see him using characters from a separatist religious group, Mennonites. Most of those who know Mennonites consider them to be good and gentle people though perhaps eccentric and naive. Burke seems to take a similar tack. Annie is portrayed

25. Ibid.
26. Burke, *Jesus out to Sea*, 26.
27. Ibid., 29.

as a beautiful innocent, Doc is a rough, burned-out idealist, and the final unnamed Mennonite character in *The Village* bears a resemblance to the martyrs so revered in the Anabaptist tradition. Burke seems to use Mennonite pacifism to heighten and contrast the violent nature of his protagonists. However logical, it is still surprising to see prominent Mennonite characters in Burke's award winning and popular fiction.

Magazines

Occasionally, Mennonite theology, the denomination, or an individual in the Mennonite church is mentioned in magazines. What follows is a sample of several occurrences from both ecumenical and secular, non-Mennonite publications.

Life, May 6, 1946, Lauds COs' Efforts at Mental Hospital Reform

During World War II, many Mennonite men refused to fight and opted instead to go into Civilian Public Service (CPS) as conscientious objectors (COs). Mennonites represented the largest religious group among COs during World War II. They served in many capacities, but perhaps the role for which they are most noted was as orderlies in mental health hospitals. Mennonite Central Committee (MCC) sponsored CPS units at twenty-three state mental hospitals during the war. In the course of their service during these years, the COs became aware of the atrocities perpetrated on institutionalized mental patients. Being men of extreme conscience, they refused to accept the way things were and began to advocate reform.

Although others had exposed the injustices happening in various psychiatric hospitals before, it took the many reports coming from COs in the 1940s to focus public attention on the plight of the mentally ill. This exposure led to significant change in the way Americans care for mental patients.[28]

Arguably the most influential expose was written by Albert Q. Maisel and published in *Life* magazine on May 6, 1946 when *Life* was a very popular national weekly photo journal. The title of the article was, "Bedlam, 1946. Most U.S. Mental Hospitals are a Shame and a Disgrace." It was sixteen pages long with fifteen illustrations and highlighted two mental hospitals, one

---

28. Taylor, *Acts of Conscience*, 1.

in Ohio and one in Pennsylvania. Many Mennonite COs were working in each of these institutions. As a direct result of the *Life* article the heads of both of these hospitals were forced to resign. In turn, Pennsylvania allocated eighty million dollars for a new mental health hospital. That same year, 1946, Congress passed the National Mental Health Act. In 1947 MCC established Mennonite Mental Health Services to operate small mental health hospitals. Then, between 1947 and 1956, Mennonites began three facilities for persons with mental illness one each in California, Kansas, and Maryland.[29]

Many consider this to be one of the finest hours of the Mennonite church. Members of the general public stood up and took notice of these humble men, serving in squalor and advocating for reform. While their neighbors were fighting to defeat Hitler's Germany overseas using the force of arms, these pacifist servants were fighting another battle at home, against equally difficult odds, using only the force of moral persuasion. Both groups were successful, but one achieved unprecedented reforms at much less cost in terms of lives and treasure lost.

La Vie Honors Neal Blough

The October 22, 2009 issue of *La Vie*, a weekly French Catholic magazine, commemorated the five-hundredth anniversary of John Calvin's birth by recognizing the one hundred most influential Protestants in France. Mennonite worker Neal Blough made the list. For the previous thirty-four years he has worked at the Paris Mennonite Center under Mennonite Mission Network. According to Blough, "Mennonites [in France] have a history as long as that of the Reformed [Church] and Lutherans, which is not the case for other Free Church Protestant traditions." The magazine article said Mennonites represent "a small but essential minority."[30] These are words of high praise, especially coming, as they do, from Catholics who centuries ago persecuted and killed Mennonites.

Additional words of praise came from an ecumenical Protestant magazine.

---

29. Ibid., 2.

30. Mennonite Mission Network, "Protestant Props - French Magazine Honors Mennonite."

PRINT MEDIA

The Christian Century Praises MC USA's Corinthian Plan

In the twentieth century, Mennonite Church USA (MC USA) officials estimated between fifty and one hundred Mennonite pastors had no medical insurance. This reality prompted denominational leaders to embark on an effort to provide medical insurance for all pastors, regardless of ability to pay, through a self-funded plan with a strong mutual aid component call The Corinthian Plan (TCP). TCP had its official start in a delegate action taken at Assembly in Atlanta in 2003 which authorized the Health Access Initiative. Additional actions by delegates at the denomination's biennium gatherings in Charlotte in 2005 and San Jose in 2007 paved the way for TCP. After many years of research, study, organizing and hard work, MC USA successfully established a denomination wide health insurance program for all of its pastors, regardless of their congregations' ability to pay. These actions came years ahead of the Affordable Care Act, which became law in December, 2009.

This initiative did not escape notice outside the denomination. Amy Frykholm, writing for *The Christian Century*, a progressive, ecumenical magazine based in Chicago, wrote:

> Whatever the outcome of the Corinthian proposal, every Mennonite [Church] USA congregation in the country will have grappled with the problem of health insurance in a concrete way. Each will have considered the tension between self-interest and care for neighbor. Each will have decided on what sacrifices it is willing to accept for the greater good. The tenor of the Mennonites' conversation and the honesty with which they have faced the dilemma is a model for the nation. If nothing else, we need more Mennonites to show up at town hall meetings.[31]

A subsequent issue of *The Christian Century* on November 17, 2009 noted, "With a flood of enrollments and inquiries in late September, a mutual aid health-care project in the Mennonite Church USA is expected to start on January 1 . . . . More than 450 congregations expected to lend assistance to pastors of smaller congregations will generate more than $500,000 for the project's Fair Balance Fund . . . the assistance will go to more than 50 congregations and their pastors [who previously had no medical insurance]."[32]

---

31. Frykholm, "Health-Care Option," 31.
32. Frykholm, "Mennonite Health-Care Plan," 16.

The Corinthian Plan was also mentioned in a Religion News Service article which appeared in an online edition of *The Washington Post*. The article described the religious exemption clause in Obamacare which allows certain religious groups, formed before 1950, to opt out of the health insurance requirement. According to Kathleen O'brien, this provision was written into the law with the Amish and certain Mennonite groups in mind, particularly those which use mutual aid to cover their health care expenses. O'brien describes it as a "precursor of Obamacare." She interviewed Duncan Smith, interim director of the Corinthian Plan who said, "It flows from the spiritual desire to avoid becoming 'too worldly,' or 'becoming too much of your culture.... It isn't so much about being anti-government, as it is a sense of 'We should take care of ourselves.'"[33]

The Corinthian Plan is a model for practicing mutual aid in the twenty first century which exemplifies the best of Mennonite theology and practice. Other Christian leaders and denominations have taken notice.

The American Spectator, Is there a Mennonite Takeover Afoot?

Mark Tooley, who writes a regular column in *The American Spectator*, a politically conservative secular monthly magazine, perceives the Mennonites are taking over. Begun in 1967 by editor R. Emmett Tyrell Jr., and reporting on news and politics, *The American Spectator* is published by the non-profit American Spectator Foundation and has a circulation of about fifty thousand. In the October, 2010 issue a column by Mark Tooley appeared under the heading "The Nation's Pulse." In the article he implies neo-Anabaptists, of whom he names Stanley Hauerwas, Greg Boyd, Shane Claiborne, and Jim Wallis, are taking over the "Evangelical Left" which is now echoing an Anabaptist message of pacifism.

Tooley, who leads the Institute on Religion and Democracy in Washington, D.C. and wrote *Taking Back the United Methodist Church*, may be worried an Anabaptist understanding of the separation of Church and State might challenge the State's practice of power. Tooley noted with concern that the Swiss-based Lutheran World Federation apologized to the Mennonites for persecuting pacifist Anabaptists four hundred years ago. He bemoaned "how mainstream liberal Protestants and Evanglicals now share essential Anabaptist pacifist and pseudo-separatist beliefs."[34] He claimed

33. O'brien, "Obamacare Religious Exemption Hard."
34. Tooley, "Mennonite Takeover?."

that while traditional Mennonites will not serve in the military or serve in public office they do affirm the State's right to go to war, whereas the "new neo-Anabaptist movement is more aggressive, demanding that all Christians, and society, including the state, bend to pacifism."[35] In the title to his column, Tooley wonders whether Mennonites are poised to take over the Evangelical Left. He noted with concern, "Neo-Anabaptist rhetoric is especially pervasive at many evangelical schools, suburban mega churches, intellectual and hipster circles. Its themes permit a naughty sense of rebellion without having to stray too far from Christian orthodoxy."[36]

Tooley's characterization of Mennonites as "hip" is intriguing. Movie critic and self-proclaimed Christian hipster Brett McCraken, in his book *Hipster Christianity*, explores the term "hipster." He claims, "The only real requirement to being a hipster is a commitment to total freedom from labels, norms, and imposed constraints of any kind. And this attitude must be very public, which is why hipsters are fairly easy to spot."[37] He traces the origins of the term "hip" through its heyday in the 1960s when being countercultural became hip. In that sense, perhaps Mennonites, who have always resisted popular culture, are hip. In his attempt to pinpoint the amorphous group known as hipsters, McCraken says they are encouraged by the writings of Tony Campolo, Jim Wallis, Ron Sider, Shane Caliborne, and N.T. Wright. Stuart Murray labeled many of these same authors as neo-Anabaptists.[38] McCraken says hipster Christians are enamored with being "missional," which asserts the church exists for the world, not for its members. Another definition of missional states, "The focus shifts from a 'come in and be blessed!' view of church to a 'go out and serve' perspective."[39] One of the top priorities of the Mennonite Church USA is to be missional, and his description of service oriented small churches fits the MC USA profile. McCraken pokes fun at what he calls the "senior switch" in which a freshman arrives on campus as a staunch Republican and leaves as a Democrat after reading neo-Anabaptist Greg Boyd's *Myth of a Christian Nation* and books by other authors, such as Mennonite theologian John Howard Yoder. Perhaps Tooley is on to something when he calls Mennonites hip, at least in the sense McCraken defines the term.

35. Ibid.
36. Ibid.
37. McCraken, *Hipster Christianity*.
38. Murray, *The Naked Anabaptist*, 166-67.
39. McCraken, *Hipster Christianity*, 152.

PART I—HOW MENNONITES HAVE BEEN PORTRAYED

Runner's World, April, 2012, Running with the Amish, by Bart Yasso

Later this book delves into the exploits of two famous Mennonite athletes, but there had never been a famous Amish athlete, at least not until Bart Yasso, a well-known marathoner and frequent columnist for *Runner's World* discovered a group of Amish and Mennonite runners in Lancaster County, Pennsylvania. Writing in the April, 2012 issue of *Runner's World*, Yasso explains, "Practically in my back yard, I had discovered a semi-secret society of, if not running savants, at least raw running talent. The Mennonites were good runners, but the Amish—with their even harder lives, and even stricter rules—were clearly a cut above. I felt a little like Christopher (Born to Run) McDougall tracking down the legendary Tarahumara Indian runners in Mexico's Copper Canyon. I wondered, with a little more training, just how good could these guys be?"[40]

In this five-thousand word article, Yasso describes his Anabaptist running mates, explains their belief in the importance of adult baptism, and helps his readers distinguish between the Amish and Mennonites. He writes, "Both groups hold fast to the principles of their forebearers—hard work, humility, modesty, community togetherness verging on clannishness, self-reliance, and a skeptical view of modernity—but whereas the Old Order Amish drive buggies and wear suspenders, Mennonites (at least most of them) drive and wear just about whatever they want. To make a crude and overly simplistic analogy, Old Order Amish are like Ultra-Orthodox Jews, and Mennonites are a more acculturated, reformed branch."[41]

Although he never gives the names of the Amish runners, Yasso mentions three Mennonite college alumni Jim Smucker, Todd Weaver, and Terry Yoder. He describes the group's nighttime runs over back lanes and unpaved roads, under the light of the moon. At one point he describes speaking to a group of Amish and Old Order Mennonites where the women are wearing coverings. He goes on to explain many of the intricacies of Amish ways, sometimes contrasting them with Mennonite practices, and highlighting the forgiveness extended after the tragic Nickel Mines schoolhouse shooting.

Runner's World has a worldwide circulation of more than one million. As the name of the article implies, Yasso's readers learn more about the

---

40. Yasso, "Running with the Amish," 96.
41. Ibid., 99.

Amish than about Mennonites, but their education regarding Anabaptists comes from a very unlikely source.

The Christian Century, March 5, 2014, Denver Mennonites Move Toward Lesbian Ordination

In the Episcopalian Church, a liberal wing of mainline Protestantism, ordaining a homosexual bishop is old news. However, the fact that the Mennonites were moving toward the ordination of a woman in a same-sex covenanted relationship was highlighted on the third page of *The Christian Century*'s news section as a worthy bit of information. The brief article reported First Mennonite Church, Denver licensed Theda Good, who serves as their pastor of nurture and fellowship, for ministry. Licensing is the first step toward full ordination in Mennonite Church USA (MC USA). The article alludes to the turmoil this has caused in other parts of MC USA, described in the article as the largest Mennonite body in the U.S. Keith Harder, moderator of the conservative Lancaster Mennonite Conference is quoted as saying, "Now the struggle is how we live together?" Pastors throughout MC USA worry that the denomination is no longer being faithful to scripture.[42]

Theda Good's licensing by Mountain States Mennonite Conference, one of MC USA's regional conferences, has challenged the denomination and shaken things up not only in Lancaster, but in Ohio, and Virginia. It remains to be seen if this twelve year old denomination, comprised of twenty-one area conferences and five agencies, can stay together.

This article, objectively reported with quotes from those supporting and questioning the action, highlights the struggles of a small and relatively conservative religious group wrestling with an issue which many parts of the broader Christian church resolved, or split over, more than a decade ago. It specifically mentions the merger of the Mennonite Church and the General Conference Mennonite Church in 2002 to form MC USA, while reiterating the churches traditional understanding of marriage.

Perhaps, *The Christian Century* reports this bit of news, which it picked up from the Religious News Service (RNS), because one of the magazine's senior editors, Richard A. Kauffman, is himself part of Mennonite Church USA which has several congregations in the Chicago area.

42. Evans, "Denver Mennonites Move," 16.

PART I—HOW MENNONITES HAVE BEEN PORTRAYED

Newspapers

The Rockingham Register, 1861

In his text *Shenandoah Religion*, Bridgewater College professor Stephen L. Longenecker, reflecting on faith in the Shenandoah Valley of Virginia, writes:

> In January 1861, the *Rockingham Register* praised local German neighbors for 'orderly and honest lives,' and one month later, as Virginians prepared to vote for a succession convention, its editor defended German neighbors from accusations that they were not 'sound on slavery.' The commentator reported that 'we have mingled' with Germans for years and asserted that 'a people more loyal to the Constitution and the laws, cannot be found anywhere.' Dunkers and Mennonites, he noted, were 'a worthy and loyal community' that abstained from slaveholding despite their prosperity, but also withheld criticism of slaveholders and did not interfere with slavery, code words implying they did not assist runaways. Antebellum Anabaptists had enjoyed the respect of the mainstream despite their avoidance of it.[43]

It appears from this editor's comments that one's perception of Mennonites largely relates to whether one agrees with them or not. Those who supported the South and the institution of slavery were quick to denounce Mennonite pacifists who refused to fight for the Confederacy. Mennonites have experienced this response for centuries.

The Floyd Landis Tour de France victory and subsequent cheating scandal

There have been thousands of newspaper articles in the past few years about Floyd Landis, the 2006 winner of the prestigious Tour de France bicycle race, who was stripped of his title because of cheating by taking performance enhancing drugs. An earlier discussion in this text highlighted the fact that Landis, although raised in a Mennonite home, is not himself a Mennonite. However, many of these articles, including several national Associated Press pieces, note his Mennonite heritage. One, which appeared in *The Washington Post* before the 2006 Tour de France began, described his childhood bike riding as an escape from his strict religious upbringing.

43. Longenecker, *Shenandoah Religion*, 176-77.

Another Associated Press article, which ran in Harrisonburg, Virginia's *Daily News-Record*, noted Floyd's Mennonite heritage and commented he was the most willful of Paul and Arlene Landis' six children raised in Lancaster, Pennsylvania. In an interview with the Associated Press, referring to his parents' view of his sport, Landis noted, "They weren't really all that thrilled about it. Their life was based around working . . . always hard work . . . and the rest of the time spent in church."[44] Landis' mother Arlene and sister Charity wear white prayer coverings traditionally worn by Mennonite women. In the Associated Press article, Landis went on to recall how he had worn sweat clothes rather than tight fitting racing gear so as not to offend the conservative sense of modesty in the community where he lived and trained until the age of twenty, when he moved to California. On the Sunday of Landis' amazing and unlikely victory, the *Daily News-Record* quoted from an Associated Press article saying, "Back at the Martindale Mennonite Church that Landis' family still attends, the Rev. David Sensenig explained 'Celebrating individual accomplishments is frowned upon in the faith.'"[45] The article highlights Mennonites' willingness to be counter-cultural, stating Landis "carried over a piece of the past that would forge a champion—the willingness to go it alone."[46]

Although Floyd Landis was disgraced for having cheated and lied about his use of performance enhancing drugs, many may still draw inspiration from his parents' humble Mennonite faith.

The Bluffton College baseball team tragedy

Many major news stories appeared after the March 2, 2007 tragedy in which five members of the Bluffton University men's baseball team were killed when their bus mistakenly exited I-75 near Atlanta, Georgia on an HOV lane and plummeted nineteen feet off the elevated overpass onto the highway below. Although Bluffton University was founded in 1899 as Central Mennonite College and is affiliated with Mennonite Church USA, only 20 percent of its students are Mennonite. Thus, most of the persons involved in this terrible tragedy were not Mennonite. The articles tell the broader public little about Mennonites.

---

44. Associated Press, "Landis Kept 'Believing,'" 3.
45. Ibid.
46. Ibid., 23.

PART I—HOW MENNONITES HAVE BEEN PORTRAYED

The Washington Post Comic Page,
August 20, 2010 and June 29, 2013

Beginning in June, 2010 Pulitzer Prizewinning writer Gene Weingarten began collaborating with his son Dan to produce a daily comic strip for the pages of *The Washington Post* called *Barney & Clyde*. Although Weingarten, whose roots are in the Jewish tradition, is a self-professed atheist, he often writes about faith, usually in a humorous way. On Friday August 20, 2010, just two months after the start of this original comic strip, he published a cartoon which gave a surprisingly astute summary of the Mennonite faith.

Barney & Clyde ©2010 Weingartens & Clark, Dist. by *The Washington Post* Writers Group Reprinted with permission

According to the cartoon, Mennonites "worship Jesus and practice pacifism." This statement accurately describes a Jesus centered people who not only preach, but practice pacifism. He contrasts these characteristics with the young girl's newly-invented religion which aspires to worship money and practice greed. The accurate implication drawn from this comic strip is Mennonites do not worship money but rather are generous. Granted Weingarten chose Mennonites because he needed a word play on the made up word "Mammonite." Nonetheless he chose a religious tradition which is diametrically opposed to "unconscionable greed." The astute reader will also hear an unspoken reference to Jesus' words, as recorded in Matthew 6:24 in the King James Version, "Ye cannot serve God and mammon." Those familiar with Mennonites will recognize this reference as part of Jesus' Sermon on the Mount which is central to Mennonite faith and practice. Weingarten goes on to poke fun at Catholics, from whom the early Anabaptists and other reformers split over many issues including the sale of indulgences.[47]

A *Shoe* comic strip, written by Gary Bookins and Susie MacNelly, appeared in the pages of *The Washington Post* on June 29, 2013 which also mentions Mennonites. *Shoe* characters are birds that inhabit a diverse "Treetop" community. The strip revolves around P. Martin "Shoe" Shoemaker, editor of the Treetops Tattler-Tribune. Another character, Roz, is the waitress at Roz's Roost, a local diner where many of the strip's characters meet. In this particular strip, Shoe is sitting at the diner's counter working at his laptop computer when he tells Roz about his new novel which concerns a "strict Mennonite sect."[48] He is of course, referring to the Amish, most commonly pronounced Ah-mish but, which some pronounce A-mish. The strip's punch line is that the novel is titled A-mish and Andy, a parody of the popular radio and T.V. show Amos and Andy, which aired in the U.S. from the 1920s through the 1950s. From this brief, two frame comic, readers learn the Amish are a sub-set of Mennonites who are more strict in their religious practice. Again, uncharacteristically, Mennonites are the subject of a comic strip.

The Philadelphia Inquirer, Glen D. Lapp's Murder

Another major news story involved the death of Glen D. Lapp, a Mennonite Central Committee volunteer and medical aid worker serving in Afghanistan. He was one of ten persons allegedly kidnapped and killed by Taliban fighters on August 5, 2010. Lapp's picture appeared on the front page of *The Philadelphia Inquirer* along with a story which spoke of a costly Mennonite commitment to serve, even in the midst of conflict:

47. G. and D. Weingarten, *Barney & Clyde*, C-6.
48. Bookins and MacNelly, King Features, June 29, 2013.

PART I—How Mennonites Have Been Portrayed

In 2008, the practicing Mennonite Christian had left... Manheim Township to volunteer through the Mennonite Central Committee, a nationwide group whose aid missions largely originate from an office in Akron, Lancaster County.... Lapp, one of two of the Mennonite organization's volunteers working in Afghanistan with partner agencies, had been part of an "eye camp" medical team that had been delivering treatments and tests for eye diseases... .The Mennonite group describes itself as a Christian relief, development, and peace-building organization active in 60 countries worldwide. Lapp was a member of the Community Mennonite Church of Lancaster. He had begun volunteering with the aid group in 2006, when from a desk in Akron he helped coordinate disaster relief to the U.S. Gulf Coast after Hurricanes Katrina and Rita, Walker said. Lapp was a graduate of Johns Hopkins University and Eastern Mennonite University.[49]

Lapp, who died at the age of forty, represents Mennonites at their best, willing to die while serving others, but unwilling to kill, even in self-defense.

The New York Times and *Fox News*—the Esh Family Tragedy

The deaths of eight members of the Esh family, Beachy Amish Mennonites from Burkesville, Kentucky, became a national news story. They died before dawn on March 26, 2010, while en route to a wedding, when the van they were driving collided head-on with a tractor-trailer after the tractor crossed the highway's median. A friend, soon to be in-law, and the truck driver were also killed, bringing the death toll to eleven.

The New York Times report opened with the words, "For years, John and Sadie Esh lifted up their Mennonite community in central Kentucky with mellifluous gospel singing. Their congregation of 20 families likewise embraced them when their son Johnny died and again when their house burned down."[50] It later noted the family had recorded four gospel albums and had children serving abroad as missionaries. Three thousand people attended the funeral at a converted warehouse in Marrowbone, Kentucky. Pictures of somber mourners, men in plain coats, and women wearing cape dresses and prayer coverings, plastered the pages of newspapers across America. The strength of their faith and the support of the eighteen-family community in which they lived nestled in the hills of south-central

49. Panaritis, "Lancaster County Man Glen D. Lapp," 1.
50. Robbins, "Crash Devastates," A11.

Kentucky, were a major part of the story carried by hundreds of newspapers. *Fox News* broadcast the story on nationwide television.

Like the unfathomable immediate forgiveness extended by the Amish after the Nickel Mines tragedy in 2006, the unshakable faith of this close-knit Marrowbone Christian Brotherhood baffled outsiders looking in. *Fox News* reported,

> Even as some fought back tears of grief, members of the close-knit Mennonite community said they were convinced the deaths were somehow God's will. 'It's a little like a tapestry,' said Kai Steinmann, 25. 'If you focus on one piece, it looks black and bad, but it has to be a part of a bigger whole.' . . . [Kentucky] Gov. Steve Beshear said the entire state grieved. The Kentucky Senate observed a moment of silence on Friday for the victims . . . . Senate President David Williams . . . said the victims were his constituents and that he knew the family well. 'These were wonderful people,' an emotional Williams said to a somber Senate chamber. 'They were hardworking. They were great citizens.'[51]

Melodie Davis, web content manager for Mennonite Church USA's outreach web site Third Way Café (TWC), noted the public visits TWC for information about Mennonites. She reported page views spiked at 2040 on March 26, compared to just 300 views on a typical day. Heavier traffic continued at the TWC site for several days following the Esh accident.[52]

The emotion and empathy displayed for this family resonated with the public and demonstrates the spiritual inspiration many draw from these quiet, humble disciples faithfully following their Lord. However, not all newspaper coverage of the Mennonites has been favorable.

The New York Times, The Misdeeds of Theologian John Howard Yoder

As is noted elsewhere, John Howard Yoder is without question the preeminent Mennonite theologian of the twentieth century. Yoder's *The Politics of Jesus*, published in 1972, reinterpreted Jesus' message and purpose. Yoder conclusively demonstrated Jesus was a pacifist and thus his followers should also reject the use of violence. His powerful arguments transformed many seminaries around the world.

51. Loller, "Mennonite Family."
52. M. Davis, "What's New."

PART I—How Mennonites Have Been Portrayed

Yet, John Howard Yoder, like all of us, was not perfect. In fact serious allegations of inappropriate contact came forth against Yoder which, in 1984, forced his resignation from a teaching post at what is now Anabaptist Mennonite Biblical Seminary in Elkhart, Indiana. More recently, in 2013, these allegations reemerged and resulted in Mennonite Church USA undertaking a process to aid in the healing of Yoder's female victims.

Mark Oppenheimer, writing for *The New York Times*, picked up this theme in a feature which appeared in print on October 12, 2013 in the New York edition titled: "A Theologian's Influence, And Stained Past, Live On." Oppenheimer calls Yoder a Mennonite Christian and "America's most influential pacifist theologian."[53] But notes, "[Theologians] should not be louts or jerks. By that standard, few have failed as egregiously as John Howard Yoder . . ."[54]

The article is critical of Yoder but generally positive about Mennonites. Oppenheimer makes it clear Yoder's indiscretions, which involved inappropriate contact with female acquaintances, did not involve sexual intercourse. Although the article accurately portrays Yoder as a brilliant but flawed individual, the Mennonite Church is not degraded or mocked. Rather, by calling Yoder a Mennonite Christian it is clear the author considers Mennonites to be a branch of the Christian faith, much as one might refer to an "Evangelical Christian." Likewise when Oppenheimer calls Yoder a "pacifist theologian" the reader would assume this is not uncommon for Mennonites, although it isn't clear that pacifism is normative Mennonite theology.

The denomination, Mennonite Church USA, is described as undertaking a fresh initiative seeking reconciliation, restoration, and healing for Yoder's female victims. Oppenheimer, referring to the denomination's earlier efforts at holding Yoder accountable, quotes theologian Stanley Hauerwas' memoir, *Hannah's Child*, calling the Mennonite Church's response to the allegations against Yoder a "testimony to a community that has learned over time that the work of peace is slow, painful, and hard."[55] These are all admirable qualities, especially in light of the sexual scandals and allegations of institutional coverup which have rocked the Roman Catholic Church in recent decades.

With the reference above, Oppenheimer links one of America's most prominent theologians, retired Duke Professor Stanley Hauerwas, with

---

53. Oppenheimer, "A Theologian's Influence."
54. Ibid.
55. Ibid.

Yoder and Mennonites. He also provides his readers with another glimpse into Mennonite theology when he says they consider actions more important than beliefs. Thus, he explains, Yoder's actions cast a shadow over his profound theological ideas. Yet, Mennonites, by engaging a denominational task force to reexamine these allegations, are not shying away from this controversy. The article also mentions Yoder's writing about the value of suffering for one's faith, an ideal which resonates strongly in Mennonite and Anabaptist circles through writings such as the *Martyr's Mirror*.

The Washington Post, November 24, 2013, Pennsylvania Dutch Shoofly Pie

The Mennonites and Amish of eastern Pennsylvania, commonly called Pennsylvania Dutch which is a misnomer derived from the name of their German home-Deutschland, have long been associated with the molasses confection known as shoofly pie. For those unfamiliar with this cultural delicacy, shoofly pie is essentially a breakfast cake made with lard, flour, brown sugar, and molasses. There are two types, wet or dry bottom. The dry bottom resembles a coffee cake, while the wet bottom has a gooey texture and is moist throughout.

In 2013, on the Sunday before Thanksgiving, an article appeared in *The Washington Post* food section titled, "Sweet memories, and the storied pie that stirred them."[56] In a nostalgic, preholiday piece the author reflects on her childhood memories of eating shoofly pie created in her Bethlehem, Pennsylvania grandmother's kitchen. The article includes a large photo of a delicious looking shoofly pie and references to the Amish and Mennonite German immigrants who arrived in Pennsylvania in the eighteenth century. The author refers to his grandmother's well-worn *Mennonite Community Cookbook* from which the shoofly pie recipe came. That particular cookbook was published by Herald Press, MennoMedia's trade book imprint and the publisher for both Mennonite Church USA and Mennonite Church Canada.

Washington Post readers do not learn much about Mennonites from this article except: many Mennonites from German heritage came to the U.S. and settled in Pennsylvania in the eighteenth century; they are closely affiliated with the Amish; together the Amish and Mennonites are sometimes called Pennsylvania Dutch; and they are good cooks, at least they have created a specialty pie which is still popular. The idea of the Pennsylvania

---

56. Martell, "Sweet Memories," R4.

PART I—How Mennonites Have Been Portrayed

Dutch also conjures images of plain people which hearkens back to a simpler time. This concept plays into the author's attempt to create nostalgia for the comfort foods our grandmothers made. It also works to create a longing for a special family holiday at Thanksgiving. Therefore, at least indirectly, the author's descriptions of shoofly pie, and the people who created it, beckons the reader to a deeper experience of family and community, the latter being a significant value among Mennonites, one often visible to, and longed for by outsiders. So, although the author's reference to pie making is a culturally specific trait not shared by all Mennonites, the significant place of family and community, to which the author alludes, is a more universal Mennonite value.

The Supreme Court Hears Conestoga Wood Specialties Case, Obamacare, 2014

Thousands of newspapers have written articles about two businesses challenging the requirement, set forth in the 2010 Affordable Care Act commonly known as Obamacare, to provide contraceptives and abortifacient drugs to their employees through all company provided healthcare plans. The two businesses objecting the most strenuously are Hobby Lobby, owned by David Green, a Baptist billionaire from Oklahoma, and Conestoga Wood Specialties, owned by the Hahn family, members of Weaverland Mennonite Conference, an Old Order group. Hobby Lobby is a chain of five hundred stores with more than thirteen thousand employees, while Conestoga Wood Specialties makes cabinets from its base in Lancaster County, Pennsylvania employing nine hundred and fifty people. Both of these companies object not to all contraceptives, but to those which destroy a fertilized egg, such as intrauterine devices (IUDs), and to all abortifacient drugs, sometimes called "morning-after pills" which they view as akin to abortion. They do so on religious grounds, arguing it is against their strongly held beliefs and claiming this mandate violates the 1993 Religious Freedom Restoration Act, which reaches back to the First Amendment of the U.S. Constitution which forbids Congress from making any laws which curtail freedom of religion. The cases, Kathleen Sebelius v. Hobby Lobby and Conestoga Wood v. Kathleen Sebelius, U.S. Supreme Court, No. 13-354, 13-356, which pit religious freedom rights against a woman's reproductive rights, have been consolidated to come before the Supreme Court together.[57]

57. Yates, "Silence Is Golden," A4.

Print Media

Obamacare has an exemption clause which allows certain religious groups, formed before 1950, to opt out of the health insurance requirement. According to Kathleen O'brien, writing for the Religion News Service, this provision was written into the law with the Amish and certain Mennonite groups in mind, particularly those which use mutual aid to cover their health care expenses. O'brien further explains, "Mennonites are not opposed to the concept of either health care or health insurance, In fact, the central governing body, the Mennonite Church USA, has been operating its Corinthian Plan since 2010. . . . In one way it was a precursor of Obamacare, in that it did not exclude people with pre-existing conditions."[58]

From these articles, and countless others like them, readers learn Mennonites are strongly opposed to abortion and in this regard hold a belief similar to the Evangelical Christian family which owns Hobby Lobby. They would not realize most Mennonites hold to a consistently prolife position which opposes not only abortion but infanticide, euthanasia, and capital punishment, a position much different from the majority of Evangelicals. They would also come away with the impression Mennonites are willing to stand up to the government for what they believe. This is generally true, in that Mennonites and Anabaptists have been willing to die for their beliefs, particularly their refusal to bear arms and kill others in combat. Traditionally, however, Mennonites have avoided lawsuits preferring rather to resolve differences outside of the courts. This case is an anomaly in that regard. The Hahns' costly legal battle is being funded by the Alliance Defending Freedom, formerly known as the Alliance Defense Fund, founded in 1994 by a group of conservative Christian leaders, including James Dobson, founder of Focus on the Family, and Bill Bright, founder of Campus Crusade for Christ (now known as Cru).[59]

The detail about this being an Old Order Weaverland group did not appear in the public media cited, but rather was a detail gleaned from a Mennonite publication. The general public often does not understand the basics of the Mennonite faith. They would be completely baffled by the many factions and subgroups within the Anabaptist movement.

Readers of the newspapers which picked up the Religion News Service article about the religious exemption, would learn about the Amish and Mennonite practice of mutual aid along with some details about MC USA's Corinthian Plan.

58. O'brien, "Obamacare Religious Exemption."
59. Cassidy, "Conestoga Wood."

CHAPTER 3

Visual Media

Drama

Voltaire's *Candide* features a virtuous Anabaptist, 1759

Voltaire has been called the most representative figure of the Age of Enlightenment. He seemed to admire Anabaptists. Like many scholars who lived and worked at that time, when the Church felt threatened by scientific discoveries being made distinct and apart from biblical revelation, Voltaire had little regard for the Church, either Catholic or Protestant.[1] Today, Voltaire is known as much for his literary work (novels, poems, and plays) as for his skill as a scientist, historian, philosopher, and political satirist. Many remember him as the author of a popular novella *Candide (or The Optimist)* which has been crafted into a comic operetta with music by Leonard Bernstein and lyrics by Stephen Sondheim.

As a boy, raised in an affluent family, Voltaire studied the Greek and Latin classics and developed an ambition to write, but his father insisted he study law. At the age of sixteen he left school and traveled to Holland where he may have encountered Anabaptists. By 1718 he was back in Paris where his play *Edipus* was performed with great success. Soon thereafter, Voltaire was imprisoned for eleven months because his satirical poem offended the Duke of Orleans. This experience turned Voltaire against the whims of arbitrary government. He was especially skillful at exposing

---

1. A. Kreider, *Tongue Screws*, 10.

institutional abuse through parody, allegory, and satirical wit. Such inflection permeates *Candide*.[2]

Candide, which first appeared in 1759, is considered to be Voltaire's greatest work, a masterpiece of ferocious satire and irony. In this brief novella, titled after the leading character, an optimistic but illegitimate young man is cast from the protection of his home and sets out to discover the meaning of life. Hitherto his teacher, Dr. Pangloss, had convinced Candide that he lived in "the best of all possible worlds" and everything that happened, happened for a reason. Dr. Pangloss convinced Candide it is best not to question why but to accept one's fate. As Candide travels he encounters many intriguing characters and endures tragedies too numerous to count. Nearly everyone he meets is a cheat and a scoundrel except one, Jacques, the Anabaptist. Jacques appears early in this novella which contains thirty brief chapters. He shows up in chapter three titled, "How Candide Escaped from the Bulgarians and What Became of Him." Here the reader meets "an honest Anabaptist named Jacques" who comes to Candide's aid when Candide is being treated badly because he does "not believe the Pope is the Anti-Christ." Voltaire describes the scene thus, "Jacques saw the cruel and ignominious treatment of one of his brothers, a fearless two-legged creature with a soul; he took him home, cleaned him up, gave him bread . . . [and money] and even offered . . . him . . . work."[3]

In chapter four Candide throws "himself at the feet of his charitable Anabaptist, Jacques" who is moved to compassion by Candide's request and pays for Dr. Pangloss's medical treatment when no one else can or will help. Jacques even hires the now disfigured Pangloss to work for him as a bookkeeper. Yet he argues against the Dr.'s fatalism, with regard to war and man's evil state, saying, "Men must have corrupted the nature a little, for they were not born wolves, and have become wolves. God did not give them twenty-four–pounder cannons or bayonets, and they have made bayonets and cannons to destroy each other."[4]

Jacques makes one more appearance in chapter 5, when, while traveling aboard a ship with Candide and Dr. Pangloss, they encounter a violent storm. In an encounter reminiscent of Anabaptist martyr Dirk Willems' rescue of his persecutor who had fallen through the ice, Jacques tries to help the ship's crew but is deliberately and violently struck by a sailor.

2. Voltaire and Block, *Candide*, x.
3. Ibid., 115.
4. Ibid., 118.

However, the force of the blow causes the sailor to fall overboard. With the sailor clinging to part of a broken mast, Jacques rescues him, only to fall overboard himself while "in full view of the sailor, who allowed him to drown without condescending even to look at him."[5] Voltaire ironically points out "no good deed should go unpunished."

Voltaire nearly always refers to Jacques as an "Anabaptist." He is twice described as "honest," once as "charitable," and finally as "virtuous." No one else in the story receives such praise. Surely Voltaire respected the Anabaptists, perhaps because they shared his disdain for the corrupt institutional church or maybe because they lived out their faith in acts of love and charity, like the character Jacques. Voltaire also gives his readers a glimpse of Anabaptist theology when he describes Jacques as a man who rejected infant baptism and refused to participate in war.

As noted earlier, Voltaire's Candide has been transformed into a contemporary operetta. Unfortunately, that version completely omits this virtuous Anabaptist Jacques. Thus the general public, which is unlikely to read *Candide*, but might see it performed in its theatrical version, will remain unaware of Voltaire's virtuous Anabaptist or the religious group he represents.

Oscar Wilde's *The Importance of Being Earnest* Mentions Anabaptists, 1895

Oscar Wilde has been called "the most quoted playwright after [William] Shakespeare."[6] Indeed, *Barnes & Noble Book of Quotations*, makes reference to Oscar Wilde thirty-nine times, compared to thirty-eight quotes by Shakespeare, and forty-nine by George Bernard Shaw.[7] Wilde's brief and controversial life encompassed the latter half of the nineteenth century as the British Victorian Era waned. Yet, his acerbic observations about the quest for status, class pretentions, and hypocrisy are just as relevant today.

What is perhaps Wilde's most significant work, *The Importance of Being Earnest*, makes reference to the Anabaptist practice of adult baptism, and more specifically rebaptism of those christened as infants. Wilde published the play in 1898 but it was first performed in 1895. Set in England it features nine characters in three acts. The principal men, Algernon Moncrieff and John (Jack) Worthington, are friends pursuing life and love. They

---

5. Ibid., 118.
6. Belford, *Oscar Wilde*, inside jacket cover.
7. Fitzhenry, *Barnes & Noble Book of Quotations*, 409–11.

are both carefree with the truth, taking on aliases, and inventing people and places which allow them to escape from their responsibilities. These two friends use the same pseudonym, Ernest, whenever they are carousing under an assumed identity. Jack takes on the identity of his fictitious younger brother Ernest when he is in the city but retains his given name, Jack short for John, when he is in the country. Algernon invents a fictitious invalid friend Bunbury, whom he uses as an excuse to get away into the country. While Jack is visiting Algernon under the assumed name Ernest, he falls in love with a young woman, Gwendolyn. She reciprocates his love with particular admiration for his name—Ernest. She feels no other name is suitable for her future husband.

Meanwhile, Algernon assumes the identity of Jack's alter ego younger brother Ernest while visiting Jack's country estate. There Algernon falls in love with Cecily Cardew, the granddaughter of Thomas Cardew, Jack's adopted father, who appointed Jack as her guardian. Cecily reciprocates Algernon's affections. She too is particularly enamored with his name Ernest. Thus, each man has fallen in love with a woman who knows him by the assumed name Ernest. Each woman insists they could never marry anyone not named Ernest. To escape this dilemma they each decide to perpetuate the deception and make it permanent by getting rebaptized or christened, and legally taking on the name Ernest. Thus the Reverend Doctor Canon Chasuble, Jack's Anglican priest, enters Act Three with the intent to rebaptize both Algernon and Jack. The complete dialogue about their desired rebaptism follows. An additional character, Lady Bracknell, who is Algernon's outspoken aunt and Gwendolyn's mother, expresses her displeasure at this practice.

> Chasuble – Everything is quite ready for the christenings.
>
> Lady Bracknell – The christenings, sir! Is not that somewhat premature?
>
> Chasuble – [Looking rather puzzled, and pointing to Jack and Algernon.] Both these gentlemen have expressed a desire for immediate baptism.
>
> Lady Bracknell – At their age? The idea is grotesque and irreligious! Algernon, I forbid you to be baptized. I will not hear of such excesses. Lord Bracknell would be highly displeased if he learned that that was the way in which you wasted your time and money.

> Chasuble – Am I to understand then that there are to be no christenings this afternoon?
>
> Jack – I don't think that, as things are now, it would be of much practical value to either of us, Dr. Chasuble.
>
> Chasuble – I am grieved to hear such sentiments from you, Mr. Worthington. They savour of the heretical views of the Anabaptists, views that I have completely refuted in four of my unpublished sermons. However, as your present mood seems to be particularly secular, I will return to the church at once . . .[8]

Lady Bracknell expresses her displeasure at the very idea of an adult being rebaptized. She finds it "grotesque and irreligious." For her, only infants should be baptized and to be rebaptized is irreligious in that it negates or doubts the efficacy of infant baptism, thus casting doubt on the power of the Church and its rites. Chasuble, the priest, on the other hand was willing to baptize both of these adult men but finds their change of heart to be unconscionable. He apparently objects to Jack's comment "it would [not] be of much practical value . . . " supposing his attitude to be secular. He compares Jack's changed opinion with regard to baptism to those of the "heretical Anabaptists."

Wilde's forte is wit and satire. Since these words condemning Anabaptists are spoken by the hypocritical Lady Bracknell and Rev. Dr. Chasuble, who represent British society and the established church respectively, he himself may have held a much more favorable opinion of Anabaptists. This supposition seems accurate since Wilde's homosexual lifestyle came under sharp criticism from both the established church and the law. Wilde was charged with gross indecency for having written *Dorian Gray* and was imprisoned for two years. Perhaps he identified with the Anabaptists, who were also persecuted and imprisoned.[9]

There have been several film adaptations of Wilde's *The Importance of Being Earnest*. One of the most popular was the 2002 Miramax Films motion picture starring three Academy Award winners in Judi Dench as Lady Bracknell, Colin Firth as Jack, and Reese Witherspoon as Cecily. Oliver Parker, who wrote the screenplay and directs, remains faithful to Wilde's 1898 script while adding elements cut in preparation for the original stage production.[10]

---

8. Wilde, *The Importance of Being Earnest*, 140-41.
9. Belford, *Oscar Wilde*, 172.
10. Wikipedia, "The Importance of Being Earnest," online, 7.1.

Disappointingly, however, all references to Anabaptism, which appeared in the 1898 text, were expunged from the film's screenplay, perhaps because a twenty-first century moviegoing audience would not be familiar with the term Anabaptist. In contrast, an Englishman seeing the original play in 1895 would have understood Wilde's reference to Anabaptism. Wilde's contemporaries would most likely have belonged to the Anglican Church, the official church of England, and therefore would have been well acquainted with the Book of Common Prayer. As has already been noted, article thirty-eight of the Thirty-Nine Articles of Religion contained in this important Anglican book disparages Anabaptists for their practice of holding all things in common.

Wilde's timeless observations, wit, and wisdom continue to enchant and entertain audiences today and in a small way, they expose a broad audience to the central Anabaptist practice of adult baptism. Unfortunately, only those who read the original play, or see it performed in its entirety, get a glimpse of Anabaptism. All this goes to prove the importance of being earnest in citing primary sources.

Art

The Vatican owns troves of priceless art, much of it commissioned by the Catholic Church for use in worship. The Sistine Chapel is one of the best known examples of Catholic religious art. Commissioned by Pope Julius II, Michelangelo painted twelve thousand square feet of the chapel ceiling between 1508 and 1512.

In contrast, Mennonites, arising from the Radical Reformation, rejected icons, stained glass, and devotional art, which are typically displayed in Catholic churches and cathedrals. Until very recently, Mennonite places of worship were simple and unadorned. Many remain so.

Swiss-German Mennonites were driven from their homeland by persecution and many settled in the Netherlands. There, a Mennonite pastor and his wife were the subject of a painting by the great Dutch master Rembrandt. Some sources, including the one quote below, argue the renowned painter was a Mennonite.

Part I—How Mennonites Have Been Portrayed

Rembrandt Harmensz van Rijn (1606-1669), The Mennonite Minister Cornelis Claesz Anslo in Conversation with his Wife, Aeltje Gerrhsdr Schouten, 1641. Oil on canvas, 173.7 X 207.6 cm[11]

Although there is no documentary evidence, there is reason to connect Rembrandt's tender conception of Christ during the first years of his mature period with the teachings of the Mennonite sect. According to Baldinucci, one of the artist's seventeenth-century biographers, Rembrandt was a Mennonite, and we have seen that he was in contact with Cornelis Anslo, a famous Mennonite preacher of Amsterdam.

In 1641 Rembrandt made an etching of Anslo, and in the same year he made the impressive double portrait of the preacher and his wife. In Rembrandt's day, the Mennonite sect was a liberal one which discarded the sacerdotal idea, accepted no authority outside the Bible, limited baptism to believers, and held to freedom of conscience. They emphasized precepts which support the sanctity of human life and man's word, and, following the Sermon on the Mount, they opposed war, military service, slavery, and such common practices as

11. Rembrandt, "The Mennonite Preacher." Used with permission.

insurance and interest on loans. Compared with the severe Calvinists, the Mennonites represented a milder form of Christianity in which, according to the literal sense of the Sermon on the Mount, the leading principle was 'Love thy neighbour'.[12]

Thus, almost four centuries since Rembrandt painted Anslo, his art hints at Mennonite ideals. Yet, those precepts are hidden to all but serious students and those with inquisitive minds who must dig deeper to learn about Mennonite faith. Several other artistic expressions, including films, also capture the spirit of Mennonite discipleship.

Film

Witness (1985) – A Passing Reference to Mennonites

The 1985 blockbuster film *Witness* contains a passing reference to Mennonites. When Samuel (Lukas Haas), the young son of an Amish widow, witnesses a brutal murder in a Philadelphia train station, homicide detective John Book (Harrison Ford) must flee with the boy back to Lancaster County for his protection. There Book learns about the Amish and falls in love with the widow Rachel (Kelly McGillis). When the murderers track them down, Book must confront them in order to save the boy and his mother. When detective Book arrives at the Amish farm, he gives up his handgun to Rachel. Her father-in-law, Eli Lapp, uses it as an object lesson to teach young Samuel that handguns are meant to kill humans and the Amish do not believe in killing. Finally, in an act of peaceful resistance, the mayhem of the climactic shootout is stopped by the collective nonviolent action of the Amish community working in solidarity with John Book against the last remaining murderer.

Directed by Australian Peter Weir, the film achieved both critical and public acclaim. In 1985 *Witness* was not only a blockbuster, it was nominated for eight Academy Awards, including Best Actor for Harrison Ford. It won Best Editing and Best Original Screenplay. *Witness* is one of the few full-length feature films set among the Amish. The film portrays Amish culture without being condescending, but rather with the keen eye of a respectful tourist.

When John Book arrived among the Amish he had been shot and was in need of medical attention. Yet, because he was in hiding he refused

12. Web Gallery of Art.

hospital treatment and instead received the homeopathic poultice and herbal tea remedies practiced by his Amish hosts. When, after two days, he recovers from a life threatening infection, the first thing he does is ask Rachel where he can find a phone in order to contact and warn his police partner. At first she sighs, then smiles and says, "The Gunthers across the valley. They're Mennonites. They have cars and refrigerators." Wanting to remain anonymous Book replies, "No, I mean a public phone."[13] This passing comment reveals Mennonites live in close proximity to the Amish and have relationships with them.

The movie implies a level of trust between the Amish and Mennonites. It does not go so far as to state their shared faith and values. Rachel calls the Gunthers by name and knows both their faith and lifestyle. She does not think of them exclusively as "The English," a name the Amish give to most outsiders. The mention of Mennonites in *Witness* did not go unnoticed by the public. A Mennonite pastor, planting a church in an urban setting, commented a visitor came to his church after seeing *Witness*. She was attracted to the peaceful, idyllic portrayal in the film and began exploring Amish faith and culture. In the process, she learned about Mennonites and ultimately became a member of that Mennonite congregation.

Matewan (1987) – Mennonites Provide Inspiration

In *Matewan*, an unseen Mennonite conscientious objector provides inspiration for the central character in the film. *Matewan*, directed by independent American filmmaker John Sayles, creates a powerful fictitious depiction of the actual "Battle of Matewan." In that battle, seven detectives hired as muscle for the coal company are killed, along with two townspeople. It was one of the most violent events in "The Coal Wars" of 1920 to 1921. Joe Kenehan (Chris Cooper), an earnest union organizer, arrives in Matewan, West Virginia to help the townspeople improve their lives by standing up to the tyrannical Stone Mountain Coal Company. Matewan is a company town, owned and operated by the mining company which leases it back to its citizens, one shovel at a time. It is a tale of the working people uniting against oppressive capitalists; of whites and blacks; natives and immigrants, reluctantly embracing each other in a monumental struggle against a common enemy.

Religion plays an important part in the film. Joe, the union organizer, is a self-professed Communist, or "Red," with little regard for faith. Joe

13. *Witness*, Weir.

Visual Media

mentors a young boy, Danny Radnor (Will Oldham) affectionately known as 'the preacher," who explores the church's role in either helping the common folks or further oppressing them. Danny notes there are two churches in this remote Appalachian town, the Missionary Baptists and the Free Will Baptists, which he calls, "hard shell" and "soft shell Baptists." He is removed from the pulpit of the Missionary Baptist church when he gets too close to the truth while relating Jesus' parable of the workers in the vineyard, each paid a full day's wage, no matter when they began working. Later, drawing on his knowledge of the Bible and the company goons' lack thereof, he recounts the Bible story of Joseph and Potiphar's wife to tip off his fellow coal miners that one of them has been falsely accused.

Joe realizes he is up against impossible odds in his struggle to organize a union which would be able to stand up to the Stone Mountain Coal Company, yet he is adamant in advocating peaceful protests and negotiations. In contrast, the company, using hired guns from the Baldwin-Felts Detective Agency, is itching for a fight to justify retaliating and obliterating these union organizers. The townspeople are quick to oblige and take up arms against the company, despite Joe's admonitions against violence. We learn Joe was imprisoned for two years during World War I at Fort Leavenworth in Kansas as a conscientious objector. He came to his pacifist convictions not through religious faith, nor through a humanistic appreciation of Jesus as a teacher, but because of his Marxist understanding of class warfare. While in Leavenworth he meets several Mennonite men, also imprisoned as COs, who provide the inspiration he needs to continue his struggles peaceably. He tells another coal miner it was against these Mennonites' religion to fight, trim their beards, or even wear buttons on their prison issued uniforms. Joe describes their merciless treatment as they were hung by shackles from their wrists for eight hours a day with their toes barely touching the floor. Despite their swollen hands and bleeding fingers, they held to their convictions and kept their principles, even biting the re-sewn buttons off their uniforms when their hands were too mangled for the task. In awe Joe says, "But them fellas, they never lifted a gun in their life. I never found any braver in my book."[14]

Although the Mennonite men are never named in *Matewan*, they provide the inspiration for the film's central character's noble actions. The men being described were probably two Hutterite brothers, Joseph J. and Michael Hofer, who were held in Leavenworth in 1917. Both died in late

---

14. *Matewan*, Sayles.

1918 in military hospitals. The exact cause of their death remains unclear. They may have died of Spanish Flu or pneumonia but there is no doubt the brutal treatment they received while imprisoned contributed to their deaths.[15] Mennonites are depicted as conscientious objectors, different in dress, highly principled, and extremely brave. The film ends in a gun fight. After it is over, one of the detectives comes face to face with the barrel of a shotgun held by the boy preacher. He cowardly begs for his life. When the boy lowers his aim, the man runs away, thrashing through a stream in a mad dash to escape town. This scene highlights the cowardice of those who hide behind a gun, and a hired gun at that, and the film's pacifist protagonist, the brave Mennonite COs who died rather than compromise their principles. However, unlike the COs he met in prison, Joe Kenehan had not embraced the Mennonite faith, only their principled pacifism. He does not follow Jesus, just the brave example of his fellow prisoners who were following Christ's example of sacrificial love.

In 1987 *Matewan* and Haskell Wexler were nominated for an Academy Award for Best Cinematography, a category which he won that same year in the Independent Spirit Awards. *Matewan* was nominated for four other Independent Spirit Awards including Best Director, Picture, Screenplay and Supporting Actor (James Earl Jones and David Strathairn). John Sayles and *Matewan* are also featured in Angel Ismailos's film *Great Directors*, presented at the Venice International Film Festival in 2009. *Matewan* contains one of the most inspiring references to Mennonites in a full-length feature film produced by someone outside the church.

The Silence at Bethany (1988)

The Silence at Bethany is one of the few full-length feature films about Mennonite culture and faith. Produced by PBS for its American Playhouse series, it was shown at the prestigious Sundance Film Festival in 1988, then released in theaters before its public television debut. *The Silence at Bethany* was directed by Joel Oliansky who is perhaps best known for writing Clint Eastwood's jazz film *Bird* and the 1981 T.V. miniseries *Masada*, and for directing Richard Dreyfuss and Amy Irving in *The Competition* in 1980. Joyce Keener wrote the screenplay and served as the film's executive producer. In 1988 it earned the Christopher Award, presented annually since 1949 to honor media which "affirm the highest values of the human spirit." This

---

15. Homan, *American Mennonites*.

award was established by the Christopher organization which was founded by Father James Keller, a Maryknoll priest. The award strives to encourage the pursuit of creative excellence in arenas with the potential to positively influence a large audience.

The film, set in 1939 in rural Pennsylvania, tells the story of a young man, Ira Martin, played by Mark Moses, who leaves the city and returns to his family's farm. Having sown his wild oats, Ira is seeking stability by re-establishing his Mennonite roots. He is welcomed into the tight-knit Mennonite community and soon marries Pauline (Susan Wilder), a prominent farmer's daughter. Ira's leadership is apparent and soon he is selected by lot to be the congregation's pastor. Instead of calm, Ira finds turmoil under the heavy hand of the church's bishop (Tom Dahlgren) who is also Pauline's uncle. The church's conflict centers on the business practices of a member who feels he must sell milk on Sundays in order to meet his financial obligations. Ira is caught between the conservative and liberal elements of the congregation and has to make decisions with serious consequences for all in the community.[16]

The film opens with the line "Are you at peace with God and your neighbor?" This phrase is often repeated as the bishop prepares the congregation for communion. In the opening scene, an attractive young waitress, who represents "the world" flirts with Ira Martin and invites him to take her to the New York World's Fair. In one of the best lines in the film she tells Ira, "You don't know plain people like I do. They think we're the odd balls." Yet Mennonites are not portrayed as odd in the film, only different.

Those who see *The Silence at Bethany* will learn much about Mennonites, at least the Mennonite faith as it existed in rural Conestoga County, Pennsylvania around 1940. They will experience the beauty of four-part a cappella singing and learn Mennonites do not participate in war. They will learn about the importance of community, the tradition of selecting ministers by lot, and the practice of the "holy kiss." Those who listen closely will learn of the *Martyrs' Mirror* and the Anabaptist belief that spiritual conversion may happen gradually over time and is best evidenced by obedience. The film simply and elegantly presents a realistic portrayal of Mennonites.

It received positive reviews. Speaking of his experience at the 1988 Seattle International Film Festival (SIFF), critic Jeff Meyer wrote,

---

16. *Silence at Bethany*, Oliansky. This film was difficult to find and borrow but the Lancaster Mennonite Historical Society in Pennsylvania has a copy.

PART I—HOW MENNONITES HAVE BEEN PORTRAYED

> There are things to look for in the SIFF schedules. One of the better signs, at least for me, has been that the film is an "American Playhouse Theatrical Release," i.e., sponsored by the PBS television program of the same name. These are released in theaters first, then on TV (the one that comes to mind is *A Flash of Green*). They are almost always understated, intelligent dramas that involve one intellectually as well as emotionally. *Silence at Bethany* is no exception.... One of the more refreshing elements of *Silence at Bethany* is in how the Mennonites are portrayed. Films like *Witness* always portray Quakers or Mennonites as spiritual hermits, constrained from emotions and habits which are considered "normal" by most of us by their faith and customs. All the characters in *Silence at Bethany* lack the Cecil B. DeMille oratorical hang-up; they discuss love, necking and each other with the candidness you would expect from people living in a farm community.[17]

Film critic Jeff Meyer confuses Quakers with the Amish. He mistakenly refers to how Quakers and Mennonites are portrayed in *Witness*, but that film is about the Amish. It does not mention Quakers, and gives only a small reference to Mennonites. Although Quakers, the Amish, and Mennonites are all a part of the historic peace churches, the Quakers are not from the same Anabaptist root as the Amish and Mennonite traditions. This is further evidence of how little the general public knows about Mennonites, except perhaps, what intriguing film subjects they are.

Another film reviewer, Hal Erickson, also praised *Silence at Bethany* saying, "Scrupulously avoiding stereotypes and patronization, *Silence at Bethany* is a well-balanced study of a rarefied (and rapidly disappearing) American lifestyle."[18] Erickson clearly values the artistic quality of the film. He also seems to be lamenting the loss of a quaint way of living which many associate with the Amish and, to a lesser degree, Mennonites.

Jesus' Son (1999) – Drug Addict Inspired by a Mennonite Couple

You would not expect an artsy film about two heroin addicts to find its inspiration from the Mennonites, but *Jesus' Son* does. The film, which closely follows the novel of the same name by Denis Johnson, is set in the midwest with closing scenes in Phoenix, Arizona. It is about a warmhearted young

17. Meyer, "The Silence at Bethany." Online
18. On Line Video Guide.

man who gets lost in the 1970s era of free sex and mind altering drugs. Billy Crudup plays F.H. while Samantha Morton stars as Michelle, the second half of this young and restless couple. Directed by New Zealander Alison MacLean, *Jesus' Son* was released in 1999 with an all-star supporting cast including: Dennis Hopper, Holly Hunter, Jack Black and Denis Leary.

F.H. (which is an abbreviation for a vulgar nickname) is a lost soul searching for meaning in life. A visit by a pair of Jehovah's Witnesses gets him thinking deeply about life and death but his new-found friend Michelle doesn't want to hear it. She is more interested in sex and drugs. She soon gets F.H. hooked on heroin. The wild crowd with whom they hang out involves them in an accidental fatal shooting, a bizarre home robbery, a deadly drug overdose, the nurture of newborn rabbits, and various hallucinogenic episodes. When Michelle gets pregnant, they have to run the gauntlet of a bevy of Catholic protestors carrying signs outside the abortion clinic they are entering. Once inside she has a procedure done. In what is one of the funniest scenes in the film, F.H. is subjected to watching a vasectomy film while waiting for Michelle. As he is leaving the clinic F.H., in a narrative voiceover, remarks, "The Catholics doused me with holy water but I didn't feel anything, at least not for a couple of years."

After getting clean, through an intensive residential rehabilitation program followed by weekly Alcoholics Anonymous meetings, F.H. moves to Phoenix to work in a senior center. While walking to and from his job he overhears a woman's voice hauntingly singing a gospel melody, "Farther Along." The song speaks of being "faithful til death." It recognizes pain and suffering but looks forward longingly to a time when, "our toils [will] all be forgotten." This song provides the soundtrack for the remainder of the film. Enchanted, he goes up to the house and peers in the window in a voyeuristic manner, but it is clear something deeper is happening. He does this repeatedly, until it becomes a part of his daily routine. When he first sees her with her husband he says, again in a narrative voiceover, "Seeing them in their get-up, I understand. They were Amish, or more likely Mennonites." Later he enters their unlocked front door while she is singing out of view. Soon after, her husband arrives and takes him to be a burglar. He calmly offers, "Take what you need" to which F.H. hurriedly leaves without speaking.

At an earlier Alcoholics Anonymous meeting one of his fellow addicts recounted how he had often looked through the curtains at normal people going about their lives and longed to be on the other side of the curtain, living a normal life. For F.H., this Mennonite couple, whom he observes singing, saying grace, and eating together, represent an ideal norm to which he aspires. In the final scene, while F.H. is looking in on the couple, he reaches magically through the glass windowpane separating him from them and touches the back of the top of her head, as if in a healing gesture. A look of happiness comes over his face, such as he has been describing and for which he has been searching throughout the film. As the credits begin to roll, F.H. strolls blissfully down the road to the fading sounds of "Farther Along."[19]

Three religious groups are depicted in the film. The viewer never fully sees the faces of the pair of young men proselytizing for the Jehovah's Witnesses. They provide a springboard for the lead character's existential musings but are quickly dismissed. The Catholics are seen carrying signs and protesting F.H.'s and Michelle's entry into an abortion clinic. The Catholics are depicted as angry and judgmental. The third religious group is Mennonites.

The lead character in *Jesus' Son* considers this Mennonite couple, in their distinctive dress, to be the norm to which he aspires. They represent an idealized state, a loving existence in peaceful relationship to God, each other, and their neighbors. This Mennonite couple provides the inspiration for F.H.'s continued recovery and ultimate redemption.

From this film, the audience learns Mennonites live in Phoenix, not just Lancaster County, Pennsylvania. They dress distinctively, are devout people, and enjoy singing. An observant viewer would notice the simple way their home was decorated and the presence of a hand-embroidered quilt on the bed.

Although not a box office hit, *Jesus' Son* was produced with high artistic values and received favorable reviews, and some acclaim. It was presented at the Telluride Film Festival in 1999, and in the following year Billy Crudup was nominated for Best Actor at the Independent Spirit Awards.

Stellet Licht/Silent Light (2007) – A Mexican Film with Plautdietsch Dialogue

In *Silent Light*, Mexican director Carlos Reygadas crafts an unlikely alliance between the modern media form of film and an isolated community of low-German speaking Mennonites in northern Mexico. He uses a largely non-professional cast of Mennonites from Mexico, Canada, and Germany who vocalize in an obscure language spoken by only three-hundred thousand

19. *Jesus' Son*, Maclean.

people on the planet. This fictional tale, in which a married male member of the Old Colony Mennonites becomes romantically involved with an unmarried woman from the same community, is remarkable both in its form, moving very slowly, almost imperceptibly, and in its substance. Reygadas has created a piece of art and preserved a glimpse into the faith and life of these simple and hardworking people.

The original intent of the film, with its painstakingly slow dialogue and film sequences, was not meant to reach a mass audience. It has not. But it has won a measure of critical acclaim, garnering the Jury Award at the prestigious Cannes Film Festival in 2007. At lesser events it won twenty-eight more awards including Best Direction, Cinematography, and Film. In 2008, it was chosen to represent Mexico in the Academy Award competition in the category Best Foreign Language Film. Roger Ebert, arguably the most famous film critic in the world before his death in 2013, named it one of the ten best films of the decade.

The opening scene begins with the stars swirling around a constant North Star before focusing on a beautiful sunrise between two trees. The sequence lasts more than six minutes during which the viewer's eyes adjust from total darkness, under a star-swept sky, to brilliant sunlight illuminating an isolated people. As morning arrives, the birds, insects, and animals come to life with a beautiful symphony of sounds. The vociferous animals contrast sharply with the people, who are largely silent. Although quiet, the steely resolve and rock solid faith of these Old Colony Mennonites is clearly evident.

The audience gets to know Johan (Cornelio Wall), his wife Esther (played by Miriam Toews, an ex-Mennonite from Manitoba, Canada and author of *A Complicated Kindness*) and their seven children through their rituals of prayer before meals, bathing at a local watering hole, and harvesting corn for their livestock. The film's artistic cinematography is noteworthy, particularly when Johan visits his mechanic and again when he meets his lover, Marianne (Maria Pankratz). [20]

The cruelly slow pace of the film makes it hard to watch, perhaps because Westerners have grown accustomed to Hollywood's split-second, action-packed thrillers. It is also difficult to understand. The key to the film, alluded to in Johan and Esther's yearning to set the clock back and begin again, is revealed in the direction from which the sun rises and in which it sets in the opening and closing scenes. It is an Adam and Eve story in

20. *Silent Light*, Reygadas.

reverse, with two fallen lovers and a heartbroken spouse restored to a Paradise such as existed before the Fall.

Reygades may have chosen to set his film in this Mexican Old Mennonite Colony because of the extreme contrast between his gentle and somber subjects and their surrounding culture with its frivolity and fiestas. In doing so, he has given his viewers a rare but respectful glimpse into the inner workings of this isolated group. Although few religious practices are depicted, apart from silent grace and the a cappella droning singing at Esther's wake, it nonetheless exudes the simple and sturdy faith of the colony.

Some have accused Peter Weir, director of *Witness*, of exploiting the Amish and introducing a corrosive influence upon them. To his credit, Weir did not use Amish actors, although one former Amishman served as a consultant during the filming, nor did he film any Amish. In contrast, Reygades's cast is almost entirely Mennonite. While *Witness* benefited Amish businessmen by promoting tourism in Lancaster County, *Silent Light* is unlikely to bring many visitors or economic resources to this isolated region of northern Mexico.

Kaw (2007) – Made-for-T.V. Movie Portrays Mennonites

Kaw, set in rural Pennsylvania, is a low budget, B-level horror film about a small town terrorized by a swarm of ravens hungry for human flesh. It turns out the Mennonites were responsible for the crazed birds.

When Sheriff Wayne Merkle (Sean Patrick Flannery) and the local doctor (Rod Taylor) look into the death of a local farmer they are baffled by the victim's wounds until they discover other bodies with similar markings. It soon becomes clear the town is under siege from a flock of murderous ravens.

The viewer meets Rachel, wearing a covering and speaking with a Pennsylvania Dutch accent, as she delivers milk to the local diner, Betty's Cookhouse. This restaurant later becomes a place of refuge for the main characters of the film in the climactic battle against the crazed birds. Because Rachel smiles and is attractive, the audience comes away with a good impression of her, although she is clearly different from the rest of the townspeople. The birds kill her very early in the film while she is returning from running errands in town.

Three other characters from the Mennonite community have a more prominent, albeit malevolent, role in the film. Jacob is the obstinate leader of this Mennonite farming community. Other Mennonite characters include Oskar (John Ralston) and his teenage daughter Gretchen, who attends the local public high school where she plays on the girls' basketball team. Gretchen is friends with Cynthia (Kristin Booth), the Sheriff's wife. Jacob decries this fraternization with the "English" saying, "God is punishing us for such friendships." He bemoans the community's gradual shift from strict separation to co-mingling with the townspeople and learning their ways. Jacob demands the community repent and return to the "old ways" in order to escape the "curse" God has brought upon them.

As the plot develops, it becomes clear the Mennonites are hiding something from their neighbors. Oskar pleads with Jacob to tell someone about their problems to which he replies, "What we do is nobody else's business."[21]

Jacob and Oskar, whose fake beards and plain dress look comical, seem to be a cross between the Amish and Mennonites. They look Amish but drive cars, although the cars are older black vehicles without any chrome. At one point Gretchen tells the school bus driver, "We are not Amish, we are Mennonite as you know full well." He derisively replies, "Why don't you go make a quilt, bake a pie, or raise a barn."

At Jacob's first appearance he is holding a hammer in a manner which is threatening toward Cynthia, the sheriff's wife, who is also Gretchen's friend. He refuses to accept a scrapbook she brings as a gift for Gretchen because it contains photos which the Amish, and some Old Order Mennonites, consider sinful. Cynthia overhears a conversation between Jacob and Oskar and misinterprets it as a death threat against her. In her haste to run away, Cynthia falls into an abandoned well, the same place Jacob and Oscar have been throwing dead animals. While attempting to burn the cattle carcasses, Jacob accidentally douses Cynthia with gasoline and almost lights her on fire until he discovers her in the bottom of the well and rescues her.

It turns out the Mennonite farmers' cattle died from Mad Cow Disease. When the birds ate the rotting bovine flesh they too became infected and crazed. Jacob saw this double plague as a curse from God given as punishment for fraternization with the English. At one point Cynthia rails against Jacob saying, "You blame me for this?" Oskar too resists Jacob and pleads, "We cannot keep this to ourselves." Later, when he is confronted by Doc, Oskar confesses his mistake in hiding this disease from them and not seeking their help, saying, "We have wronged you [townspeople]."

Mennonites are portrayed as intolerant, secretive, harsh, and threatening. However, this is due largely to a series of misunderstandings between

21. *Kaw*, Wilson.

them and the townspeople, who blame the Mennonites for the bird attacks. The film writer needed a group who could be portrayed as "other," outsiders who could be blamed for this tragedy. Perhaps, the Amish are too well loved and too far removed from society to fulfill that role, so the director chose to use Mennonites. This portrayal of Mennonite farmers is not surprising since those seen as different are often portrayed negatively by those in the mainstream. It is easy to fear and mistrust those you do not know or understand.

Television

The Simpsons – "Those Shiftless Mennonites"

Anabaptist writer and blogger Tim Nafziger calls *The Simpsons* "the best satire of contemporary American culture." He goes on to claim, "For those interested in Mennonites involved in mass culture, it is also a case study of a family morphing from immigrant Mennonite experience to pop culture celebrity in four generations."[22] In his blog Tim describes the ancestry of Matt Groening, the creator of the wildly popular Fox network animated series about the dysfunctional Simpson family. The parents, Homer and Marj Simpson, and their three children, Bart, whose name is an anagram for brat, Lisa, a child genius, and infant Maggie, share a home in the city of Springfield with Grandpa Abraham. Matt Groening's great-grandfather Abraham Groening was a part of the Mennonite immigration from the Ukraine to Hillsboro, Kansas in the 1870s. He became a leading member of the Gnadenau Krimmer Mennonite Brethren church. In 1908, his son, Matt's grandfather, Abram Abraham or A. A. Groening was one of the first thirty-nine students to attend the newly opened Tabor College, which was meeting in the Mennonite Brethren Church in Hillsboro. Because the Groenings spoke both High German and Plautdeutsch, they were targets of persecution during World War I. As a pacifist, he fled to Canada to avoid the draft. There he married, began a family, and had a son named Homer. When Homer reached adulthood he worked in advertising but also dabbled in filmmaking, writing poetry, and drawing cartoons. He married Margaret (Marg) Wiggam and abandoned his father's pacifism to become a pilot and fight in World War II. Homer and Margaret's son Matthew

---

22. Nafziger, "The Groenings." Online.

Abram Groening, born in 1954, went on to create two hit cartoon series, *The Simpsons* and *Futurama*.[23]

Nafziger notes, "The [*Simpsons*] is preoccupied with religious—and some might say also sacrilegious—themes. From Reverend Lovejoy—of complex denominational identity, to neighbor Ned Flanders—the born-again, Bible-believing neighbor, Groening wrestles with complex issues of faith and meaning in all his characters."[24] Of particular interest is a show titled "Old Yeller Belly," the nineteenth episode in the fourteenth season, which aired on May 4, 2003. When Bart's treehouse is destroyed, he recruits the Amish to rebuild it but insists it have electricity. Since the Amish builders don't use electricity, they are unskilled in its installation. As a result the treehouse burns down yet again. The Amish are portrayed as industrious and are contrasted with their Mennonite neighbors when Bart's sister Marj says, "Oh, those Amish are so industrious, unlike those shiftless Mennonites." Marj makes those comments based on prior impressions, despite the fact it was the fault of the Amish craftsmen that the treehouse is destroyed a second time. At that point the scene shifts to a group of "Mennonite" men depicted shooting dice and smoking cigarettes. This is clearly an inside joke which those unfamiliar with the Amish and the Mennonites would not understand. However, it demonstrates yet again the link in the public's mind between the Amish and the Mennonites. There are other references in *The Simpsons* to Groening's German speaking ancestors but no other found references to Mennonites.

In Matt Groening's other animated show, *Futurama*, there is a drunken robot character named Bender. Perhaps this is another inside joke with a double meaning referring not only to a drunken binge but to a common Mennonite surname.

The Office – a Mennonite pastor performs a wedding

A Mennonite pastor makes an appearance in an episode of *The Office*, a hit U.S. television series adapted from a British show of the same name, performing a wedding entirely in German. *The Office* is produced by Greg Daniels, who also wrote for *Saturday Night Live* and, coincidently, *The Simpsons*. The television show debuted on NBC in March, 2005 and stars Steven Carell as Michael Scott, the Scranton, Pennsylvania sales branch

23. Ibid.
24. Ibid.

PART I—HOW MENNONITES HAVE BEEN PORTRAYED

manager for a fictitious paper company, Dunder Mifflin. Michael's assistant branch manager, Dwight Schrute, played by Rainn Wilson, is a power hungry psychopath with Germanic ancestry.

In "The Surplus," the tenth episode in season five, Dwight's jealousy of the wedding planned for co-workers Angela and Andy takes a cynical turn. Dwight convinces them to have their marriage ceremony on his family farm in Pennsylvania. He sets up chairs and decorations, and hires a German speaking Mennonite minister to perform the ceremony. He invites the bride and groom to a rehearsal at the Schrute Farm, then talks Andy into sitting down to watch and enjoy the ceremony, placing himself in the groom's role for the rehearsal. The rehearsal, which is really a legitimate wedding performed in German which only the minister and Dwight understand, is a legally binding ceremony uniting Dwight and Angela in marriage. When she learns of his trickery she throws the improvised twine ring in his face. Another inside joke occurs when Dwight and the pacifist Mennonite minister begin fighting after Angela rejects him.

The significance of this episode is that it involves a plainly dressed, German speaking Mennonite minister, a contrivance necessary for Dwight to pull off his trickery. The scuffle afterwards is only funny if the audience knows Mennonites do not typically fight, which they do not learn from the episode.

These T.V. references to Mennonites are few and far between and teach the audience next to nothing about Mennonite faith and practice except to associate them with the Amish and German language.

There is a Mennonite athlete who has become a T.V. star whose accomplishments and faith have made a significant national impact but not in the U.S., rather she has been called "Canada's heavy metal queen."[25]

Cindy Klassen – Canada's most decorated Olympic athlete

Speed skater Cindy Klassen is a devout Mennonite and, during her Olympic run, the darling of Canada. She won more medals in a single Olympics (five at Turin in 2006) than has any other Canadian athlete. This extraordinary accomplishment led Jacques Rogge, President of the International Olympic Committee, to name Klassen the "woman of the [2006] Games."

With six medals, including an earlier bronze medal earned at the 2002 Olympics in Salt Lake, Klassen is the most decorated Canadian Olympic

25. Castello, "The Medals Plaza."

athlete of all time. She holds three world speed skating records in the one thousand, fifteen hundred, and three thousand meter races.

During the Turin games in 2006 she was frequently the subject of CBS broadcasts and much has been written about her accomplishments, often with references to her character and faith. Piazza Castillo, writing for Canada's weekly newsmagazine *MacLean*, noted her humble character saying, "It may be more of that Mennonite aversion to self-aggrandizement, but Klassen is understated even by that standard."[26]

Klassen is quick to attribute her accomplishments to God and name her personal relationship with Jesus Christ as the most important thing in her life. Her web site, www.CindyKlassen.com, has a scripture reference, I Thessalonians 5:16–18, prominently displayed in her biography which serves as the home page. It reads, 'Rejoice always; pray without ceasing; in everything give thanks; for this is God's will for you in Christ Jesus.'

Cindy grew up Mennonite Brethren, is a member of the McIvor Church, and a 1997 graduate of the Mennonite Brethren Collegiate Institute in Winnipeg, Manitoba, Canada, her home town. It was there in 2006 where she gave her testimony via video at a Billy Graham Evangelistic Association's rally. She said, "Having Jesus at the center of my life and as my friend has made such a huge difference in my life. I have Him there to lean on and to talk to. Basically He's my friend and someone that I can go to when I am happy or when I'm sad. That has created the person I am today."[27] An earlier Wikipedia entry made mention of Klassen's Mennonite denominational heritage and her ancestor's immigration to Manitoba but those references were no longer present in 2014.[28]

She is a true Canadian national hero. In 2010, the Royal Treasury minted twenty-two million quarter coins inscribed with her image and the year of the Turin Olympics—2006. In Winnipeg they named the local recreational center in her honor.

NBC Nightly News with Brian Williams, March 29, 2011

Often, the major network news broadcasts end their nightly program with a human interest story. On Tuesday night March 29, 2011 *NBC Nightly News with Brian Williams* aired a segment, in their *Making a Difference* series,

---

26. Ibid.
27. Chismar, "Speed Skater." Online.
28. Wikipedia, "Cindy Klassen," online, introduction.

PART I—HOW MENNONITES HAVE BEEN PORTRAYED

about Mennonite volunteers rebuilding homes in Grand Bayou, Louisiana five years after hurricane Katrina. The segment ran two minutes and thirty seconds and is titled "Quietly assisting Katrina victims in Cajun country." Williams, the news anchor, led the story by pointing out he frequently visits disaster sites saying, "Often the first people we see arriving on the scene to jump in and help out, and rebuild, are the Mennonites. . . . Hurricane Katrina was no different. They arrived without fanfare and they are still there."[29]

Shifting to location in Grand Bayou, Louisiana, NBC reporter Kerry Sanders explained the efforts of thousands of Mennonite volunteers from Wisconsin and western Canada, who came for a week or two at a time to rebuild storm damaged homes with Mennonite Disaster Service (MDS). So far ninety-seven homes have been built with more on the way. Sanders began the segment saying, "Cajuns say they don't know much about the strangers who dress old school and speak Dutch."[30] He focused on the new home MDS volunteers built for sixty-five year old Dwight Reyes who had lived with his wife for the past four and a half years on a small house boat the size of a prison cell. Sanders explained, "When outsiders promised him a new home and wanted nothing in return he was skeptical."[31]

The camera showed a skiff traversing the bayou with a "Mennonite Disaster Service" emblem on its side, then a "Mennonite Disaster Service Work Site" sign, followed by an interview with Scott Sundberg, the MDS representative. It was noted Scott did not grow up Mennonite and is thus more willing to be on camera. Sundberg explained the Mennonite faith promotes a "culture of service." He compared what these Mennonites are doing in Louisiana to a traditional Amish barn raising noting "you help your neighbor." Sanders, the reporter, noted these Mennonite people are not necessarily shy but they are reluctant to be the focus of attention saying, "To be prideful is contrary to their beliefs." He noted their humility and the fact they asked not to be named in the broadcast. The women left most of the talking to the men, especially Scott Sundberg. There were many dramatic camera shots of women in traditional long skirts with head scarves painting and also working on the roof. Some women were shown crawling on the roof operating a power drill. Other women were seen using crow bars to pry up damaged sheet metal with their skirts billowing in the wind.[32]

29. Sundberg and Hadlock, "Quietly Assisting."
30. Ibid.
31. Ibid.
32. Ibid.

Visual Media

Another video, three minutes and thirty-four seconds long, is available online called "Capturing the camera-shy Mennonites" which further elaborates on Mennonite humility, faith, and practices.[33]

It is ironic that conservative Mennonites, who dress in unadorned clothing in an effort to live simply and not be noticed individually, stand out as a group. This NBC broadcast is an example of a case where the Mennonite values of hard work and helping others, coupled with their humility and starkly simple clothing, brought attention and honor to the entire group. It is reminiscent of a comment made by Dennis Bennetch, a member of the Dohner Mennonite Church in Lebanon, Pennsylvania. He noted people often come up to him to ask if he is Amish. His desire is to glorify God and bring people into God's Kingdom. "Plain attire is not enough," he says, "But with a regenerated heart it's an asset [in witnessing to others]." That was the case here as well.

Paul Schrag, editor of the *Mennonite Weekly* (now *World*) *Review*, which published an article about this NBC coverage, said "It's notable that NBC only thought MDS was interesting when it could get pictures of plain-dressed Mennos. There are plenty of MDS volunteers in Louisiana who look like average Americans, but they don't make interesting video, I guess."[34] That has been the pattern for most of the media coverage of Mennonites. Media producers are most interested in things that are unusual. Mennonites are interesting subjects because their distinct appearance makes them not like "us," rather they are "other." This often leads producers to cover stories about the Amish and Old Order Mennonites, rather than more acculturated Mennonites, but that was not the case in the next example cited.

CNN and Goshen College's National Anthem controversy

This topic was covered in an earlier chapter on Aural Media but it continues here since it moved from radio to television. The facts of the case are repeated here for clarity.

In 2011 Mennonites received a lot of national media attention over a decision by the board of Goshen College, a Mennonite school in Indiana, to stop playing the national anthem. Goshen's board reversed a decision made about a year and a half earlier when it began playing an instrumental version of the anthem, followed by a prayer, at intercollegiate sporting events.

33. "Capturing the Camera-Shy Mennonites," Online.
34. Schrag, e-mail.

PART I—How Mennonites Have Been Portrayed

That decision was made in an effort to be more welcoming to the college's non-Mennonite students, who constitute about 50 percent of the student body. Typically, members of the Mennonite church avoid oaths and military service. Many also abstain from voting, saying the pledge of allegiance, or singing the national anthem. Goshen's decision to revert back to its traditional practice of not singing the national anthem created a brouhaha in Goshen Indiana, where the college is located. In making the decision the board of directors asked President James Brenneman to find an alternative to singing the national anthem.

The *Star Spangled Banner*, written by Francis Scott Key after witnessing the British bombardment of Fort McHenry near Baltimore, Maryland during the War of 1812, became the national anthem of the United States in 1931. Goshen began playing intercollegiate sports in 1957 but did not play the national anthem on campus until an instrumental version was introduced prior to a baseball game held on March 23, 2010. The prayer of Saint Francis of Assisi followed the anthem that day.

Local media outlets picked up on the controversy about the decision to go back to *not* using the national anthem, but were initially refused interviews by college officials. However, after a brief article about this decision appeared in the June 6, 2011 issue of the *Chronicle of Higher Education*, the story was launched. It went national on June 7, 2011 when National Public Radio (NPR) broadcast a news segment about it.

The following week James Brenneman, President of Goshen College, granted an on-air interview to Robin Young, host of NPR's *Here and Now*. That five minute dialogue aired on June 13, 2011. In that piece listeners learned much about the five- hundred year old Anabaptist tradition including Mennonites' commitment to following Jesus in the way of peace and a willingness to be martyred for their faith.[35]

The story skipped from radio to television when Mark Schloneger's article, "Why I Don't Sing the National Anthem," was picked up by Cable News Network (CNN) and posted June 26th on their "Belief Blog." Schloneger was then pastor of Springdale Mennonite Church in Waynesboro, Virginia and is a Goshen College graduate. His blog quickly received more than four-thousand online comments.[36]

Schloneger was invited to do an on-air T.V. interview because of the huge public response to his posting. That interview, by CNN's Kyra Phillips,

35. Young, "Indiana's Goshen College."
36. Schloneger, "My Faith."

aired on T.V. on July 1, 2011, the Friday of the Fourth of July weekend. It was available for viewing online for a limited time but has since been removed.

Mark Schloneger explained, "I saw how the Goshen College decision was being portrayed in the media and I wanted to go deeper, to get past the liberal/conservative divide and explain the beliefs behind their decision."[37] While writing the article, which he knew would be controversial, he kept his congregation informed and felt their support and encouragement, even from those who disagreed with him. When it was completed he sent it to several national media outlets including *Fox News*, *The New York Times* and CNN but only CNN expressed interest. When Schloneger attended Mennonite Church USA's biennial convention in Pittsburgh, Pennsylvania July 4 through 9, Joe Hackman, a recent seminary graduate and the pastor of Salford Mennonite Church in Pennsylvania, along with several others, recognized him from the interview and called him "The CNN pastor."[38] Schloneger cringes at the name but cherishes his Anabaptist faith and is not afraid to humbly express he views, even when controversial.

By August 26, *Mediaite*, Abrams Media's flagship blog run by Dan Abrams, an ABC news analyst, picked up the story.[39] CNN Belief Blog Co-editor Eric Marrapodi chose this news story as one of the top five "My Faith" stories of 2011. He comments, "When Mark Schloneger, a Mennonite pastor from Waynesboro, Virginia, wrote this piece, it stirred a hornet's nest of civil religion. Commenters questioned his patriotism when he explained, "I love my country, but I sing my loyalty and pledge my allegiance to Jesus alone.""[40]

Through Schloneger's very public witness many were exposed to core Mennonite beliefs and how some Mennonites practice their faith.

Amish Reality Shows, e.g., *Breaking Amish* and *Amish Mafia*.

Several so called "reality" shows which include Amish subjects have emerged since the success of the Lucy Walker's 2002 acclaimed Cinemax documentary *Devil's Playground*. These programs include UPN's *Amish in the City* (July 2004), TLC's *Breaking Amish* (September 2012), Discovery Channel's *Amish Mafia* (December 2012), and several other spin-offs.

37. Schloneger, conversation with the author, July 5, 2011.
38. Ibid.
39. Alvarez, "Cue Outrage." Online.
40. Marrapodi, "My Faith." Online.

PART I—HOW MENNONITES HAVE BEEN PORTRAYED

Amish in the City, which did not contain a cast member portrayed as Mennonite, is discussed at length in Umble and Weaver-Zercher's book, *The Amish and the Media*.

Breaking Amish and *Amish Mafia* do include characters depicted as Mennonite. TLC's *Breaking Amish* follows five Anabaptist young adults, four Amish and one Mennonite, who move to New York City to experience a different lifestyle. Sabrina High, the cast member depicted as Mennonite, was born to Puerto Rican and Italian parents and subsequently adopted by a Mennonite family. *Breaking Amish* averaged 3.9 million viewers per episode and was the Discovery Channel's top rated new series for women ages eighteen to thirty-four.[41] The second season, which moved the cast to Sarasota, Florida, follows six young adults, five Amish and one Mennonite—Matt Bristol from Earl, Pennsylvania. His family became Mennonite when he was seven years old.

Donald Kraybill, an Elizabethtown College professor was quoted in the *Lancaster Intelligencer* saying "My own view is this is trash TV. To call these shows documentaries is a fraudulent lie."[42]

Amish Mafia debuted on the Discovery channel in December, 2012 and was renewed for a second season of eight episodes which began airing in August, 2013. It follows the exploits of supposed gang leader "Lebanon Levi," who was born Levi King Stoltzfus in Lebanon County, Pennsylvania in 1979. Levi has three assistants including Jolin Zimmerman, who is portrayed as Mennonite.

However, these programs are so staged, false, and exploitative as to give the general public no accurate depictions of Mennonite faith, life, or practices. They follow a "fish-out-of-water" formula which preys on unsuspecting young people and gives a very false sense of who these peaceful people are and how they live. Ironically, Melodie Davis, who helps manage MennoMedia's Third Way Café web site, noted a spike in web visits after these shows air. Since the Amish do not generally use the Internet, their Mennonite cousins, who are part of the Mennonite Church USA and Mennonite Church Canada, include accurate information about Amish and Mennonite beliefs and practices on their Third Way Café web site. In an August 2, 2013 blog post on Mennobytes, Melodie referred to a huge surge in traffic on the Third Way Café on November 12, 2012 which she

---

41. "Amish 'Reality' Shows Keep Coming," 1.
42. Ibid.

attributed, with a fair degree of certainty, to the airing of the season finale of *Breaking Amish*.[43]

Although the general public gets little accurate information about Mennonites from these reality T.V. shows, some have their interest peaked and do go on to discover much about Anabaptist faith from other sources.

ABC's *Modern Family*, January 8, 2014 – A Mennonite Joke.

Modern Family, the award winning ABC comedy series about three blended families linked by the patriarch Jay (Ed O'Neill), aired an episode titled "And One to Grow On" on Wednesday, January 8, 2014, which included a joke referencing Mennonites. Two of the main characters, Mitchell (Jesse Tyler Ferguson) and Cameron (Eric Stonestreet), who portray a gay couple, are planning their wedding and seeking a venue. They are enamored with the Carriage House and sit down with the establishment's booking agent. While discussing terms Mitchell asks the agent, "Is this price per person?" to which he replies. "Yes, excluding alcohol, cake, and music." Mitchell responds, "What's that, the Mennonite package?" The agent comes back with, "I think you'll find our prices are competitive."[44]

Mitchell is clearly not interested in renting the space without alcohol, cake, and music. His response to the booking agent is negative, asking in affect, "Do I look like a conservative, religious person to you?" The joke implies Mennonites keep their celebrations simple, avoiding the expense and frivolity of alcohol, cake, and music. It may also be implying Mennonites are cheap, always looking for the least expensive option. In that regard, "Mennonite" may be a more culturally acceptable substitute for a much older tradition of using the word "Jewish" to imply cheapness. Hotels, and other establishments, often feature specials such as a "Honeymoon Package" or a "Golfers' Weekend" but would likely not have one based on religious preference. The joke likely went over the audience's head, since few of the show's estimated 12.6 million viewers would know much about Mennonites. Some would likely confuse the term with Methodist or Mormon. In any regard, the implication is negative, implying certain religious groups avoid celebrating and are cheap.

Yet, *Modern Family* is a cultural phenomenon. Having first aired in September, 2009 it is now in its fifth season. It earned four consecutive

43. M. Davis, "News About "Mennonites." Online.
44. Mancuso, "And One to Grow On."

PART I—HOW MENNONITES HAVE BEEN PORTRAYED

Emmy awards for "Outstanding Comedy Series" tying *The Dick Van Dyke Show* as the only other comedy to win this award for four consecutive years. *Modern Family* also won a Golden Globe Award for the "Best T.V. series – musical or comedy." [45] Who would have thought the shows comic writers were acquainted with Mennonites?

---

45. Wikipedia, "Modern Family," online, 4.2.

CHAPTER 4

The Ngram and a Summary of Part I

BEING SMALL IN SIZE, Mennonites seldom appear in popular media, certainly far less frequently than Jews, Latter-Day Saints (Mormons), and many other religious groups. There is now a research tool called the Ngram which is able to quantify such relationships with regard to print media. This powerful tool, developed by Harvard University, Google, and others, will be described in greater detail at the conclusion of this book. For now suffice it to say, it enables researchers to compare sociological trends by tracking the frequency of the occurrence of certain words over time using a database of five hundred billion words from more than five million books published between 1500 and 2008. By stripping the words of their context, they were able to avoid the copyright infringements normally associated with published literature.

Using the Ngram (see Figure 1 below)[1] to compare the occurrence of the word "Catholic" to the word "Jew" it is evident that Jews, numbering 1.3 million, are mentioned relatively more frequently in literature, by a factor of ten, when compared to the much larger body of fifty-one million Catholics.[2] Elaborating further, there are forty times more Catholics than Jews. Ignoring the percentages listed to the left in Figure 1, notice there are six horizontal bars in the graph, each representing an equal interval. Throughout the period covered, 1800 through 2000, the word "Jew" consistently hovers between the

---

1. This, and the other word comparison graphs which appear in this text, were copied from Google Books Ngram Viewer which makes them available freely, and allows for their publication.

2. Russell, "Database Tracks Popularity of 500b Words." Online.

69

first and second horizontal bar, while the line of the word "Catholic" moves between the second line to above the sixth line, but most frequently oscillating around the fifth horizontal line. Thus, in general terms one could say the word "Catholic" appears three times more frequently than "Jew" (five divided by one point five). However, since there are forty times more Catholics than Jews, to express this relationship in relative terms one would divide the ratio, three, by forty to get an accurate comparison. Again, in general terms, the number forty is more than a factor of ten larger than the number three. Thus the word "Jew" is ten times more prevalent in literature, in terms of relative size, than the word "Catholic." Expressed another way, for every Jew there are ten times more references to Judaism in literature than references to Catholicism for every Catholic.[3]

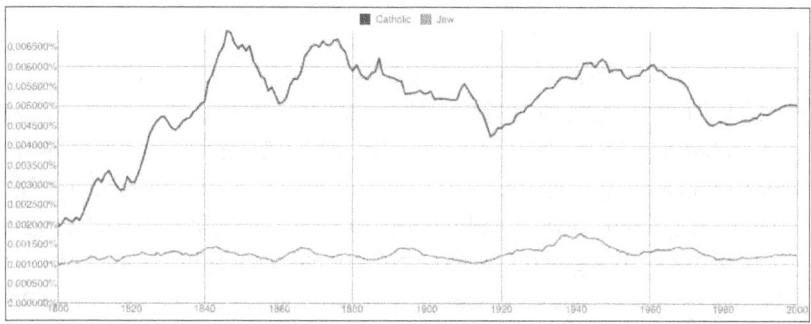

An Ngram word search comparing use of the words "Catholic" and "Jew."

There is also much anecdotal evidence which indicates unique religious groups are frequently portrayed in media. The Jews have been the subject of countless plays, films, and books. Shakespeare's *The Merchant of Venice* (circa 1596), *Fiddler on the Roof* (1971), *Schindler's List* (1993), and James Michener's epic novel *The Source* (1965) are but a few noteworthy examples. Catholics are also keen subjects for writers and filmmakers who usually portray priests negatively while mocking religion and Catholic dogmatism or missiology. Two films, *The Mission* (1986) and *Doubt* (2008), come immediately to mind. Latter-Day Saints are also seen as a distinct religious community and have been depicted in many books, dramas, films and T.V. shows. *September Dawn* (2007) recounts the 1857 Mountain Meadow Massacre perpetrated by a Mormon militia which killed about one hundred and twenty men, women, and children on a wagon train headed west to California.

3. Google Books Ngram Viewer.

The Ngram and a Summary of Part I

There is even a hit Broadway musical called *The Book of Mormon*, a satire of organized religion from Trey Parker and Matt Stone, the creators of the diabolical T.V. cartoon sensation *South Park*. It opened on Broadway in the spring of 2011 to rave reviews and led the Tony Awards with wins in nine categories. From 2006 through 2011, HBO aired *Big Love*, a drama about a fictitious polygamous fundamentalist Mormon family. TLC followed with a similarly themed reality show called *Sister Wives* which follows the Brown family with patriarch Kody Brown, his four wives, and their seventeen children. It first aired in 2010 and continues in its sixth season.

The significance of these references is they represent religious groups which are distinct from the dominant white Anglo Saxon Protestants (WASPs). These groups are "religious others," or sects, and are easy targets for media to exploit and sensationalize because they are frequently misunderstood and sometimes separate themselves from the dominant culture by withdrawing into their own enclaves. Although most Mennonites could also be called WASPs, they are distinct enough in faith and practice to be seen as "religious others." Mennonites are sometimes classified as a sect by those in the dominant culture.

What is it about Mennonites which makes them interesting subjects in books, art, and film? Certainly the reasons have changed since the 1500s when Mennonites were reviled. At that time the Anabaptist practice of adult baptism was considered heretical. Since then it has become the norm for many Christian denominations, including the largest Protestant group—Baptists. Even so, suspicion of those who keep themselves separate from the main community is still present today, as evidenced in the portrayal of Mennonites as antisocial in the film *Kaw*.

Jodi Nisley Hertzler, author of *Ask Third Way Café: 50 Quirky and Common Questions About Mennonites*, thinks the public's fascination with Mennonites is "partly because the Amish and Old Order groups are so very visibly distinct and have fairly successfully separated themselves from the surrounding culture. People are genuinely curious about the minutiae of this alternative lifestyle.... Popular trends toward gardening, simple living, and sustainability have also brought these groups into focus."[4]

Kenneson's definition of the term "sect" provides categories to classify Mennonites' cultural, religious, and linguistic differences as depicted in movies and on television. An examination of the three component parts of Kenneson's definition—sociological (culture), theological (religious

---

4. Quoted by M. Davis, "From Holy Kiss to Quilt Designs," 7.

PART I—HOW MENNONITES HAVE BEEN PORTRAYED

thinking), and ecclesiological (group practice)—help explain how Mennonites are similar to and different from Jewish people and Latter-Day Saints. The three components of Kenneson's use of the word "sect" provide the rubric to place each media reference to Mennonites included in this book into one of these three categories, based on its predominant characteristics. For example in the films *Silent Light, Jesus' Son, Centennial,* and *Kaw,* the Mennonite characters are defined not by their religious beliefs and ethical practices but by their clothes and culture. Thus, these four references were placed in the sociological group. The first three were positive, meaning they portrayed Mennonites favorably, while the fourth, *Kaw,* was characterized as negative since it blames Mennonites for the town's problems and paints them as antisocial. Some references, such as Rembrandt's painting of the Mennonite pastor and his wife, were considered neutral. The following tables map each reference into one of these three areas and categorize them as positive, negative, or neutral. One entry, *Centennial,* appears in two tables.

Table 1 - Summary of **Positive** Mennonite Depictions in Media

Sociological (culture)	*Theological (beliefs)*	*Ecclesiological (practices)*
Rockingham Register	Christian Century, healthcare	Life Magazine
Silent Light		James Lee Burke's writings
Jesus' Son	La Vie	
Centennial	Barney & Clyde	Abraham Lincoln
Washington Post shoofly pie	The NY Times on Yoder	Matewan
		Candide
Runner's World		Cindy Klassen
		NBC Nightly News
		Catch-22

The Ngram and a Summary of Part I

Table 2 - Summary of **Negative** Mennonite Depictions in Media

Sociological (culture)	Theological (beliefs)	Ecclesiological (practices)
Kaw	Martin Luther/ Lutherans	*The Simpsons* (in jest)
Communism in Central Europe	Anglicans	*Amish Paradise* (in jest)
	Catholics	Floyd Landis scandal
	Centennial	
	Enthusiasm	*Modern Family* (in jest)
	The Spectator	
	Silence at Bethany	

Table 3 - Summary of **Neutral** Mennonite Depictions in Media

Sociological (culture)	Theological (beliefs)	Ecclesiological (practices)
Witness	*Tillie: A Mennonite Maid*	The Esh Family tragedy
The Office		
Rembrandt's art	*Christian Century*, gay ordination	*The Philadelphia Inquirer*. Glenn Lapp

Looking at these three tables, it is noteworthy there were fewer neutral references to Mennonite theology discovered and reported here. If one agrees theologically with the Mennonites they are generally portrayed positively and vice versa. With regard to ecclesiology, or church practices, the depictions were generally favorable and those which were negative were mainly poking fun at Mennonites. Sociologically, Mennonites are shown in a positive, negative, and neutral light. However, the emphasis was more often on their practices, e.g., pacifism (*Matewan*, James Lee Burke's writings), humility (Cindy Klassen), and practice of social justice (*Life* magazine, *NBC Nightly News*), and not on Mennonite cultural distinctives, such as clothing (*Jesus' Son*) and Germanic culture (*Silent Light*, *Kaw*). As we shall see in Part II, even the best Mennonite theologians are ethicists at their core. Mennonites are known for their communal practices, derived from their theology but rooted in doing, not being.

More than three dozen non-Mennonite portrayals of Mennonites in media were examined. It is interesting this small group has repeatedly emerged in the mainstream consciousness, both in Europe and America, since their beginnings in the early 1500s through the present. A cursory review of church confessions and statements by prominent church leaders demonstrated Catholics and Lutherans reviled Anabaptists, while Anglicans specifically warned their parishioners against them by pointing out doctrinal differences. There was some justification in condemning Anabaptists. As noted earlier, an Anabaptist group led by Jan van Leyden violently took over the town of Münster on March 30, 1535 and imposed a revolutionary rule in which all things, some speculate even wives, were held in common. This revolt was brutally suppressed, its leaders were killed, and their bodies were hung in cages from towers on the city square as an example to others.

According to church historian Franklin Littell, "The continued misunderstanding of Anabaptism can be explained in a very brief statement: *the writings and records of the movement were successfully suppressed, whereas the polemics of their enemies circulated and were early translated into various languages (including English)*."[5]

After Münster, Anabaptists rejected the use of the sword in God's kingdom, embracing pacifism under the leadership of Menno Simons. For most government officials this was unacceptable. However, both Abraham Lincoln, himself a devout Christian, and General Stonewall Jackson were tolerant of these conscientious objectors, even during wartime.

Jumping forward one hundred and fifty years to the present, when National Public Radio stations broadcast a popular Saturday night program there were a few Mennonite jokes gracing the airwaves while an unusual gangster rap parody made a fleeting reference to Mennonites.

A leading Renaissance thinker admired the Anabaptists, although he despised the established Catholic and Protestant Churches. A Communist

---

5. Littell, *The Origins of Sectarian Protestantism*, 148. Emphasis in original.

The Ngram and a Summary of Part I

apologist was disappointed in the Anabaptist movement, which had such a revolutionary beginning, while a Catholic scholar painted all Anabaptists with a broad stroke as immature enthusiasts, perhaps because of the debacle at Münster. One of the most influential antiwar novels of the twentieth century contains a prominent Anabaptist military chaplain, while another beloved American writer of historical fiction grew up among the Amish and Mennonites and occasionally writes about them. An American award winning murder mystery writer created at least three Mennonite characters who are central to the moral meaning of his violent tales.

Newspapers and magazines acknowledged the remarkable lives or deaths of individual Mennonites, or the tragedies stoically endured by some Mennonite families. The editor of the *Rockingham Register* newspaper was not as charitable as many in the Shenandoah Valley in the mid-1800s who looked upon their Germanic Mennonite neighbors and noted their "orderly and honest lives." *Life* magazine acknowledged the remarkable contributions of Mennonite conscientious objectors in bringing about reform in the U.S. mental health system. A Pulitzer Prize winning humor columnist for *The Washington Post* even contrasted Mennonite piety with crass materialism for comic effect. One contemporary ecumenical magazine noted the diligent efforts of a Mennonite faith group attempting to address the problem of uninsured leaders among them, while another politically right leaning periodical conspiratorially asked is there a "Mennonite Takeover?" of the evangelical Christian world in the works. Not only did the article portray Mennonites as more powerful than they actually are, it equated being Anabaptist to being "hip," a far different characterization than Mennonites typically receive.

Looking at the visual arts, Rembrandt surprisingly painted a Mennonite pastor and his wife and perhaps embraced their faith. In two films Mennonites provide the central character's inspiration, while one very popular film, focused on the Amish, barely mentioned Mennonites. Two films used close-knit Mennonite colonies as the setting for human drama. Another with an exotic location used a little-known German dialect. The sixth and final film depicted Mennonites as the cause of great calamity to the community. The producer of one T.V. show is very knowledgeable of Mennonites but recognized his audience is clueless about them, while a second T.V. show used them as a gimmick.

A look at T.V.'s portrayal of Cindy Klassen, a young Mennonite Brethren Canadian who exemplifies the best of Mennonite qualities, along with a series of unrealistic Amish reality shows, a negative joke on *Modern Family*, and a two minute and thirty second video segment aired on *NBC Nightly News with Brian Williams*, which positively depicted Mennonite beliefs and practices, wrapped up this survey.

One's perception of Mennonites often depends on whether or not one agrees with them. At other times, Mennonites are simply an oddity which provides someone with a scapegoat or subject to parody. This survey demonstrated that religious leaders, writers, artists, and filmmakers the world over have often despised Mennonites; but at other times Mennonites have been tolerated, and occasionally they have been a source of inspiration.

Following centuries of persecution in Europe and their eventual migration to America, it is only in the last century that North American Mennonites have begun to emerge from their farms and sectarian communities to exert influence over the broader society. Still, they remain a small Protestant denomination, with distinct beliefs and practices, largely unknown by others. In the next section we will look at a few prominent examples of Mennonite writers, musicians, and filmmakers who have made ever so slight inroads into popular culture while retaining at least a semblance of Mennonite identity.

PART II

How Mennonites Have Used Media to Shape Identity and for Outreach

Introduction

Part I of this book examined many representatives from the small set of media (films, books, magazines, etc.) which mentions Mennonites, or Mennonites *in* media. Part II looks at Mennonites *and* media, exploring those persons of the Mennonite faith who have exerted influence by reaching into the broader culture through media.

Since their beginnings in sixteenth century Europe, Anabaptists have used media to shape their religious identity and reach out to others. Early Anabaptist writings were seldom published but rather were circulated in manuscript form. Many printers refused to handle Anabaptist writings because of the severe threat of persecution and physical harm. Government and religious leaders confiscated, banned, or burned many Anabaptist books along with their authors. In this way, Anabaptist ideas and writings were suppressed and kept from the broader society.[6] Those writings which have endured, such as Pilgram Marpeck's *Vermahnung* (1542) and the writings of Balthasar Hubmaier, Michael Sattler, and Menno Simons, were most often read by theologians and scholars but not more broadly.

6. Ibid., 148.

Similarly, during World War I, Federal authorities confiscated one-hundred and fifty copies of a church tract on nonresistance, produced by the Mennonite Publishing House in Scottdale, Pennsylvania. Around the same time Archibold Yoder of Ohio was arrested for trying to convince someone not to enlist in the military. Thus Mennonites have continued to use media to spread their heretical ideas of loving enemies, to the chagrin of those in authority.[7]

A renaissance of scholarly Anabaptist studies began in Europe in the mid-nineteenth century with the publication of several books on Mennonite history by scholars Carl A. Cornelius and Ludwig Keller. Most church historians rejected Keller's premise that Mennonites were a part of a larger evangelical movement in church history but he inspired further scholarship by Mennonites. American Mennonite historian John Horsch was one such person influenced by Keller's work.[8] These seeds of scholarship took root and came to bloom when Harold S. Bender began publishing *The Mennonite Quarterly Review (MQR)* in 1927. But even then, the *MQR* did not reach beyond Mennonite scholars into the general public.

Although there have been and still are many Mennonite writers, thinkers, musicians, and artists, few have risen to the level of media stars, that is, persons recognized by the general public both for their media presence and their faith. By way of comparison and contrast with another "outsider religious group," in addition to the well-known and much loved music of the Mormon Tabernacle Choir, eight popular, media savvy Mormons come immediately to mind: Mitt Romney, governor of Massachusetts and 2008 and 2012 Republican Presidential candidate; Donny and Marie Osmond, the 1970s brother and sister pop music sensation and T.V. hosts; Ken Jennings, reigning all-time *Jeopardy* champion; Jon Hedder, who starred in the titular role of the 2004 quirky hit film *Napoleon Dynamite*; Stephen Covey, author of *The Seven Habits of Highly Effective People*; U.S. Senator Orin Hatch (R-Utah); and Glen Beck, politically conservative pundit and T.V. show host. There are no comparable media stars in the Mennonite community. Two athletes, Floyd Landis and Cindy Klassen, were the subjects of much media (Part I) centered not only on their accomplishments but also on their Mennonite upbringing. However, Landis and Klassen were media subjects and not media shapers, which is the focus of Part II.

Perhaps one reason few Mennonites have embraced media is because of a theological reluctance to become entangled in what was, and for many continues to be seen as, a worldly, and thus forbidden, endeavor. According to research

---

7. Preheim, "Conflicts of Conscience," 6.
8. Toews, *Mennonites in American Society, 1930-1970*, 87.

conducted by J. Howard Kauffman and Leo Driedger, "In 1972 Mennonites were in the closing stages of a controversy over whether they should use television; many families were reluctant to do so."[9] Nonetheless, there are several Mennonites who have exerted a degree of influence through media and have left a lasting impression upon the broader culture concerning who Mennonites are and what they believe.

Although, Mennonites are not known for their media personalities, they are known for their four-part a cappella singing and their books. Two of the most influential books by twentieth century Mennonite authors are *The Politics of Jesus* and the *More-with-Less Cookbook*, both of which will be explored in Part II of this text. When John Howard Yoder published *The Politics of Jesus* in 1972 Christian seminaries stood up and took notice of Anabaptism, some for the first time. However, the message of a radical faith committed to following Jesus, loving enemies, and living simply didn't reach beyond academia to the general public until 1976 when Doris Janzen Longacre compiled and published the *More-with-Less Cookbook*. These two books, perhaps more than any others, greatly extended the influence of Mennonite theology and practice. Dr. Christopher Marshall, head of the School of Art, History, Classics, and Religious Studies at Victoria University of Wellington, New Zealand, reflected on the influence of these two books on he and his wife with these words, "To say we were converted by a cookbook would be going too far. But it was the *More-with-Less Cookbook*, together with John Howard Yoder's *The Politics of Jesus* which my wife Margaret and I read as university students that first triggered our interest in the Anabaptist tradition . . . Both gave expression, in different ways, to the same fundamental conviction that to be a Christian means following Jesus; . . . and that taking Jesus seriously means a lifestyle of simplicity, service, and peacemaking."[10]

As Mennonites become more mainstream and culturally assimilated, it becomes increasing difficult to identify who is Mennonite and who is not. The authors and artists cited here all self-identify as Mennonite. Hildi Froese Tiessen, reflecting on the Sixth Mennonite Writers Conference held at Eastern Mennonite University in Harrisonburg, Virginia in the spring of 2012, noted, "Mennonite writers locate themselves in the worldly present and most of their Mennonite readers are in the same place. So we are left with tracings . . . what remains of what doesn't remain . . . the absent present."[11]

---

9. Kauffman and Driedger, *The Mennonite Mosaic*, 266.
10. Roth, *Engaging Anabaptism*, 41.
11. Clemmer Steiner, "Self in Mennonite Garb," 23.

CHAPTER 5

Toward a Mennonite Theology of Media

A Peculiar People

During periods of severe persecution Anabaptists withdrew from society as a means of self-preservation. At other times their separation was the result of a truce mediated with ruling authorities to limit their cultural and theological influence on the native people. Mennonites have also secluded themselves by choice, often withdrawing into self-sustaining colonies. In part, this was to obey what they saw as clear biblical injunctions toward holiness and against worldliness.[1] One of the primary texts containing this injunction is Peter's command, found in 1 Peter 2:9, quoted here from the King James Version, "But ye are a chosen generation, a royal priesthood, an holy nation, a *peculiar people*; that ye should shew forth the praises of him who hath called you out of darkness into his marvelous light."

When the "hippies" of the 1960s rejected the dominant culture they did so individualistically, each one finding their own form of dress and expression. In contrast, Mennonite nonconformity has not been expressed individually, but collectively. Thus, although Mennonites have traditionally dressed very differently than "the world," they dressed in conformity with their group. Mennonites embraced a sense of godly otherness, manifest in a distinct form of dress and practice, which made them a "peculiar people." Today, the Amish retain these distinctive forms of clothing and lifestyle to a much greater extent than most Mennonites. Yet, even within the progressive Mennonite Church USA denomination many members have a clear

1. Umble and Weaver-Zercher, eds., *The Amish and the Media*, 166.

sense of Christian discipleship which calls them to live and think counterculturally. This is seen in disparate ways. In some it leads to a missionary zeal; others respond to Christ's call to "come and follow me" with peace activism, anti-consumerism, solidarity with the poor or immigrant, or embracing stewardship of the whole Earth. Books published by Mennonite authors such as *Simply in Season, More-with-Less* and *Living More with Less* all document this Mennonite tendency to "live simply so others can simply live." Mennonites remain a peculiar people, although it is less obvious in outward appearances than it once was.

This tendency toward separation has shaped how Mennonites have engaged with media and their neighbors. A significant historic event which has had a lasting impact on how Mennonites view the world and media was their time in Russia.

Another important point of understanding, with regard to Mennonites and media, is the tension held in the Mennonite faith between orthodoxy (right theological thinking) and orthopraxy (right practice or ethics).

A Lived Faith and its Relationship to Media

The Mennonite faith is a lived faith. It is not based primarily on complex theological constructs but rather on simple obedience to the commands of Christ. A key part of this "lived faith" is discipleship characterized by self-denial. Barry Callen describes it thus, "It is the self-denial that allows a believer to say "no" to some ways of thinking, acting and being, thus opening the door wider for the saying of "yes" to another, to God, and to the call of God's grace for sacrificial ministry in the world. Asceticism leads to greater love and thus service to others..."[2]

Callen points out the purpose of discipleship is not to be negative but rather to build up the church toward spiritual health so it can be about the work of extending God's kingdom in the world.[3] Yet petty prohibitions against cultural practices were common among Mennonites. That sense of self-denial and peculiarity was often demonstrated in a rejection of worldly entertainment. In 1972 three percent of Mennonites did not read newspapers or magazines, 14 percent were not reading books other than the Bible, 5 percent were not listening to radio, 15 percent were completely avoiding T.V. and 19 percent were not listening to recorded music. More than a de-

2. Callen, *Radical Christianity*, 132.
3. Ibid., 133.

cade later, in 1989, with the exception of an 8 percent increase in television viewing, these statistics were largely unchanged.[4]

By and large, until fairly recently the vast majority of Mennonites avoided movies and other "worldly" distractions. A booklet distributed among Mennonites in 1921, written by Clayton F. Derstine, named motion picture theater and stage productions in its title as *Hell's Playground*. In 1930 an article appeared in the Mennonite Conference periodical *Gospel Herald* by Herald Press which added opera to the trio of forbidden theatrical spectacles calling them "soul seductive institutions." This cultural resistance continued in 1940 when a Mennonite denominational publisher, Herald Press, printed the booklet *The Menace of the Movies* which was widely circulated among Mennonites. It argued motion pictures place too much emphasis on sex and crime while discounting honest work and glorifying immorality. Furthermore, it claimed the worldly attitudes promoted in films contributed to moral delinquency. The booklet was popular enough to be reprinted in 1943.[5]

This shunning of film and theater was rooted in a desire to live faithfully in obedience to Christ and the Ten Commandments. Those who avoided photography, believing it violated the commandment against graven images, saw motion pictures as an extension of this forbidden technology.[6] For others it was simply the subject matter of secular films which was incompatible with the isolated rural lifestyle of most Mennonites. They believed it threatened their innocence, modesty, and simplicity. Most Amish and Old Order Mennonites continue to forbid moviegoing, although their young people may sneak into theaters before being baptized into the church.[7]

On July 29, 1954, Virginia Mennonite Conference leaders took action condemning "compromises with world standards of life, including pleasure seeking and questionable entertainment."[8] Movies were not expressly forbidden by this resolution but they were clearly implicated. This attitude began to shift a decade later when televisions became commonplace in American homes.

Millard Osborne, former Conference Minister for South Central Mennonite Conference, tells of his moviegoing experience in his self-published

---

4. Kauffman and Driedger, *The Mennonite Mosaic*, 265.
5. Kraybill, "Motion Pictures." Gameo. Online.
6. Umble and Weaver-Zercher, eds., *The Amish and the Media*, 48.
7. Kraybill, "Motion Pictures."
8. Blosser, et al. *Minutes of the Virginia Mennonite Conference*, 27.

memoir *Along the Road*. In a brief story called "Going to the Movies" he recalls his first film experience as a teenager in 1950 when he saw *Cheaper by the Dozen*. He writes, "Entering the theater felt strange to me . . . I must admit I delighted in the comedy, but still found myself dealing with nudges of conscience. I do not remember telling my parents anything about going to this movie."[9] Sixteen years later, while serving as pastor of a Mennonite church, Osborne took his entire family to see Julie Andrews in the 1965 award winning film *The Sound of Music*. Writing in his memoir he recalls driving to a theater an hour away from their home in Lebanon, Oregon to see the film, "So to avoid any unnecessary talk among those who would not have wanted their pastor and family going to a movie theater . . . we kept that experience a moviegoing family secret."[10]

Julie Andrews' singing in *The Sound of Music* attracted many Mennonites and began to erode opposition to film among denominational leaders. In 1970, *The Cross and the Switchblade*, a powerful testimonial film based on David Wilkerson's ministry among New York City gangs, and evangelist Billy Graham's 1975 entry into the industry with *The Hiding Place*, based on Corrie Ten Booms' experiences hiding Jews during the Holocaust, expedited the demise of the Church's opposition to movies. In 1973, a team of independent Mennonite businessmen, including Merle Good, proprietor of People's Place and Good Books, produced their own full-length feature film *Hazel's People* which depicted Mennonite life and faith. Since then, many Mennonites have grown to appreciate the power of film and embraced cinematography. The Mennonite Church USA produced its own films through Third Way Media, which until 2011 was a division of Mennonite Mission Network when it merged with the Mennonite Publishing Network to form MennoMedia. Many pastors and church leaders watch movies not only for their own enjoyment and intellectual stimulation but as a window into popular culture. Some quote from popular films during their sermons in an effort to reach out to the community in their church's missional efforts.[11] Even so, many leaders, in Mennonite and other Christian denominations, continue to criticize Hollywood films for their graphic depiction of drug use, excessive violence, sexual situations, nudity, and profanity. According to Kauffman and Drieger's research, in 1989, 62 percent of Mennonites were not watching video cassettes at home. Films shown in movie theaters

9. Osborne, *Along the Road*, 43.
10. Ibid., 45.
11. Kraybill, "Motion Pictures." Gameo. Online

were not included in Kauffman's survey.[12] However, Conrad Kanagy did include movie viewing in his 2006 Church Member profile and found only 10 percent of Mennonites watched movies at home or in the theater at least weekly.[13]

Some consider the Amish to be Luddites, or technophobes rejecting all modern conveniences, but in reality they embrace those technologies which enhance their businesses without threatening their way of life. They test new technologies against the community's Ordnung or church rules for communal living. According to Amish scholar Donald Kraybill, "The Ordnung evolved gradually over the decades as the church sought to strike a delicate balance between tradition and change. Specific details of the Ordnung vary across church districts and settlements . . . A respected Ordnung generates peace, love, contentment, equality, and unity. It creates a desire for togetherness and fellowship. It binds marriages, it strengthens family ties to live together, to work together, to worship together, and to commune secluded from the world."[14]

Deciding which technologies to use and which to reject is an intricate process of community, not individual, discernment. This process, with its concurrent willingness to submit to the decision reached by the group, called Gelassenheit, meaning yieldedness, by the Amish, is unfamiliar to many. Rather, most Americans value their independence and self-reliance. This ability, to communally discern the value of any given technology and decide collectively whether to embrace it or reject it, is a unique gift the Amish can offer to the rest of the world.

In the latter half of the twentieth century Mennonites began to emerge from their cultural isolation. Some saw great potential for new forms of media, such as the radio, for evangelism and outreach. Mennonites were ready to embrace media as mission.

Embracing Media as Mission

Burton Buller, former director of Third Way Media, which at the time was an agency under Mennonite Mission Network within MC USA, wants the church to engage with the broader culture. He points out how Jesus effectively used parables referencing things familiar to his listeners and wonders

12. Kauffman and Driedger, *The Mennonite Mosaic*, 265.
13. Kanagy, *Road Signs for the Journey*, 106.
14. Kraybill, *The Riddle of Amish Culture*, 98.

if the Mennonite church is doing as well in connecting to its neighbors.[15] He challenges the Mennonite Church asking, "Could it be that God, as he did for Peter, is lowering a sheet filled with "the unclean"—computers, VCRS, TVs and video games—to challenge us to look beyond the walls we have built for ourselves? . . . When . . . we seek to engage [media] for kingdom purposes, we begin to imagine how it might be used in helping us to more effectively fulfill our mandate to 'teach all nations,' including our own.[16]

Buller goes on to note, 'We are called to live in the odorous kingdom of the world and to embrace it enough that we understand it at a deep enough level to impact it with the good news.'"[17]

For televangelist Billy Graham, addressing people one on one with the gospel or speaking to millions using television or the Internet is essentially the same. Some Mennonites are reluctant to accept that premise. While Graham was quick to recognize the power of television as a tool for evangelism, some Mennonite pastors, steeped in an Anabaptist tradition which values community, feel the Internet and television are too individualistic and thus not suited to sharing the gospel. Nonetheless, religion is big business on the Internet, ranking third behind sex and financial services online.[18]

To that end Mennonites are beginning to understand the power and importance of media, and how the form of media used in communications affects how recipients "hear" the message. Shane Hipps, former pastor of Trinity Mennonite Church in Phoenix, Arizona, is leading the way in cautioning Christians about technology's impact. He has written two books on the subject, *The Hidden Power of Electronic Culture*, published by Zondervan in 2005, and *Flickering Pixels: How Technology Shapes Your Faith*, published in 2009. In both he writes about the interrelationship between media and message and urges prudence and discernment in relation to the use of media, cautioning his readers about media's power to shape and distort the message.

Hipps advises against a glib approach which seeks to proclaim the unchanging message of the gospel using new methods without discerning their power, saying such a mindset discounts the impact of the form of media on the message. He asserts, "The forms of media and technology—regardless of their content—cause profound changes in the church

15. Buller, "Does Techno-Faith Have a Future?," 12.
16. Ibid., 2.
17. Ibid.
18. Ibid., 20.

and culture."[19] Hipps states, "When we fail to perceive media as an extension of ourselves, they take on godlike characteristics, and we become their servants . . . When we become aware of the specific ways in which technology and media serve as extensions of ourselves, much of their power is dispelled. We are returned to being owners of technology rather than those who are owned by it."[20]

Hipps notes the church has been significantly shaped by the printed and spoken word, which have been the dominant media forms since the time of the Reformation and the beginnings of Anabaptism. The age of print was logical and linear, giving rise to a sense of objectivity, repeatability, and uniformity. This reinforced the church's message of a grand meta-narrative based on scripture and was reflected in the post Reformation church's emphasis on right doctrine and individual Bible study. In contrast, today's post-modern society, saturated by electronic media, is bombarded by contradictory messages which often undermine the church's message. Knowledge is seen less as a building, with scripture as the foundation from which all truth is derived, but more as a web with multiple interconnections rooted in experience. Electronic media are attuned to stories and visual images. They employ circular logic, rather than the linear logic of print media.[21]

Hipps goes on to explain, "An image shows us the world as it is—an array of mystery and ambiguity. It does not explain or organize the world as language can. As a result, we are becoming increasingly tolerant of ambiguity and mystery—the very things images can best depict."[22]

Although the effects of electronic media can revert to relativism and undermine the church's message of Biblical truth, media can also enhance a creative—right brain—encounter with God and shift emphasis from an individual to a corporate approach to faith. Electronic media can enhance the mystery of God by retrieving an Eastern Orthodox understanding of spirituality and restoring Jesus, rather than Paul, as the central figure of the gospel.[23]

---

19. Hipps, *The Hidden Power of Electronic Culture*, 23.
20. Ibid., 37.
21. Ibid., 69.
22. Ibid., 80.
23. Ibid., 82.

Hipps declares "We need to develop healthy relationships with our technologies. This means nurturing a conscious awareness of their power, our longings, and the way both of these shape us."[24]

Pressed by this reality, Mennonite colleges and seminaries now offer courses which explore the intersection of faith and media. Eastern Mennonite Seminary has a newly developed online course in communication called, "Christ in a Communication Culture: Communicating in Today's Global, Digital, Relational World." Instructor Julie Gochenour says, "We are most like God because of our ability to communicate."[25] Increasingly that communication is not face to face but mediated through some form of technology. The church must continue to embrace these technologies, and fashion them for their own purposes, or face irrelevancy.

---

24. Ibid., 113.
25. Gochenour, "Seminary Offers Class." Online.

CHAPTER 6

Tracts, *Martyrs Mirror*, Signs, and Bookracks

Mennonite Tracts, Spreading the Gospel, and Other Heretical Ideas

Anabaptists identify the "Constantinian shift" as the time in the fourth century when Roman Emperor Constantine adopted the Christian faith thus displacing paganism as the official state or imperial religion. He provided material resources, lavished favors on the Christian Church, and began a process, which centuries later would result in the Holy Roman Empire, bringing all of Europe into an alliance centered on civil religion. This state/church alliance, begun by Constatine, is known as "Christendom."[1]

As paganism, and other religions, was suppressed and ultimately outlawed, the Jews became the only dissident religious community within the extensive Holy Roman Empire for centuries. Later on, pockets of Christians arose who refused to accept the biblical interpretations thrust upon them by the established church. These dissident groups, who dared to read the Bible for themselves, were suppressed, persecuted, and killed. The mighty power and efficiency of the Holy Roman Empire eradicated any challenge to its religious hegemony by threats and brutal acts of violence. Nonetheless, despite the best efforts of the State to eradicate them, dissident communities continued to emerge and spread. The simple tools they used to spread their ideas were preaching and teaching. The invention of the printing press by

1. Murray, *The Naked Anabaptist*, 51.

the German Johannes Gutenberg around 1440, changed everything. This new media greatly amplified the power of the written word allowing it to travel faster and farther than ever before. Prior to the printing press it took a professional scribe a full day to produce forty pages printed by hand. A printing press can produce ninety times more copy (three-thousand six-hundred pages) in the same amount of time. By 1500 there were twenty million volumes in print, produced by presses in operation throughout Europe. A century later their output had risen tenfold to an estimated one-hundred and fifty to two-hundred million volumes. The printing press allowed Martin Luther to become a bestselling author, selling hundreds of thousands of books in his lifetime.[2]

Anabaptism began early in the sixteenth century during this furtive time. Using the printing press, Anabaptists mass produced tracts, thus spreading their views and linking widely disparate communities. The sheer volume of these tracts frustrated attempts to suppress them.[3]

It is clear, from similarities noted at the trials of various accused Anabaptists, that many in this group had in their possession a common scripture portion—an abbreviated Bible—which they had printed, then carried and hid on their persons. Many of the works of early Anabaptist writers and thinkers have been lost, yet some remain. In 1525 Balthaser Hubmaier wrote a sixty-eight page booklet in defense of adult baptism called *On the Christian Baptism of Believers*. He wrote other tracts defending the movement against the anti-Anabaptist writings of his mentor, Zwingli of Zurich, and Oecolampadius, the state-church pastor in Basel.[4] Through the power of the printing press, these writings were soon in the hands of many Anabaptists and those who sympathized with them.

Thus from the very beginning of the Anabaptist movement, its leaders harnessed the power of the printing press, which represented the latest form of media, to amplify their message to great effect. More than a century later, Anabaptists would once again harness the power of the printing press to solidify their identity as a people persecuted for their faith in the tradition of the Apostles and early church fathers who had been killed for their beliefs.

---

2. Wikipedia, "The Printing Press," online, introduction.
3. Murray, *The Naked Anabaptist*, 136.
4. Dyck, *Introduction to Mennonite History*, 52.

Martyrs Mirror, Thieleman van Braght, and Colonial Printings

Contrary to the impression many have of Anabaptist history in Europe, Mennonites were not always harassed and persecuted for their faith. In the Netherlands, Mennonites went from being isolated and regarded as heretics to being integrated and accepted. Mennonites became successful businessmen and industrialists as well as accomplished in the arts and other intellectual pursuits.[5]

It is in this context of assimilation and a "lukewarm faith" that Dutch Mennonite Thieleman van Braght compiled what was to become *Martyrs Mirror*. The full title of this remarkable book, first published in 1660, is: *The Bloody Theater or Martyrs Mirror of the Defenseless Christians who baptized only upon confession of faith, and who suffered and died for the testimony of Jesus, their saviour, from the time of Christ to the year A.D. 1660*. The term "defenseless," as used in the title, refers to an Anabaptist understanding of Jesus' words, recorded in Matthew 5:39-39 (NIV) within the Sermon on the Mount, when he said, "You have heard that it was said, 'Eye for eye, and tooth for tooth.' But I tell you, do not resist an evil person. If anyone slaps you on the right cheek, turn to them the other cheek also." The book records the martyrdom of the Apostles and others who died for their faith, including the early Anabaptists. Although not widely read outside of Anabaptist circles, this books is significant and therefore included here because it served to shape the identity of this pious group, provided inspiration for faithful living, and promoted a willingness to die for Christ.

The *Martyrs Mirror* has since been revised, expanded, and translated into many languages. The 1685 edition contains one hundred and four illustrations made from copper etchings by artist Jan Luyken. The depiction of Dirk Willems turning back to save his pursuer who has fallen through the ice remains one of the most enduring images Mennonites use to express their practice of peace and nonresistance, even toward their enemies.

---

5. Visser, "Aspects of Social Criticism and Cultural Assimilation," VII.

PART II—HOW MENNONITES HAVE USED MEDIA

Anabaptist Dirk Willems rescues his pursuer and is subsequently burned at the stake in 1569. From *Martyrs Mirror*. In the public domain.

For many Mennonite families the *Martyrs Mirror* holds a place of prominence and significance second only to the Bible. In 1745 Jacob Gottschalk of Ephrata, Pennsylvania arranged to have it translated from Dutch into German to better serve the needs of the growing Mennonite colonies in America. The task took fifteen men three years to complete. When it was finished and printed in 1749 it numbered 1582 pages of text, ten by fifteen inches in size, and five inches thick, making it the largest book printed in America before the Revolutionary War.[6] Herald Press, the Mennonite Church USA denominational publisher, lists *Martyrs Mirror* as its ninth bestseller in the decade between 2000 through 2009, with 22,499 total copies of all editions sold.[7]

Nearly three and a half centuries after the first publication of *Martyrs Mirror*, Robert Kreider and John Oyer constructed an exhibit to display the recently recovered copper plates used to illustrate the 1685 edition. They called it *The Mirror of the Martyrs*. Built in 1989, during the 1990s it traveled to fifty-five venues in North America as distinct as Amish equipment

6. Hostetler, *God Uses Ink*, 10-11.
7. Lefever, "Mennonite Media Resources Business Plan,"Appendix I.

sheds and college art galleries. "This traveling visual exhibition has perhaps stirred up more interest in the Anabaptist legacy among contemporary Mennonites and Amish than even [Harold] Bender's more academically circumscribed "The Anabaptist Vision" did in the 1940s and 1950s."[8]

With *Martyrs Mirror* Anabaptists harnessed the power of printed media to forge a major piece of literature which helped shape their identity and expand their witness. This classic text remains important to Anabaptists nearly three and a half centuries later.

Martyrs Mirror was not the only early Anabaptist book used to shape the faith community's identity. *The Ausbund*, compiled in 1540, is a collection of fifty-one hymns written by Swiss-German Anabaptists, many of whom were imprisoned and often killed for their faith. *The Ausbund* does not contain music, only the hymns' words and the name of the associated tune. Germantown Dunker printer Christopher Sower printed the first American edition of *The Ausbund* in 1742.[9] It is seldom used by Mennonites today yet remains central to Amish worship practices.[10]

Another piece of media which shaped Anabaptist identity was the *Dordrecht Confession*, written in 1632 and reprinted countless times. American Mennonites, seeking to preserve their religious identity in a new land, were anxious to have this confession available in English. They translated it from Dutch and arranged for its printing. In 1727 it was published under the title *The Christian Confession of Faith of the Harmless Christians, in the Netherlands known by the name of Mennonists* becoming the first Mennonite book printed in America.[11] Others followed.

In 1717, Henry Funk emigrated from Europe to America settling north of Philadelphia where he farmed, milled, and served as a bishop in Franconia Mennonite Conference. An important Mennonite scholar, in 1744 he published *Ein Spiegel der Taufe* (*Mirror of Baptism*), a very popular ninety-four page treatise on the scriptural and practical aspects of baptism.[12]

Christopher Dock, a Mennonite schoolmaster in eastern Pennsylvania, is remembered for writing the first American treatise on pedagogy called *Schulornung (School Management)* which he published before the

---

8. Biesecker-Mast, *Separation and the Sword in Anabaptist Persuasion*, 61.
9. Hostetler, *God Uses Ink*, 12.
10. Friedmann, "Ausbund," Gameo. Online.
11. Hostetler, *God Uses Ink*, 8.
12. Ibid., 9.

American Revolution.[13] Indeed, each of these publishing feats; *Martyrs Mirror, The Ausbund, The Christian Confession of Faith of the Harmless Christians, Mirror of Baptism* and *School Management*, were accomplished by Mennonites in the American colonies before the first English Bible was printed in America. That ocurred in Philadelphia in 1782.[14]

Property Signs

The term "quiet in the land" is grounded in Mennonite experiences while living in separate colonies in Prussia prior to their migration to Canada and the U.S. The term has also been applied to the Amish, rural Mennonites, and even to some members of one of the most progressive expressions of the Mennonite Church, MC USA. A simple expression of faith, favored by some of the "quiet in the land," is the use of signs on the edges of farms and homesteads. They are intended as an outreach to neighbors. These ads are usually brief scripture quotes which are simple and straight to the point. For example, "Submit to God, resist the Devil" James 4:7 expresses the theme of discipleship, which is central to the Mennonite faith. Other signs are more encouraging such as "Have you thanked the Lord today?" while still others have an evangelical bent, e.g., "Eternity where?" They are often positioned on the edge of a Mennonite's property, adjacent to the road where they are clearly visible to passersby. Some are crudely made and hand painted. Others are more professional in their appearance.

Paul and Arlene Landis, parents of cyclist Floyd Landis, used this quiet form of witness when the worldwide press showed up on their front step asking how they were handling Floyd's surprising Tour de France victory. Several photos of the Landis home in Lancaster County showed the three signs displayed in their front yard.

13. Ibid., 12.
14. Ibid., 14.

Tracts, *Martyrs Mirror*, Signs, and Bookracks

Charity, Paul and Arlene Landis in front of their Farmersville, Pennsylvania home on July 24, 2006 with a magazine featuring Floyd on the cover. Photo by Dale D. Gehman, used with permission.[15]

Mennonites are not the only faith community to use this form of witness but they are perhaps the most proficient at it. A small survey, conducted by the author, of property owners displaying religious signs in and around Rockingham County, Virginia, revealed all were Mennonites or formerly Mennonite. One Mennonite denomination centered in Pennsylvania has a systematic gospel sign ministry begun by Dennis Bennetch.[16]

Before creating the Cable News Network (CNN) Ted Turner got his start in his father's Atlanta billboard advertising business. Although he would likely not understand the cultural reference, Dennis Bennetch is the Ted Turner of roadside gospel signs. When interviewed, at sixty-five years of age, his passion for sign evangelism was palpable. Bennetch, a member of the Dohner Mennonite Church in Lebanon, Pennsylvania, wants to glorify God and bring people into God's Kingdom. "Plain attire is not enough," he says, "But with a regenerated heart it's an asset." Bennetch says people often approach him and ask if he is Amish. He uses such opportunities to give

---

15. Rhodes, "Cyclist Wins World's Top Race," July 31, 2006.
16. Bennetch, telephone conversation, March 26, 2011.

a quick church history lesson then turns the conversation to faith in Jesus Christ. But his evangelistic method of choice is the roadside gospel sign.

For more than twenty years Bennetch has been involved in a "gospel sign system" which places standardized green, white, and yellow lettered metal signs, each measuring eighteen inches tall by twenty-four inches wide, on the edge of a church member's property in plain view of passing motorists. Most, but not all, contain a short scripture reference, e.g., 'Be tender, forgive, Ephesians 4:32' or 'Return unto the Lord, Isaiah 55:7.' Others have a religious theme and point to scripture, e.g., 'There is mercy with the Lord, see Psalm 130:7.' Bennetch explained some messages are negative, e.g., 'God destroyed Sodom,' while others are neutral, e.g., 'Sing praises to God.' Still others contain a positive message about God's love. There are one-thousand three hundred different messages in circulation. In each location two signs, with different messages, are placed back to back on a wooden display board. Bennetch recalled making as many as two-hundred signs in a single month, but he was reluctant to estimate how many have been distributed. He did not want to boast but said, "It's a little like numbering Israel. You don't do it." Bennetch retired from the Gospel Sign Ministry governing board in 2005 but remains active in the work. He has little patience for Christians unwilling to share their faith and said, "I don't understand how some people can be so quiet." He hopes these signs "with a message of repentance and hope, get people looking and thinking." [17]

The Gospel Sign Ministry is overseen by five men from churches in the Eastern Pennsylvania Mennonite Church. This group was granted release from Lancaster Mennonite Conference in 1968 and adheres to the 1921 Mennonite Confession of Faith. In 2010 it had seventy-seven congregations with a total of 5,333 members. The ministry uses volunteer labor provided by their church youth who cut four by eight foot sheets of painted aluminum and then apply reflective vinyl letters. James L. Kreider, the group's marketing manager, has records from the past four years indicating they produced and sold two-thousand and two hundred signs. He estimates there are more than five thousand signs on display in thirty U.S. states, British Columbia, Ontario, and Guatemala. The vast majority of these signs are being displayed by Mennonites, although there are a few Baptists participating too.[18]

Families are encouraged to buy two signs for $17.50 each and place them in a wooden frame on the edge of their property. Once the frame is

---

17. Ibid.
18. J. L. Kreider, telephone conversation, March 27, 2011.

in place, a group of young men from the church travel along a "sign circle" route approximately twenty to twenty-five miles in diameter, rotating the signs with a fresh message each month. Sometimes signs need to be replaced because they had been vandalized. Others are retired when they become too weathered. Kreider explained the impact of the signs saying, "Sometimes people stop at a house with a gospel sign out front and ask for help with a spiritual need. At other times they ask for money. I guess they think if you have a sign you're a compassionate person."[19]

Gospel Sign in Augusta County, Virginia. Photo by the author.

Roger Hertzler, a CPA living in Halsey, Oregon, has a similar ministry called Watchman Gospel Signs. Hertzler's inspiration came from the life and evangelistic ministry of the late George R. Brunk II, an itinerant Mennonite evangelist home based in the Warwick River Mennonite Church in Newport News, Virginia, and from one of Brunk's disciples, Ralph Palmer. Hertzler recommends Martha Shenk Palmer's book *A Sower Went Forth*, which is a biography of her husband Ralph.[20] Hertzler grew up Mennonite but now worships with another Anabaptist group. He estimates he distributed one thousand gospel signs last year and more than three thousand in

19. Ibid.
20. Hertzler, "Watchman Gospel Signs." Online.

the six years of his involvement in this ministry. His philosophy is "Put out a fishing line and the hungry ones will bite."[21]

The missionary impulse to reach out with the Gospel message was a defining characteristic of the early Anabaptist movement. Years of persecution and cultural isolation dampened this impulse among some Mennonites, while acculturation has diminished this evangelical bent among others. One Mennonite institutional response to the desire for spiritual outreach was "bookrack evangelism" through Choice Books.

Choice Books, "Bookrack Evangelism"

Choice Books began in its present form in 1965 when the Mennonite Board of Missions transferred responsibility for its "bookrack evangelism" program, then called Life-Line Books, to Mennonite Broadcasts (later Mennonite Media, Third Way Media, and MennoMedia) in Harrisonburg, Virginia.

The goals of the program from the beginning were to "assist persons in developing a better understanding of the Christian gospel" and "provide information and alternatives from a Christian perspective for many of life's problems."[22] Choice Books is a form of Christian outreach to unchurched and nominally Christian people, rather than a ministry of nurture and discipleship for Mennonite and Anabaptist groups. It was, and is, an extension of the Mennonite impulse, exhibited since the beginnings of the movement, to share their faith with others. The method used is to place inexpensive Christian literature in unexpected places so as to make it readily available to persons who would not visit a Christian bookstore. Thus, by 1972, the rotating display racks began showing up in drug stores, supermarkets, and even the Pentagon. In later years airports became a particularly fruitful location for displays.

Growth was rapid. 1968 saw a growth rate in excess of 100 percent going from 28,554 books sold to 66,950. Such explosive growth rates continued with 58 percent in 1969 and 52 percent in 1970, while the number of displays also increased dramatically from seventy in 1966 to two-hundred and forty-five in 1970. The number of books distributed in a ten year period between 1967 and 1977 was 3,610,794.[23] In 2010, more books were sold in a single year than in the first decade of Choice Books operation, num-

21. Hertzler, telephone conversation, March 28, 2011.
22. Pellman, *Mennonite Broadcasts*, 205.
23. Ibid., 216.

Tracts, *Martyrs Mirror*, Signs, and Bookracks

bering 5,112,343 volumes through eleven thousand permanent displays nationwide.[24]

Choice Books is not primarily about promoting Mennonite books, although Herald Press imprints have numbered among the best sellers, particularly in the early years. In 1977 the sale of 6,275 copies of *Real People* by A. Martha Denlinger and published by Herald Press placed it fifth on Choice Books' top ten list. In 2010, the top seller was *Know Your Bible* by Paul Kent with Barbour Publishing which sold 63,072 copies.[25]

Initially Choice Books needed the financial support of the Mennonite Mission Board to obtain publishers discounts and thereby keep prices low. Over the years Choice Books has relied less on volunteers and mission dollars and more on an astute business plan. In 1998 Choice Books became a limited liability corporation operating under a board of directors, independent of any Mennonite church or mission agency.

---

24. "Choice Books Sells 5 Million Books Again," 1.
25. Ibid.

CHAPTER 7

Music and Radio

Music and Joseph S. Funk

Certain ancient Greeks wondered which among the forms of media were the most powerful. They saw a close relationship between music and morals. In his *Republic,* Plato went so far as to propose a ban on dramatic poetry because of its supposed negative influence on its audience. Music is closely linked with the communication arts of writing and painting, but it is of a more visceral media which cannot be fully contained in representational form. According to media guru Thomas de Zengotita,

> The consensus of the wise is that music is unique among the arts because it operates on the same plane as the unmediated, the given. It belongs to sensation itself, to bodily existence and, for that very reason, it elevates that existence in a way no other art can match. Music takes hold of you on levels of being that precede intentional articulation, levels of being that contain what you cannot put into words. And that is why words, when they are sustained by the immediacy of music, have a unique power. They represent, they articulate—and they penetrate, they fill dumb bodies with meaning.[1]

The power of music has not gone unnoticed among Mennonites. Even as the Mormons are known for the Mormon Tabernacle Choir, Mennonites have become known for the quality of their unaccompanied four-part singing. The hymns of faith sung in Mennonite gatherings are sometimes

---

1. De Zengotita, *Mediated,* 97.

simple, unadorned harmonies. At other times they are intricate and elaborate, even when sung a cappella.

The a cappella multi-part singing, which many associate with Mennonites, is a fairly recent phenomenon.

> Mennonite Church (MC) congregations of North America, as well as some of the more conservative groups, long promoted four-part *a cappella* singing, which, according to Walter E. Yoder, began "about 1875 in the more progressive congregations and was gradually adopted by all of our churches during the 1890s. The church really came into four-part singing after they had been taught in singing classes and the church adopted the English language and the Gospel songs." Four-part singing of German chorales in congregations of Mennonites in Russia began in the mid-19th century, when the practice was introduced with "Ziphern" (numbers) on the musical staves, similar to the North American method of shaped notes.[2]

The thrust toward a cappella singing came from a prohibition, in effect until the early 1900s, against the use of musical instruments in worship. All musical instruments, that is, except the human voice.

Joseph S. Funk, born in 1778 in Franconia, Pennsylvania into a German speaking Mennonite family, entered that void and filled it with something beautiful. He devised a system to teach singing using songbooks printed with four shaped notes and later seven shaped notes. In addition to his skill as a musician and teacher, he was also the first Mennonite known to have owned and operated a printing press.[3] Funk was appointed by Virginia Mennonite Conference to a three person committee which, in 1847, published the first English edition Mennonite hymnal. Funk's most famous songbook, *Harmonia Sacra*, published in 1832 and now in its twenty-fifth edition, is the oldest hymnal in continual use in the United States. The songbook's complete title is *The Harmonia Sacra, being a compilation of the genuine church music, comprised of a great variety of metres, harmonized for three and four voices: together with a copious explication of the principles of vocal music. Exemplified and illustrated with tables. In a plain and comprehensive manner. By Joseph Funk and Sons.* Nearly one hundred thousand copies of *Harmonia Sacra* have been sold and demand for it continues. Ben

---

2. Bender et al., "Church Music," Gameo. Online.
3. Hostetler, *God Uses Ink*, 20.

PART II—HOW MENNONITES HAVE USED MEDIA

Hibbs, editor of the prestigious *Saturday Evening Post*, called Funk's work "of genuine national significance."[4]

By 1890, four-part singing was widely accepted in North American Mennonite congregations. From the late 1800s through the mid-1900s, many churches organized singing schools and in 1913 Bluffton College was the first Mennonite school to dispatch an a cappella choir into the community for performances.[5]

Harmonia Sacra is yet another example of Mennonites innovating and using print media to shape the faith identity of their communities and for outreach. Although slow to adopt new forms of media, by the mid-1900s Mennonites saw the tremendous potential for outreach using radio.

Radio and *The Mennonite Hour*

Former Mennonite pastor Shane Hipps skillfully describes the power of radio saying, "With radio, we began to share simultaneous oral experiences on a scale never before known to human culture. . . . [It] was a reversal of the fragmentation of individualization brought on by the print age: a book is consumed on one's own private time, but to participate in the radio event, everyone must huddle around the radio receiver at the same moment and listen. Just as in tribal cultures, the radio allows shared songs, experiences and stories to emerge, but with radio, these extend far beyond the perimeter of the local campfire."[6]

For some Mennonite preachers, the communal nature and broad expanse of radio, as described by Hipps, was an attractive tool to share the gospel.

Perhaps the earliest use of radio by Mennonites was *The Calvary Hour* begun in November 1936 by William G. Detweiler, then pastor of Pleasant Hill Mennonite Church in Sterling, Ohio. *The Calvary Hour*, which consisted primarily of preaching and Bible exposition, continued independent of any church-wide institution. After William's sudden death in 1956, the broadcast continued under the direction of his twin sons Bill and Bob Detweiler for more than fifty years. During much of that time, Bill Detweiler served as pastor of Kidron Mennonite Church in Kidron, Ohio (1957 to 1994) while preaching every other week on the broadcast, alternating with

    4. Ibid., 24.

    5. Lofton, "Those Famous Mennonite Harmonies," 9.

    6. Hipps, *The Hidden Power of Electronic Culture*, 71.

Music and Radio

his brother Bob. The radio program ceased operations on December 30, 2007. Although popular, *The Calvary Hour* preached an Evangelical Christian message with very little Mennonite content. It never reached beyond radio into other forms of media, nor was it embraced by a denominational entity. It took the organization of Mennonite Broadcasts, Inc. to lead the church to broaden its vision and embrace radio as mission.[7]

It is ironic that a church-wide media ministry would emerge in Virginia when as far back as October 1924 Virginia Mennonite Conference took action in the form of a resolution stating, "We deem it wrong to have the radio in our homes." The action was further strengthened in 1931 when the bishops required members to remove radios from their homes and dispose of them.[8]

Nonetheless, compelled by an evangelical zeal to preach and teach others about Christ, on March 4, 1951, Mennonites in Virginia began a weekly radio broadcast of a program called *The Crusaders for Christ*. In March, 1952 the name was changed to *The Mennonite Hour* in order to identify it as a "missionary project of the church." Norman Derstine was the first announcer for the program which was comprised of sacred, four-part a cappella singing and two testimonies from students at Eastern Mennonite College. By the end of 1955, Mennonite Broadcasts, Inc. (MBI) was incorporated as the parent organization for *The Mennonite Hour*. From 1963 through 1972 more than one hundred radio stations carried *The Mennonite Hour* which reached a high of one hundred and thirty-five stations in 1972. MBI added other radio programs, such as *Heart to Heart*, and ministries, including home Bible studies, publishing endeavors, and a "book rack evangelism" program which would become Choice Books. In 1964 MBI produced four 60 second Family Life T.V. spots aired over 267 stations across the U.S. MBI became Mennonite Media, renamed itself Third Way Media, then, in 2011, merged with Mennonite Publishing Network to form Menno Media.[9] Although the forms of media continue to change and programs evolve, the Mennonite Church was reluctant to embrace media as mission.

---

7. McFarland, "Calvary Hour," Mennonite Church USA Archives. Online.
8. Pellman, *Mennonite Broadcasts*, 13.
9. Ibid.

PART II—HOW MENNONITES HAVE USED MEDIA

Contemporary Music

There are many fine musicians and musical groups with Mennonite members.[10] Mennofolk, a loose organization for Mennonite musicians, lists eighty-eight musicians or musical groups on their web site including: Andru Bemis, Chuck Neufeld, Goldmine Pickers, Heather Kropf, Rachel Ries, Reunion Vocal Band, Jonathan Reuel, Steel Wheels, and Brad Yoder. Jim Croegaert, the group Shapiro, and opera singers Anthony Brown and Madeline Bender are not on the Mennofolk list but could be added. Few of them are professional musicians, and fewer still have risen in the public's consciousness to the level of media stars. An example of an excellent, but not well known, songwriter is D. Gerald Derstine, a.k.a. J. D. Martin. Although raised Mennonite he is a bit less public about his Mennonite faith. Perhaps his best known religious song, *Jesus, Rock of Ages,* appears in the Mennonite Publishing House's *Hymnal: A Worship Book,* number 515, which is used extensively in Mennonite and Brethren Churches, but did not reach a broader audience.

There are two singing groups with at least one Mennonite member on the cusp of being famous. Over the Rhine, comprised of a German Mennonite Lindford Detweiler and his Swedish Lutheran wife Karin Berquist, is perhaps the most popular music group with a Mennonite member. With roots in a working-class neighborhood outside of Cincinnati, Ohio for which the duo is named, Over the Rhine has been recording albums since 1989. On February 8, 2011 they were interviewed on National Public Radio concerning their fourteenth CD, *The Long Surrender.* "The first time I heard Karin's voice, I knew there was something special there," Detweiler says in an interview with *All Things Considered* host Melissa Block. "I loved the fact that her voice came from the place where her pain lived."[11]

Brian McCraken, in his book *Hipster Christianity,* names Over the Rhine's album *Ohio,* released in 2003, as one of the ten essential "albums that every true Christian hipster is likely to own."[12] Karin and Linford were named to *Paste* magazine's list of 100 Best Living Songwriters. Much of their music explores Christian themes with frequent references to redemption, grace, a Pentecostal fire, and other biblical illusions. Speaking of the

---

10. My research overlooked Jason Scott Chasez, a Mennonite member of NSYNC which sold more than fifty million albums during the band's career from 1995 through 2002.

11. Staff NPR, "Over the Rhine," National Public Radio. Online.

12. McCracken, *Hipster Christianity,* 174.

band's aspirations they say, "[We] write music that is undeniably connected to the story we're writing with our lives. We show up and wait for God to walk through the room and settle for nothing less."[13]

Karin and Linford have a large and loyal fan base but they shy away from glitzy marketing. Instead they have taken an "Aww, shucks approach . . . we still believe we have something potentially significant to contribute to the American music scene. The songs we write will eventually be what we refer to as our life's work. And we're going to work really hard to make sure the songs keep getting better."[14]

Bob Townsend, music critic for *The Washington Post*, did a feature on Over the Rhine in the Post's Style section on September 8, 2013. It included a seven inch square photo and noted Detwiller grew up in an Amish and Mennonite family in Canton, Ohio. It also mentions they met at Malone College, a small Quaker liberal arts school in Canton. Townsend writes, "Maybe you've never heard of Over the Rhine, even though they've recorded some 25 albums since the early '90s and toured with Bob Dylan and the Cowboy Junkies. But for hundreds of thousands of fans the literate music of husband-and-wife singer-songwriters Karin Bergquist and Linford Detweiler is like a secret handshake, signifying meaningful moments and important passages in their lives."[15]

Although many of their fans would recognize the Christian roots of their music, their songs convey little about particular Mennonite beliefs or practices, although social justice and peace issues are common. For Over the Rhine their music is an expression of who they are. It reflects their deepest passions and longings, including a sense of God's call upon their lives. They are both shaping and being shaped by their music. It is their medium for outreach and they have been successful in sharing their ideas and values with a multitude of fans.

Steel Wheels began in Harrisonburg, Virginia in the early 2000s as Trent Wagler and the Steel Wheels, in recognition of the bands founder, lead singer, and primary song writer. Beside Trent, the group is made up of three other Mennonite men; Jay Lapp, Brian Dickel, and Eric Brubaker. 2010 was a breakout year for the band culminating with five nominations from The Independent Music Awards including "Nothing You Can't Lose" taking top honors as "Best Country Song." Steel Wheels made their first

13. "Over the Rhine," OTR web site. Online.
14. Ibid.
15. Townsend, "Over the Rhine, Comfortable 'under the Radar,'" 5.

appearance on National Public Radio's Mountain Stage aired on April 13, 2011. The program aired live and included a twenty-one minute segment of songs from their new CD, *Red Wing*.[16] That album spent thirteen weeks on the Americana Music Association's Top 40 radio charts, topping out at number fifteen as well as cracking the top ten on the Euro-Americana charts. It was ranked the number two independently released album, as charted by the Americana Music Association, and number seventy on the top one hundred Americana albums of 2010.

In the spring of 2012 they released *The Steel Wheels: Lay Down, Lay Low* which ranked 29th on the Americana Music Association's radio chart for the week of May 7, 2012.[17] The album placed the band in the top forty chart for Bluegrass music for nine weeks, with its lively blend of traditional music, bluegrass, gospel and blues. Each of the four members is active in a Mennonite church. On May 10, 2012 National Public Radio (NPR) chose *Rain in the Valley* by Steel Wheels as their "Song of the Day." Claire Marie Blaustein, writing in the NPR blog, says, "The new album is stronger in its use of the band's vocal talents, reminiscent of the four-part singing of the Mennonite communities where several of them once lived."[18] In describing the featured song, *Rain in the Valley*, she calls it "a heavy hymn" and describes Steel Wheel's music this way, "[It] passes from voice to voice, in waves overlapping defiance and fear, drenching the whole song in sound, and leaving the listeners hoping to get washed away."[19]

They appeared a second time on the *Mountain Stage* on February, 16, 2014 which was recorded at the Culture Center in Charleston, West Virginia before a live audience. Steel Wheels also graced the cover of the widely read musical performance industry magazine Pollstar.[20]

These four young Mennonite men know who they are and where they come from. Trent's father was a leader among the General Conference Mennonites. The band makes an annual "Spokesongs" tour entirely by bicycle averaging five hundred miles and ten concerts while carrying themselves and all of their equipment via pedal power. They also perform other benefit concerts to raise support for Mennonite Schools and relief organizations.

---

16. Blauser, "The Steel Wheels on Mountain Stage," National Public Radio. Online.
17. Schrag, "Mosaic," 10.
18. Blaustein, "Steel Wheels," National Public Radio. Online.
19. Ibid.
20. KTTZ, "The Steel Wheel on Mountain Stage," Texas Tech University. Online.

CHAPTER 8

Art, Performance, and Television

HISTORICALLY MENNONITES ARE CLOSELY aligned with the Reformed church in their thinking with regard to art. Both groups rejected the ornate art, icons, and statuary found in the Roman Catholic Church. Both objected to the use of religious art in their services of worship. Rather they emphasize simplicity, sincerity, and humility. In contrast art seems artificial, pretentious, and wasteful to them.[1] Yet Mennonites have created significant art on religious themes which can inform the public about their Mennonite faith.

Artist - Warren Rohrer

Warren Rohrer is arguably the most well-known and influential Mennonite artist since Jan Luyken created the copper plate lithographs used as illustrations in *Martyrs Mirror*. Rohrer's works grace the collections of both the Metropolitan Museum of Art in New York and the Philadelphia Museum of Art. They have been on display in thirty-one solo exhibitions in galleries throughout eastern Pennsylvania and New York, including Eastern Mennonite College, from which he graduated in 1950 with a BA in Bible Studies. Rohrer went on to earn a BS in art education from neighboring James Madison University in 1951.

Rohrer, born in Smoketown, Pennsylvania in 1927, was heavily influenced by his upbringing on a Mennonite farm in rural Lancaster County,

---

1. Bender et al., "Art," Gameo. Online.

Pennsylvania. He attended Lancaster Mennonite High School and what was then Eastern Mennonite College. During the summer of 1946 he volunteered with Mennonite Central Committee and accompanied a shipment of cattle being transported to Poland to replenish the herds lost during World War II.

An art critic for *The Philadelphia Inquirer*, after viewing a 1960 solo exhibit in the Robert Carlen Gallery in Philadelphia, wrote, "Warren Rohrer's canvases are a combination of romanticism and expressionism." The gallery patron called him "an interesting young abstractionist." [2]

In 1961 Eastern Mennonite College (now University) commissioned him to create a wood block portrait of Menno Simons. Dr. Irvin B. Horst, professor of art history, contacted Rohrer about the project and cautioned, "If it is to sell to our people it will have to be sufficiently representational to be appreciated."[3] This print is in wide use in Mennonite congregations.

Warren Rohrer. Print from a woodcut of Menno Simons, 25 x 19 inches, 1961. Commissioned by Eastern Mennonite College, Harrisonburg, Virginia. Photograph by the author.[4]

2. Rosenberg et al., *Warren Rohrer*, 63.

3. Ibid., 64.

4. This print is on display at the Eastern Mennonite University Historical Library and in many other locations.

Art, Performance, and Television

At Warren Rohrer's request, when he died in 1995 at the age of sixty-seven, Mennonite historian John L. Ruth gave a meditation at his memorial services held at Community Mennonite Church in Lancaster, Pennsylvania and at the Martin Locks Gallery, Philadelphia, Pennsylvania. In the eulogy Ruth quotes Rohrer saying, "I'm engaged in a dialogue between what I'm indebted to and what I'm rejecting . . . I'm not a Mennonite, but I consider myself a Mennonite."[5]

Rohrer's career as an artist and art teacher took many forms, but he is perhaps best remembered for his abstract but highly structured oil on canvas paintings which emerged from his fascination with the Fibonacci number sequence (1, 2, 3, 5, 8, 13). This sequence, first discovered in the Middle Ages, occurs repeatedly in nature as the spiral pattern of sea shells, leaves, and branches. Rohrer used the sequence to dictate proportional changes in hue and tone. Susan Rosenberg, in her book which published a collection of Rohrer's painting created between 1972 and 1993 writes, "Rohrer explicitly describes his life's work as an investigation of origins, linking the local wellspring of his painting in . . . Lancaster, to the very process of artistic self-invention. From a lived experience in which nature and spirit were inseparable, he encoded his abstract paintings with the residue of place and culture remade in a pattern announcing itself as universal."[6]

Recognizing the tremendous influence Rohrer's upbringing had on him, Rosenberg gives considerable detail about his Mennonite ancestors as well as the origins, beliefs, and practices of the Mennonite faith. While Rohrer, a Mennonite ambassador among the artists of Philadelphia and beyond, strayed far from his religious roots, serious Rohrer fans, and art historians, can learn much about Mennonites from Rosenberg's book and other sources describing his art and life.

Artist - Esther Augsburger

Esther Augsburger has had a successful artistic career working primarily in sculpture. Her original art has been recognized around the world with much praise and critical acclaim. She is also well known as the wife of author, preacher, Mennonite statesman, and President Emeritus of Eastern Mennonite University (EMU)—Myron Augsburger.

---

5. Ruth, "Memorial Observance."
6. Rosenberg et al., *Warren Rohrer,* 26.

PART II—HOW MENNONITES HAVE USED MEDIA

Augsburger grew up in India, the daughter of missionary parents. She learned to sculpt with mud for lack of regular toys. Her work reflects her deep Christian faith and pacifist convictions. In 1971, she was the first person to graduate from Eastern Mennonite College with a BA in Art. In 1978 she earned her Master of Arts degree in sculpture from James Madison University. She went on to teach at EMU and established an art program at Eastern Mennonite High School.

Collectors in at least eight countries possess Augsburger's artwork: Canada, England, Japan, India, Switzerland, New Zealand, Russia; and the U.S. Several famous persons own Augsburger's art including: Former President Jimmy Carter, Reverend Billy Graham, Senator Mark O. Hatfield of Oregon; and Representative John Dellenbach of Oregon. Two of Augsburger's originals, *Love Essence* and *Guns into Plowshares*, have received worldwide recognition and are pictured below.

She crafted two versions of the sculpture *Love Essence*, which depicts Jesus washing his disciple Peter's feet, and created two pieces of each version. They are located at: Eastern Mennonite University, Union Biblical Seminary in Pune India, Service Master's headquarters in Chicago, and Warner's Christian College in Florida. The figures in *Love Essence* are faceless, representing the universality of serving others. They point to service as a religious practice dear to Mennonites.

Love Essence. **Photograph by sculptor Esther Augsburger.
Used with permission.**

One of Augsburger's sculptures strikingly communicates her Mennonite passion for peace. *Guns Into Plowshares* is a sixteen foot tall steel plow and has more than three-thousand handguns welded onto its "V" form. The District of Columbia's Metropolitan Police Department commissioned Augsburger to use pistols, obtained by the police from individuals in a buy-back program, in a work of art. Each handgun was rendered inert before Augsburger and her son Michael welded it into the sculpture. It took two and a half years to complete. From 1997 until 2008 it was prominently displayed in the center of Judiciary Square in Washington, District of Columbia. Since Judiciary Square's renovation, the sculpture was moved to storage where it remained as of this writing.[7]

Guns to Plowshares. Photograph by sculptor Esther Augsburger. Used with permission.

For more than ten years Augsburger helped organize a Christian Artists Conference in Eastern Europe which she hopes will encourage artists to share their vision and their faith with the world. In 2001, Eastern Mennonite University dedicated a freestanding fine arts studio named after Esther K. Augsburger. EMU honored her again in 2003 by naming her a Distinguished Artist in Residence. She has two honorary doctorates, one from Grove City College and the other from Eastern Baptist Seminary in Pennsylvania.

7. Morgan, "Esther Augsburger Shares Her Faith." Online.

PART II—HOW MENNONITES HAVE USED MEDIA

Performer - Ted Swartz

Ted Swartz is a not so typical Mennonite actor. Beginning in 1987, he partnered with Lee Eshleman performing comedy skits at youth retreats and in other settings. They worked together in a theater company called AKIMBO, which Swartz founded in 1991 with Barbara Graber, a professor of theater at Eastern Mennonite University. In 1992 Ted graduated from Eastern Mennonite Seminary and began a ministry which took him, not to a congregational pulpit, but to audiences across the U.S. and beyond with a business called Ted & Lee Theater Works. Together these two best friends developed biblically based plays including: *Armadillo Shorts, Fish-Eyes, Creation Chronicles, Live at Jacob's Ladder* (in partnership with Ken Medema) and *DoveTale* (in partnership with Ingrid De Sanctis).[8]

Since Eshleman's tragic death in 2007, Swartz has continued to write new material and perform with a variety of artists including the two-act play, *What Would Lloyd Do?*, about a youth pastor's struggles with his boss, a cynical lead pastor in a staid congregation. Commenting on *WWLD?* Jerry Holsopple, Professor of Visual and Communication Arts at Eastern Mennonite University said, "This show moved me more than anything I have seen in a long while. *What Would Lloyd Do?* captured the angst of a middle-aged faith where some days the questions outnumber the pre-boxed answers. This experience collides with a younger post-modern singer sparking a whole series of metaphors of life and faith. Thanks Ted for getting inside my life and wreaking havoc with both laughter and tears."[9]

In addition to his plays, Swartz performs a workshop for congregations called *Humor and Faith: A Holy Accident* in which he introduces his audience to previously unseen characters from familiar Bible stories. His perspective and humor open a unique window into the biblical narrative.[10]

Gerald Shenk, [former] professor of church & society, Eastern Mennonite Seminary says of Ted's work: "Shocking, isn't it, how someone with a seminary degree can dredge up such incredible jollity from the stiff and sturdy accounts of Jesus and his first followers? We thought we knew the scriptures pretty well until Ted came along with his tricky mirror. It turns

---

8. King, "Ted and Lee-on the Hunt for Humor and Authenticity."
9. T. Swartz, "Ted & Company's" Homepage. Online.
10. Ibid.

out that humor in fact unlocks some aspects of the story that would otherwise escape a detailed analysis. Camels and needles, indeed!"[11]

Swartz has recorded many of his shows; a dozen are available as DVDs. All of his material emerges from the biblical narrative and, like Mennonite theology, is Christo-centric. Although the audience seldom learns of Swartz's Mennonite background, for those who learn of his Mennonite faith he becomes a roaming ambassador, shattering stereotypes of dour Mennonites. One of his plays, *Can I Buy an Enemy?*, highlights Swartz's pacifist convictions by asking probing questions about how and why we choose our enemies.

In 2012 Swartz published his memoir *Laughter is Sacred Space: the Not-So-Typical Journey of a Mennonite Actor* with a foreword by Brian McLaren. He then turned it into a traveling show. In it, and in the dramatic production, he explains his Mennonite roots and his faith journey from exploring a call to pastoral ministry to embracing a role as a biblical interpreter with a bent toward the humorous.[12]

Swartz performs extensively within and outside of the Mennonite Church exposing his audience, and his readers, to his unique sense of humor as well as his values of justice and peace which spring up from his deep Mennonite faith.

Scholar and T.V. Commentator - Donald B. Kraybill

The Amish received a lot of media attention during and after the 2006 Nickel Mines School shooting. For some, they have become national heroes because of their willingness to forgive the man who brutally murdered their daughters. Because the Amish practice a strict form of separatism, they are reticent to speak to the media or allow themselves to be photographed. Therefore, their more assimilated Mennonite cousins often serve as intermediaries and interpreters of Amish culture to the broader society. For a time, Mennonite scholar Donald B. Kraybill became a bit of a television celebrity as he helped America understand this tragedy and the remarkable response of these deeply spiritual people.[13] He was even embodied in

11. Ibid.
12. T. Swartz, *Laughter Is Sacred Space*.
13. Although Donald Kraybill grew up in, and served as a pastor within the Mennonite church, he and his wife are presently members of the Elizabethtown Church of the Brethren with is located adjacent to Elizabethtown College where Kraybill serves on the faculty.

the character "Bill North" who serves as a narrator in the play *The Amish Project*, written by Jessica Dickey which and premiered in New York in 2008. After seeing the play performed by Factory 449 at the Anacostia Arts Center in May, 2014, Rebecca Ritzel describes one of the play's characters, Bill North, as "a professor of religion at a local university." In real life, he is Donald B. Kraybill, a senior fellow at Young Center for Anabaptist and Pietist Studies at Elizabethtown College. "Bill North," as Kraybill is known in the script, answers questions and speaks for the Amish adults. The pretext is that he's holding a press conference for the dozens of media types who descend on Nickel Mines after the shootings. It's clever and Kraybill, whom I called up recently to chat about the play, agreed."[14]

Ritzel notes Kraybill was consulted by playwright Jessica Dickey as she wrote *The Amish Project*, but he skipped its 2008 premier at an off-Broadway theater and has turned down multiple requests to speak at theaters staging the play. She notes he didn't see the play until 2012 when Dickey performed it as a one-woman show in the Netherlands while Kraybill was in Amsterdam for a conference. "I feel great affection for Kraybill" Ritzel writes, "He's not a publicity-hound academic."[15]

Kraybill's expertise was again heavily drawn upon in the fall of 2011, when the Amish Bergholz Clan of Ohio were attacking other Amishmen and cutting their hair and beards; Kraybill was interviewed by BBC, CNN, NPR, and dozens of newspapers.[16] He is one of several experts who are frequently quoted by reporters to give background to news stories involving the Amish. Others include D. Holmes Morton, a Harvard trained physician who specializes in rare genetic disorders affecting Old Order Amish persons, and Steven Nolt, Goshen College professor and the author of more than twelve books on Amish and Mennonite history.

Kraybill has written, co-authored, edited, or contributed to two dozen books but perhaps his best known work is *The Upside-Down Kingdom*, an examination of Jesus' radical life and teachings. In it he explains much of Anabaptist theology without ever naming it as such. Originally published by Herald Press in 1978, it was updated and reissued in 2011. With nearly one-hundred thousand copies in print it has been a very influential book and received the prestigious National Religious Book Award as Best Religious Book.

14. Ritzel, "A Grevious Tragedy, Insightfully Staged."
15. Ibid.
16. S. C. Good, "Ohio Amish Consider Renegade Group a Cult," 8.

Art, Performance, and Television

Donald B. Kraybill is arguably the foremost living expert on the lifestyles, beliefs, and practices of the Old Order Amish. A Distinguished College Professor and Senior Fellow with the Young Center for Anabaptist and Pietist Studies at Elizabethtown College, he earned his PhD in sociology from Temple University. In 1967 he earned a BA from Eastern Mennonite College. Kraybill authored or edited many books and dozens of professional articles. His Anabaptist research has been featured in journals, magazines, and newspapers, and on radio and television programs across the United States and around the world. He has been a consultant for many Amish related projects, including the two hour PBS documentaries *The Amish*, which aired in 2012, and *The Amish Shunned*, which aired in February, 2014. Kraybill has received research funding from the National Endowment for the Humanities and is the series editor of Young Center Books in Anabaptist and Pietist Studies published by the Johns Hopkins University Press.[17]

Kraybill's Amish expertise points yet again to the close link between these two Anabaptist faith traditions. As Kraybill educates people about the Amish they often learn a bit about Mennonites.

---

17. Kraybill, "Home Page" Elizabethtown College. Online.

CHAPTER 9

Film

FEW MENNONITES ARE INVOLVED in writing and producing film. This study explores those films which are not only produced or written by Mennonites, but which also tell their viewers something about the Mennonite faith or traditions. An example of an excellent film written by Mennonites is *Miracle in Lane Two*, co-written by Joel Kauffmann and Donald C. Yoder. It is the heartwarming story of Donald's disabled son, Justin Yoder, and his exploits racing soapbox cars. The Yoders live in Goshen, Indiana and attend the same Mennonite church as Joel Kauffmann. Their son Justin was born with spina bifida and was thus unable to compete in sports like his older brother. However, at the age of twelve he discovered soapbox car racing and became quite good at it. He and his family had to fight for Justin's right to compete by insisting the racing rules be changed to allow a handicapped person to use a hand break, rather than the prescribed foot pedal. In 1996, Justin was the first disabled child to compete in the All American Soapbox Derby.

Mennonites are never mentioned in the Disney produced film of this inspiring story which aired on the Disney channel in 2000 to an audience of millions. The viewer learns about Justin's deep religious faith, the nature of his disability, and his determination to compete, but they never learn he is Mennonite. Many of the film's characters have "Mennonite names," e.g., Yoder, Burkholder, and Sauder, but they are never identified as Mennonite. At one point in the film the family attends a relative's funeral. The priest is wearing a white starched clerical collar more typical of the Episcopal than the Mennonite Church. Viewers learn nothing about Mennonites watching *Miracle in Lane Two*.

The criteria established that a film must tell its viewers something about Mennonites in order to be included in this analysis. This eliminated *Miracle in Lane 2* and limited the number of movies under consideration. However, screenwriter Joel Kauffmann argued there is a direct line from the heightened awareness which Mennonite conscientious objectors (COs) brought back to their churches after serving in mental health hospitals during World War II to *Miracle in Lane 2* which sensitively portrays a child with spina bifida. Kauffmann further argued that, although not unique to Mennonites, Justin's positive self-image grew out of his Mennonite family of faith which drew on the experiences of World War II COs. Kauffmann wrote another widely seen, made-for-T.V. drama for Disney about Hanukah, but that too is not relevant to this discussion.

Historical Drama and Documentaries

The Radicals – Joel Kauffmann and Myron Augsburger

The Radicals is a first-rate, full-length feature film in the form of a docudrama centered on the life and death of Michael Sattler, an early Anabaptist leader, martyr, and author of the Schleitheim Articles. Screenwriter Joel Kauffmann based the film's script on Myron Augsburger's novel *Pilgrim Aflame* which was published in 1990. Directed by Raul V. Carrera, *The Radicals* was originally made and released in VHS format shortly after the novel was published. In 2004 the film was converted to DVD format and expanded. The additions include: an introduction to each chapter by historian John E. Sharp; commentary by Dr. Myron Augsburger, President Emeritus of Eastern Mennonite University; an abbreviated version of the seven Schleitheim Articles; and some "making of The Radicals" reflections by those involved in the original project, including actor Norbert Weisser who plays Michael Sattler, and screenwriter Joel Kauffmann. The film used hundreds of volunteers as extras, costume designers, and set builders, but included three first-rate professional actors in Norbert Weisser, Leigh Lombardi (Margaretha) and Mark Lenard (Lord Hoffman). Weisser appeared in more than thirty films, most notably in Stephen Speilberg's highly acclaimed *Schindler's List*, which won the Academy Award for best picture in 1993. Fans of the original *Star Trek* T.V. series, and the subsequent movie spinoffs, will recognize Mark Lenard as Sarek, the Vulcan father of First Officer Mr. Spock.[1]

The Radicals is not a dry documentary. It does an excellent job telling this important early chapter of Anabaptist history in the context of a very human love story between Michael and Margaretha Sattler. The film aimed to reach a broad audience by couching Anabaptist history in terms of faith, love, revolution, and risk. At times overly dramatic in its use of classical music to convey the gravitas of the situation, it nonetheless succeeds in capturing the unsettled mood of this troubled time concurrent with the Protestant Reformation and The Peasants' Revolt in the Swiss German region of Europe. That sentiment is captured in the slogan on the DVD cover which reads, "To a world of fear Anabaptists introduced freedom . . . a crime punished by death." Michael's martyrdom is portrayed in the film's climax to dramatic effect, but Michael and Margaretha Sattler's religious devotion, spiritual wisdom, and gentle spirits are depicted in an overly deferential manner as almost angelic.

Those who watch this film learn much about Anabaptism, but the word Mennonite is only heard if one listens to the extra features which include commentary by John Sharp and Myron Augsburger. *The Radicals* was produced by Sisters and Brothers Productions under the leadership of J. Ron Byler, Jim L. Brown, D. Michael Hostetler, and Joel Kauffmann, all Mennonite leaders. It is sold as a full-length feature film by Gateway Films/Vision Video as well as in a repackaged thirty minute summary form in a church history series. Although, when it was first released it played at secular film festivals, it has succeeded more as a Sunday School lesson for Protestant Christians than as a popular movie, despite its producers' intention to share their peaceful Believers' Church tradition with a broader audience. The film has been sold overseas and comes with Spanish and Portuguese language subtitles needed for Central American and Brazilian audiences. Screenwriter Joel Kauffmann estimates only about 25 percent of the DVD sales are within Anabaptist groups. The film is present on the web site *All Movie Guide*, but its page has very little information, no synopsis, no list of actors, not even a release date. None of the three primary actors' filmography lists includes *The Radicals*.[2]

---

1. *The Radicals*, Carrera.
2. *All Movie Guide*, All Media Network, LLC. Online.

Film

Burton Buller's and Jerry Holsopple's film work at Mennonite Media

Burton Buller, former Chief Executive Officer of Mennonite Media, is an award winning filmmaker. His work on the Amish and Hutterites has won numerous CINE Golden Eagle awards. He holds a Master's Degree in Mass Communication from the University of Nebraska's School of Journalism. His work has aired on PBS, The Learning Channel, and Discovery Channel to name but three.

For twelve years, from 1989 through 2001, Jerry Holsopple, a documentary filmmaker, photographer, and iconographer, worked at Mennonite Media where he produced more than two dozen videos and video curriculum projects. Since 2001 he has been a faculty member at Eastern Mennonite University in the Visual and Communication Arts department where he teaches courses on photography and digital media. Holsopple's work has garnered more than a dozen awards including the prestigious *Telly*. Five documentary films, three by Burton Buller and two by Jerry Holsopple, are particularly relevant to the materials being examined in this book.

Waging Peace: Muslim and Christian Alternatives

Burton Buller produced and narrated *Waging Peace: Muslim and Christian Alternatives*, a documentary about "overcoming mistrust, hatred and violence"[3] released in 2011. It aired on more than one hundred and thirty U.S. ABC-TV affiliates as part of their Vision and Values series.[4] The film explores peacemaking in both the Muslim and Christian faiths through the centuries with particular emphasis on cooperative efforts today. It interviews significant Christian leaders including Lynne Hybels, author and wife of Willow Creek's founding pastor Bill Hybels, Dr. Martin Marty, and Richard Cizik. Unlike most of Buller's other documentaries, this one highlights Mennonite peacemaking efforts, a cornerstone of this Anabaptist group's faith. One particularly powerful example highlighted in the film is Floradale Mennonite Church's efforts to bridge the divide between Christians and Muslims. Situated in Ontario, a group of Christians and Muslims meet in the church to fashion colorful comforters which are given to Palestinian refugees settling in their area. At another point in the

---

3. Narration by Burton Buller, *Waging Peace*.
4. M. Davis, "ABC TV Ends Successful Run of *Waging Peace*," 1.

PART II—How Mennonites Have Used Media

film, Peggy Gish, a Mennonite serving with Christian Peacemaker Teams in Iraq, tells how she was invited into a refugee family's tent pitched amid the battlefield rubble in Fallujah. After listening to their stories, "[we] hugged and kissed in good Iraqi style, and there were tears coming down our faces. We had not done anything to change their situation, but merely connected on a human level."[5] David Shenk, a Mennonite pastor, author of *A Muslim and Christian in Dialogue*, missionary, and statesman to the Muslim world, is also featured in the documentary. In contrast to other documentaries produced by Buller and Third Way Media, which focus on generic faith values by telling other peoples' stories, this documentary highlights the significant contributions Mennonites are making in an effort to be reconciled to our national enemies. In many ways it is a Mennonite promotional piece although the focus remains on the broader community and its efforts at Christian-Muslim reconciliation. One ABC viewer, Lisa, commented, "I hardly ever watch TV but caught this on ABC and it's wonderful!! I was very impressed by the Mennonite attitude of love. We need more of this."[6]

Shadow Voices – Finding Hope in Mental Illness

Shadow Voices – Finding Hope in Mental Illness was produced in 2005 by Burton Buller while he was at Third Way Media (TWM). It aired on ABC, the Hallmark Channel, and other cable outlets. It is TWM's best seller with 4,303 copies sold. *Shadow Voices* offers an inside look through a faith-based lens at what it is like to live with a mental illness from the perspective of ten people with the disease. Former First Lady Rosalynn Carter is interviewed along with doctors and other health care professionals. This fifty-eight minute video was produced in cooperation with Faith & Values Media for the Hallmark Channel and includes a discussion guide.

Fierce Goodbye

Fierce Goodbye is a forty-four minute documentary about the devastating effects of suicide. Produced in 2004 by Burton Buller and Mennonite Media for the National Council of Churches, it aired on the Hallmark Channel,

---

5. Burton Buller, *Waging Peace*.
6. M. Davis, "ABC TV Ends Successful Run of *Waging Peace*," 1.

FILM

NBC, and ABC. In the documentary, members of five families affected by suicide are interviewed. The program probes the depths of their pain and heartbreak, while offering hope and healing. It is hosted by singer-songwriter Judy Collins and deals effectively with the difficult issues of faith and forgiveness. The documentary also features Dr. Kay Redfield Jamison, professor of psychiatry at Johns Hopkins University.[7] It is impossible to estimate the number of viewers who have seen this program on television but 3,662 copies of the video have been sold.

Journey Toward Forgiveness

Jerry Holsopple directed *Journey Toward Forgiveness* which was produced by Mennonite Media for the National Council of Churches in 2001. It aired as a presentation of the Interfaith Broadcasting Commission on ABC in December, 2001 and January, 2002. Since then it has been on the Hallmark Channel and other cable networks and has sold 3,614 copies.

This documentary film tells the stories of seven people struggling with their anger in the face of horrible circumstances including: a racially motivated beating, the murder of a child, and the aftermath of a terrorist attack. Coming as it did on the heels of the September 11th terrorist attack on the World Trade Center, *Journey Toward Forgiveness* spoke to an audience struggling with how to respond to the worst attack on U.S. soil since Pearl Harbor. "The hour-long documentary powerfully demonstrates that those who are able to embark on a process towards forgiveness—though heart-rending and difficult—find it to be the path to inner healing."[8] Interviewees include: Christian development pioneer John Perkins, Lutheran pastor and award winning author Walter Wangerin, Jr., and Bud Welch who lost his daughter in the 1995 Oklahoma City terrorist bombing.

Beyond the News – Sexual Abuse

Beyond the News – Sexual Abuse, a brief twenty-one minute video produced in 1993, consists of five segments related to sexual abuse in churches, homes, and institutions. It features psychotherapist and author Carolyn Holderread Heggen, who studied at Hesston College. These true but disturbing stories

---

7. M. Davis, "Fierce Goodbye." Online.
8. M. Davis, "Journey toward Forgiveness." Online.

PART II—HOW MENNONITES HAVE USED MEDIA

are told by professional actors and scripted by Barbra R. Graber, Associate Professor of Theater at Eastern Mennonite College. The DVD, which sold 2,280 copies, comes with a study guide suitable for use with high school students and young adults. This was the first of Mennonite Media's *Beyond the News* series. Others tackled such difficult topics as AIDS, homelessness, and racism. The intent of the series was to provide churches with the resources needed to go "beyond the statistics, beyond the impersonal, beyond the sensational, beyond the comfortable to real stories, in-depth understandings, and questions to stimulate discussion, all from a faith perspective."[9] Mennonite Media produced this series as an outreach tool to promote Christian values from a distinct Anabaptist perspective. Some of those interviewed in these videos are Mennonites, but they are never identified as such. Only *Waging Peace* explicitly identifies Mennonites. Therefore, with the exception of *Waging Peace*, it is unlikely the general public will learn much about Mennonites from watching them unless they notice the production credits, or use the accompanying study guides. The importance of these documentary films is they promote Mennonite values such as peace and reconciliation without denominational self-promotion, demonstrating this small denomination is a player at the table of Christians who are producing meaningful videos on relevant topics. Beyond these documentary films, Mennonites have also been involved in the production of at least two full-length feature films.

Fiction

Hazel's People (1973), a.k.a. *Happy as the Grass Was Green* - Merle Good

Miriam Toews, in a curious bit of media cross-referencing, mentions two films produced by Mennonites in her novel *A Complicated Kindness*.[10] Describing the movie theater in the fictitious East Village, where the narrator's preacher Uncle Hans attempts to rid the town of sinful establishments, Toews writes,

---

9. Holsopple, "Sexual Abuse," video box cover.
10. One of the two films, *Menno's Reins* is a dramatic documentary of the history of Mennonites in Manitoba, produced by Dueck Film Productions in Winnipeg and released in 1976. It did not reach a broad audience outside of Mennonite circles and will not be discussed here.

> The only thing he couldn't take down was the Rogue Cinema but I was never sure why not.... Who knows, he may have left it there for American tourists... or maybe he had a dream of someday showing the movie *Hazel's People* non-stop. Or *Menno's Reins*. Those were the films (we were discouraged from calling them movies) that we were shown on a regular basis. If you think that those films were only propaganda, simplistic tales about a group of shy farmers overcoming world pressure to be normal and starting up their own whacked-out communities in harsh climates, you'd be right.[11]

Hazel's People, directed by Burt Martin, was released in 1973 just as the military draft and the Vietnam War were ending. The film's protagonist, Eric Mills (Graham Beckel), is a long haired hippie and anti-war demonstrator who witnessed his best friend John being shot and killed by police during a nonviolent protest. Eric accompanies Jim, the dead boy's brother, back to the Mennonite community near Lancaster, Pennsylvania for John's burial. There Eric finds the peace he has been seeking. "Hazel" refers to the Mennonite pastor's daughter (Rachel Thomas) who is Eric's love interest.

In *Silence at Bethany* it was the flirtatious waitress who represented the lure of the sinful world; in *Hazel's People*, Eric represents the world. In this case, Eric's idealism and newfound faith serves to renew the Mennonite community rather than to destroy it, even though they have trouble fully accepting him.

The film depicts Mennonites accurately, showcasing their distinctive dress, separation from the world, pacifism, and a cappella singing. It also effectively demonstrates the differences between the Amish and Mennonites. Some memorable lines include this one, spoken by an Amishman working alongside Eric at a barn raising, "The further you get from simple things, the further you get from godliness." At another point, pastor Eli speaks to Eric saying, "You expect too much of us Eric. We disappoint you."[12]

Geraldine Page delivers an excellent performance as the dead boy's mother. Page, a seven-time Academy Award nominee, won the Best Actress Oscar for her lead performance in 1985's *A Trip to Bountiful*. Pat Hingle is also excellent as Mennonite farmer and pastor Eli. Hingle may be best known for his role as Commissioner Gordon in the Batman films. Most of the actors in the film are genuine Pennsylvania Mennonites. It is based on a book by Merle Good called *Happy as the Grass was Green*. Good served as

---

11. Toews, *A Complicated Kindness*, 13.
12. *Hazel's People*, Davis.

the film's associate producer. Syndicated Columnist Rex Reed called *Hazel's People*, "A warm tender film with a big heart. I enjoyed it thoroughly."[13] However, seeing it after more than forty years, the film shows its age.

There are a lot of similarities between *Hazel's People* and a more recent feature film produced by a Mennonite director which is the subject of the next section.

Pearl Diver - Sydney King (2004)

Sidney King, a 2000 Goshen College graduate, has written, directed, and produced a captivating and thought provoking film centered in a Mennonite farming community in Goshen, Indiana. It is not clear until well into the film what the unusual name *Pearl Diver* means, but that is part of its charm. The story is rooted in a strong faith tradition, surrounded by bucolic farm land, and founded on the love between two sisters. This beautifully filmed and powerfully acted movie is filled with unexpected tragedies and extravagant gifts.

It opens with a flashback to the defining moment in the lives of two young girls when a desperate pair of thieves brutally murders their mother. Each girl's response to this tragedy shapes the trajectory of their lives. Time reveals their differences when their mother's imprisoned murderer comes up for parole and each girl, now a young woman, offers the opposite advice to the parole board. Hannah, a writer, living in a big city with her boyfriend, writes a letter pleading for denial. Meanwhile, her older sister Marian appears before the board dressed conservatively with her hair tied in a tight bun under a white prayer covering. She carries a sketch of Anabaptist martyr Dirk Willems. Willems escaped from prison in 1569, and when his pursuer fell through the ice, Dirk came back and offered assistance. Willems was then recaptured, imprisoned, and burned at the stake as a heretic. The Amish and Mennonites have been retelling Dirk's remarkable act of love for his enemy for centuries. Marian retells it for the parole board as a plea for clemency for her mother's killer. [14]

King raises many thought provoking questions: Is it really possible to love our enemies? Do accidents just happen or do they happen for a reason? When they do occur should one just accept them as God's will, or is it possible, or even right, to fight against the seemingly inevitable outcome

13. Ibid., jacket cover.
14. *Pearl Diver*, King.

by mustering all the physical, emotional, financial, and spiritual resources at your disposal? Is it O.K. to hurt those closest to us in the pursuit of our dreams? The question of God lingers in the background behind the actors' dialogue and actions. Where is God in all of this?

The memory of Dirk Willems' selfless action to save his pursuer from certain death is crucial to the choices these two sisters make and central to King's themes. The film is about the choices we make and how they shape our lives and communities. Choices such as to: forgive or not, stay on the family farm or move away, marry or remain single, pursue your dreams or give up on them, fight against our plight or accept it, keep a secret or find release by sharing it. Finally, it is about two sisters who choose to love each other, despite their differences.

Released in 2004, *Pearl Diver* was shown to packed audiences at the Mennonite Church USA's Assembly in Charlotte in 2005. For several years it made its way around independent film festivals (winning awards at five competitions and appearing in two others) and playing in independent theaters. Still, it never received wide theatrical distribution. It was released in DVD format in 2008.

CHAPTER 10

Books

Rosanna of the Amish – Joseph W. Yoder (1940)

With more than four-hundred and ten thousand copies in print, *Rosanna of the Amish*, ranks 6th on Herald Press' bestseller list.[1] It is the account of Rosanna McGonegal, an orphaned daughter of Irish immigrants born in 1838 and raised by Elizabeth Yoder, an unmarried Amish woman living in rural Pennsylvania. The story is a tale of a love which extends the bounds of family, faith, and culture when an orphaned dark eyed and raven haired Roman Catholic girl is embraced within a conservative, Swiss German, Amish group.

Author, Joseph W. Yoder, is the son of Christian Z. Yoder and the titular Rosanna McGonegal. As noted earlier, Rosanna McGonegal Yoder Hostetler, the author's great-niece, claims Joseph was inspired to write *Rosanna* partly in response to *Tillie, A Mennonite Maid* which he felt dishonored the Amish. "I want to write a book which shows the true picture of Amish customs and practices in religion, industry, and social life."[2] Although Yoder grew up Amish he became Mennonite, taught at the Elkhart Institute (now Goshen College), and is buried in the Locust Grove Mennonite Church cemetery near Bellville, Pennsylvania. He accomplished what he set out to do, having written an account of his mother's life which lov-

---

1. Herald Press is an imprint of MennoMedia, formerly Mennonite Publishing Network, which has produced trade books since the early 1900s under an earlier name, Mennonite Publishing House.
2. Yoder, *Rosanna of the Amish*, 10.

ingly portrays both her and her Amish community. It also provides many descriptions and observations about Amish life which educate and inform his readers.

However, the text of *Rosanna* does not mention Mennonites except in; a *Supplement*, found on page 313; in the *Books on the Amish* section, which begins on page 316; and in the *About the Author* section, pages 318 to 320. In these supplements, one learns the Amish and Mennonites share a common Anabaptist confession. He describes Mennonites as having church buildings, in contrast to the Amish practice of using private homes for preaching services. Yoder states most Mennonites have accepted modern conveniences. Although not a primary source about Mennonites, those reading *Rosanna* would learn much about the Amish and would come to understand their common faith and practices and the link between these two faith groups.[3]

Rosanna underwent revision in 1973 and was reissued again in 1995, one-hundred years after the title character's death. Although factual, it was perhaps the first in the now popular Amish romance novel tradition epitomized by the writings of Beverly Lewis and others.

Good Books, Intercourse, Pennsylvania

For many years, the Mennonite husband and wife team of Merle and Phyllis Pellman Good owned and operated Good Books out of Intercourse, Pennsylvania in the heart of Amish country. However, in December, 2013 Good Enterprises Ltd. filed for bankruptcy liquidation and ceased operations.[4] Prior to its closing, Merle served as the publisher while Phyllis was the executive editor. This is the same Merle Good referenced in the previous chapter as the associate producer for the film *Hazel's People* and author of *Happy as the Grass was Green* on which the film is based.

Since its beginning in 1979, Good Books published more than seven-hundred titles, four-hundred of which were active in 2013. They succeeded in reaching a mass market with their publications. Although the heart of their mission was to print and promote books by and about the Amish and Mennonites, the most profitable part of their retail book business came from the sale of other books. They had three books in the number one position on *The New York Times* Bestseller List, namely the *Fix-It and Forget-It*

---

3. Ibid.
4. Mekeel, "Intercourse-Based Good Enterprises Closes."

cookbook, *The Mayo Clinic Diet*, and *Me and My Dad*, a children's book by Alison Ritchie.[5] However, none of these three very popular titles tells their readers anything about the Amish or Mennonites.

According to USA Today, "*Fix-It and Forget-It*, which sold nearly three million copies, is among the top 10 bestselling cookbooks tracked on the USA Today bestselling books list since the list began in 1993."[6] But, unlike the *More-with-Less Cookbook*, which contains quotes from Menno Simons and promotes a Mennonite ideal of living simply, *Fix-It and Forget-It* tells its readers nothing about Mennonite beliefs and practices. Although many Mennonites would recognize the names and hometowns of those whose recipes are included in *Fix-It and Forget-It*, the general public would not recognize it as a Mennonite book or learn anything about Mennonites from it.[7]

Other titles printed by Good Books strongly voice Mennonite values and teachings. "The Little Book" series is particularly important in this regard. It includes more than a dozen titles on justice and peacebuilding including Howard Zehr's *The Little Book of Restorative Justice* and John Paul Lederach's *The Little Book of Conflict Transformation*. Some of these titles have sold well. Goshen College history professor John D. Roth's *Choosing Against War* is another example of the fine books published and marketed by Good Books which promote a specifically Mennonite faith perspective. *Mirror of the Martyrs*, *An Introduction to Russian Mennonites*, *A Culture of Peace*, and *From Anabaptist Seed* are all further examples of the quality texts about Mennonite faith, history, and practices which Good Books publishes and promotes.

Good Books, with its well-honed marketing skill, provided an outlet for Mennonite writers to reach a broader audience. *Sailing Acts* is such an example. Written by Eastern Mennonite University professor Linford Stutzman, *Sailing Acts* recounts his travels by sailboat retracing the Apostle Paul's missionary journeys. Although it speaks much about Paul's relationship to the Roman Empire, its readers learn nothing about Mennonites except that the author teaches at a Mennonite university. Someone is unlikely, after reading *Sailing Acts*, to seek to learn more about Mennonites. But a Mennonite engaging the broader culture with a missional mindset might find an inroad to speak with an avid sailor who does not attend church, or a professed Christian interested in the Apostle Paul, about the book *Sailing*

5. M. Good, telephone conversation, June 21, 2011.
6. M. and P. Good, "Good Books Fall 2011 Catalog," 25.
7. Ranck and Good, *Fix-It and Forget-It Cookbook*, 45.

Acts and its author's particular form of radical discipleship expressed in the Mennonite church.

Many of Good Books' titles concern the Amish and will not be included in this discussion, except when their subject is both the Amish and Mennonites. Merle and Phyllis Good co-wrote a very popular book about both the Amish and Mennonites called *20 Most Asked Questions about the Amish and Mennonites*. It looks at origins, dress, pacifism, and many other aspects of Amish and Mennonite life and has sold more than four hundred and fifty thousand copies.[8]

In November, 2013, just six weeks prior to their bankruptcy, Merle's play *The Preacher and the Shrink* opened in an off-Broadway theater for a three month run. The play examines the relationship between a Presbyterian pastor and his daughter. Good Books was a key player in the Mennonite movement toward engaging the broader culture through media—especially the printed word.

The Writings of Canadian Rudy Wiebe

Rudy Weibe, raised in a one room cabin in a Mennonite colony in Saskatchewan, has been called "one of Canada's foremost novelists." His parents migrated from Russia to Canada in 1930, and he was born four years later. A prolific author, Wiebe's works include nine novels, ten nonfiction volumes, four collections of short stories, and an autobiography. In 1973, Wiebe received the General's Award for Fiction for *The Temptation of Big Bear*. He repeated that honor in 1994 for *A Discovery of Strangers*. Then, in 2004, he won the Charles Taylor Prize for literary nonfiction for his memoir *Of This Earth: a Mennonite Boyhood in the Boreal Forrest*.

In 1961, Wiebe earned a Bachelor of Theology degree from Mennonite Brethren Bible College, Winnipeg. His first novel, *Peace Shall Destroy Many*, was published by Eerdmans a year later. It tells the story of the lives and struggles of a small group of Mennonites who fled hardships in Russia to farm in Saskatchewan. The foreword contains a brief primer on the origins of the Anabaptist movement in the sixteenth century. As a Mennonite with a background in theology, he writes with a deep understanding of the challenges faced by those within this religious tradition. In 1963, he accepted a position as an assistant Professor of English at Goshen College in Indiana. His next two novels, *First and Vital Candle* (1966) and *The*

---

8. Good, "Good Books Fall 2011 Catalog," 69.

PART II—HOW MENNONITES HAVE USED MEDIA

Blue Mountains of China (1970), were also published by Eerdmans. Robert Kroetsch, of State University of New York, calls Wiebe's third novel, which recounts his people's exodus from Russia and subsequent disbursement to places all around the world, "an epic of Mennonite wanderings."[9]

Wiebe centers many of his writings in his and his parents' life experiences as Mennonite refugees. He has also written about aboriginal and settler culture in *The Temptations of Big Bear* (1973) and the spiritual upheaval caused by marital infidelity in *My Lovely Enemy* (1983). In 2010, the University of Alberta, from which he received a Master of Arts degree in 1960, published his latest book, *Rudy Wiebe: Collected Stories 1955–2010*.

Some would consider Wiebe to be a Canadian media personality. His second novel, *First and Vital Candle*, was adapted for radio in 1967. He has given hundreds of readings and lectures all around the world and wrote the script for *Big Bear* (1998), a four-hour miniseries produced by CBC. Canada is home to a large number of Northern European Mennonites of Dutch descent who arrived via Prussia and Russia. Hildi Froese Tiessen, of Conrad Grabel University College in Waterloo, Ontario, notes Mennonite writings have been produced and received as ethnic literature in keeping with the Canadian government's emphasis on multiculturalism in the 1970s and 1980s.[10]

In part because of Wiebe's prolific writings, many Canadians have a greater understanding and appreciation for their fellow Mennonite citizens than United States citizens do. Other factors impact the favorable impression Canadians have of Mennonites in contrast to opinions in the U.S. The two countries have different views toward immigrants. Prior to 1920 both Canada and the U.S. welcomed immigrants. However, after 1920 U.S. immigration policy changed and became more restrictive, whereas the Canadian immigration laws have remained welcoming. The Canadian appreciation for its Mennonite citizens may also be because multiculturalism is embraced to a greater degree in Canada, where there are two official languages (English and French), than in the U.S. According to Driedger, "It is more popular to be ethnically distinct in Canada than in the United States."[11]

---

9. Wiebe, *The Blue Mountains of China*, jacket cover.
10. Steiner, "Self in Mennonite Garb," 23.
11. Kauffman and Driedger, *The Mennonite Mosaic*, 50.

BOOKS

The Politics of Jesus – John Howard Yoder (1972)

Perhaps no modern theologian has done more to introduce the broader society to Mennonite and Anabaptist theology than the late John Howard Yoder. And, arguably, no single Mennonite text has had a greater impact in the sphere of Christian ethics than Yoder's *The Politics of Jesus*, which is a standard text in many college and seminary ethics courses. *The Politics of Jesus* was published in 1972 by William B. Eerdmans Publishing House, a conservative Evangelical, non-Mennonite press, in the Reformed tradition whose motto is, "The finest in religious literature." It sold more than one-hundred and fifty thousand copies. Stanley Hauerwas, writing in 1993 in *The Christian Century* said, "I am convinced that when Christians look back on this century of theology in America, *The Politics of Jesus* will be seen as a new beginning."[12] In 2000 *Christianity Today* named it fifth in the list of the top ten Christian themed books of the twentieth Century.

Yoder is not alone among American Mennonite academics. Harold Bender was a Goshen College, and Associated Mennonite Biblical Seminary professor. His seminal work, "The Anabaptist Vision," which was first presented at an annual assembly of church historians in 1944, helped inspire a generation of Mennonite historians, theologians, and scholars, including Yoder.[13] However, "The Anabaptist Vision" was not circulated widely beyond those in Anabaptist circles. It was not until 1972, when Yoder published *The Politics of Jesus*, that Christian scholars became more aware of Mennonites and Anabaptists. Many Christian seminary professors began to see Mennonites as more than a mere curiosity and were less likely to dismiss them as a sect because of Yoder's brilliant writing.

In *The Politics of Jesus*, John Howard Yoder first delineates the social ethics Jesus taught. He then reclaims the universality of Jesus' teachings, including a pacifism based on love for enemies, as normative for all Christians, not just Mennonites.[14] He begins by debunking the "sixfold claim to Jesus' irrelevance"[15] which has been used by Biblical scholars and church leaders to dismiss the importance of Jesus' life and teachings and focus instead on his miraculous birth and sacrificial death. Yoder develops his arguments, beginning with the Gospel of Luke, and focuses on Jesus of Nazareth.

---

12. Hauerwas, "When the Politics of Jesus Makes a Difference," 982.
13. Bender, *The Anabaptist Vision*.
14. J. H. Yoder, *The Politics of Jesus*, 11.
15. Ibid., 5.

PART II—HOW MENNONITES HAVE USED MEDIA

According to Mark Thiessen Nation, Professor of Theology at Eastern Mennonite Seminary, "For Yoder there is nothing more crucial for getting theology right than naming the centrality of Jesus. Jesus is the Word of God made flesh. Jesus is also the Messiah, thus the fulfillment of political and redemptive expectations within the context of first century Judaism."[16]

Yoder argues that Jesus' teachings were more than mere spirituality with passing political implications. Jesus was not *just* a sacrificial lamb, nor so Divine that his humanity has no relevance for us. Yoder contends that Jesus' life, teachings, and cross inaugurated a new regime, and that we, as his disciples, are called to be like him.[17]

The third chapter of *The Politics of Jesus* addresses Jesus' teachings about the year of Jubilee. Yoder views the language of forgiving "debts" and "debtors" in "the Lord's Prayer" as a reference to the year of the Jubilee when all debts were to be forgiven. According to Mark Thiessen Nation, New Testament scholar "N.T. Wright, in his recent book, *Jesus and the Victory of God*, captures Yoder's intent . . . well: 'Jesus did not envision . . . he would persuade Israel as a whole to keep the Jubilee year, he expected his followers to live the Jubilee principle among themselves.'"[18] This ideal, as practiced among Anabaptists, is known as "mutual aid." It remains a "Shared Conviction of Global Anabaptists" who "hold the following to be central to our belief and practices: . . . shar[ing] our possessions with those in need."[19]

Yoder goes on to argue that the central tenet of Pauline literature is not individual salvation by faith but the reconciliation of groups in conflict, especially Jews and Greeks. This idea is consistent with Yoder's interpretation of the nonviolent, reconciling politics of Jesus.[20] Similarly Yoder gives a fresh interpretation to apocalyptic literature from Daniel to Revelation when he says, "When read carefully, none of the biblical apocalypses . . . is about either pie in the sky or the Russians in Mesopotamia. They are about how the crucified Jesus is a more adequate key to understanding what God is about in the real world of empires and armies . . . than is the ruler in Rome."[21]

---

16. Nugent, *The Politics of Yoder Regarding "The Politics of Jesus,"* 39.
17. Yoder, *The Politics of Jesus*, 52.
18. Nation, *John Howard Yoder*, 113.
19. Mennonite World Conference, "Shared Convictions of Global Anabaptists." Online.
20. Nation, *John Howard Yoder*, 120.
21. Ibid., 246.

BOOKS

As Mark Thiessen Nation has so aptly observed, "Yoder [was] a brilliant polemicist."[22] Nation, describing what Yoder accomplished in *The Politics of Jesus*, claims, "Yoder is not intending to call attention to some concept labeled "pacifism." Rather, he wants to enable us to hear dimensions of the gospel of Jesus that our preconceived notions prevent us from hearing."[23]

Yoder's far reaching influence was not only due to his brilliant mind and compelling biblical analysis. It also had much to do with Stanley Hauerwas, the person who became his chief disciple and in turn introduced Yoder's writings to the broader community of Christian thinkers and ethicists. Hauerwas is the Gilbert T. Rowe Professor of Theological Ethics at Duke Divinity School. In 2001, *Time* magazine named him the "Best Theologian in America."

More-with-Less Cookbook
– Doris Janzen Longacre (1976)

Who would have imagined that a cookbook comprised of five hundred recipes and hundreds of spiritual reflections would become a bestseller and in many ways a signature piece synonymous with Mennonites for many in the general public? With nearly a million copies in print, people who had never heard of Mennonites are using this practical cookbook loaded with spiritual content. The word "Mennonite," along with a representation of Mennonite Central Committee's (MCC) peace dove and cross logo recreated in beans, rice, and grains, appears in the subtitle on the book's cover which says, "suggestions by Mennonites on how to eat better and consume less of the world's limited food resources."[24]

Authored by Doris Janzen Longacre, printed by Herald Press in cooperation with a host of volunteer recipe submitters and testers under the auspices of MCC, the *More-with-Less Cookbook* was a surprising hit with the public. It is also ranked second among Herald Press's all-time bestsellers. In an article, first published in Mennonite Central Committee's *Common Place Magazine* in November 2000, J. Daryl Byler writes, "Written to challenge North Americans to consume less so others could eat enough, the book has sold an astonishing 830,000 copies since its release in 1976. "It is by far our best-selling book," says Patty Weaver, marketing manager at Herald

22. Ibid., 124.
23. Ibid., 127.
24. Longacre, *More-with-Less Cookbook*, cover.

Press."25 Patty Weaver, in a phone conversation on March 3, 2011 updated these figures saying, "The book has gone through nineteen reprintings during the past eleven years. It continues to sell well with nearly nine-hundred thousand copies [in circulation]. We will be releasing a special thirty-fifth anniversary issue of *More-with-Less* this fall."26

More-with-Less exposed the public to much in the way of Mennonite thinking and theology. The cookbook begins with two Creole proverbs and this quote from Menno Simons, "We are prepared with all our hearts to share our possessions, gold, and all that we have, however little it may be; to sweat and labor to meet the needs of the poor, as the Spirit and the Word of the Lord and true brotherly love teach and imply."27

It is difficult to precisely measure the theological impact of the *More-with-Less Cookbook* but some, including Gayle Gerber Koonz, professor at Associated Mennonite Biblical Seminaries and director of communications for a regional office of Mennonite Central Committee, consider it to have had more of an impact on the general public than any other Mennonite publication, including volumes on ethics and theology.28 Seminary professor and doctoral student Malinda Elizabeth Berry, in *A Table of Sharing*, calls *More-with-Less* a book of organic Anabaptist theology, emerging not from the branches of the seminaries, or the trunk of pastoral ministry, but from the multiple roots of ordinary Mennonites practicing their faith. She writes, "Not until I began to rub shoulders with others outside my denominational faith community [Mennonite] did I begin to realize how much my view of North American culture had been shaped *directly* by Longacre's *More-with-Less* and *indirectly* by John Howard Yoder's *The Politics of Jesus*."29

According to J. Daryl Byler, "A global food crisis in the early 1970s with food reserves at a "precarious low" created the impetus for *More-with-Less*. In the first chapter of her cookbook, Longacre writes that the 'average North American uses five times as much grain per person yearly as does one of the two billion persons living in poor countries.'"30

Longacre's ideas and simple recipes caught on and helped add a practical dimension to the lifestyle choices many Christians and other persons

25. Byler, "Earmarks of a Bestseller." No pages, online.
26. Weaver, telephone conversation, March 3, 2011.
27. Longacre, *More-with-Less Cookbook*, 6.
28. Byler, "Earmarks of a Bestseller."
29. Weaver, *Table of Sharing*, 285. Emphasis in the original.
30. Ibid.

of conscience were faced with in the early 1970s. David Swartz, in his book *Moral Minority* writes, in "Longacre's *More With Less Cookbook* [Evangelicals] learned that kitchens were moral places where a theology of simple living could be practiced."[31]

Longacre began writing a companion text called *Living More with Less* but died of cancer in 1979 at the age of thirty-nine before she could finish it. The book was completed and published posthumously. It has sold more than eighty-six thousand copies. In 2010 a new thirtieth anniversary edition was released by Herald Press. *Living More with Less* is a practical guide to living a simple, sustainable, and healthy lifestyle. Author, speaker, and justice activist Shane Claiborne says *Living More with Less* is "like a cookbook for life."[32]

According to David Heusinkveld, he and his wife came to, and remain in, the Mennonite Church because of the *More-with-Less Cookbook*.[33] In the chapter titled "Extending the Theological Table: MCC's World Community Cookbooks as Organic Theology," Malinda Elizabeth Berry concludes:

> What Longacre began through organic theologizing with *More-with-Less Cookbook* and *Living More with Less* is still nourishing those of us who are her contemporaries, those of us who were raised with these values, and those of us whose introduction to Anabaptism came through the cookbook. As a series the cookbooks offer us a model for thinking critically about alternative witness to and within culture that we can and do offer as Anabaptists.[34]

Rich Christians in an Age of Hunger
– Ronald J. Sider (1977)

When author and theologian Ron Sider published *Rich Christians in an Age of Hunger* with Intervarsity Press in 1977, it caught people's attention. Sider, who is an evangelical and the son of a Brethren in Christ pastor, spoke from a perspective seldom heard in evangelical circles. His Anabaptist upbringing significantly influenced his views. In the same article naming John Howard Yoder's *The Politics of Jesus* as the fifth in a list of the most influential religious

---

31. D. R. Swartz, *Moral Minority*.
32. Herald Press staff, "30th Anniversary Edition *Living More with Less*." Online.
33. Weaver, *Table of Sharing*, 298.
34. Ibid., 296.

book of the twentyth century, Christianity Today named *Rich Christians in an Age of Hunger* one of the top one hundred most influential religious books.[35] There are more than three-hundred and fifty thousand copies in print.

As the title implies, the book is a scathing indictment of persons professing faith in Christ yet living as if their faith did not matter in a world plagued with hunger and poverty. Part one makes a case, using graphs and statistics, that poverty is prevalent in our world, and contrasts it with knowledge that the United States is the richest nation in the world, and Christians comprise a large part of this affluent minority. Part two examines biblical perspectives on the poor and possessions arguing that God is on the side of the poor. Part three examines the causes of poverty. The book is not mere criticism. It offers practical steps individuals and communities can take to help alleviate poverty. For example, Sider encourages his readers to adopt the "graduated tithe" while explaining his personal experience implementing it.[36]

Although Sider's writings and teachings introduce his readers to Anabaptist theology, he never explicitly associates this radical way of following after Jesus as Anabaptist. Likewise, they would need to read *Rich Christians* very closely to learn anything about Mennonites. Sider never identifies himself as a Mennonite, although he and his wife attend Oxford Circle Mennonite Church in Philadelphia. Even when Sider speaks of intentional Christian communities and cites Reba Place Fellowship in Evanston, Illinois as an example, he never lets his readers know Reba Place is affiliated with the Mennonite Church.[37] He mentions Doris Janzen Longacre's *More With Less Cookbook* and her sequel, *Living More With Less*, in Appendix A as books about "lifestyle." Donald Kraybill's *The Upside-Down Kingdom* appears in the "theology, biblical studies and the church" section of Appendix A but each of these books by Mennonite authors is buried in the bibliography with dozens of others.[38] He mentions Mennonite Central Committee and Mennonite Economic Development Association in Appendix B, under the title "organizations," but again only in a long list.[39]

Although Sider, who founded Evangelicals for Social Action, is an extremely influential Mennonite theologian, teacher, and practitioner, only

---

35. Christianity-Today, "Books of the Century," 92-93.
36. Sider, *Rich Christians*, 193.
37. Ibid., 219.
38. Ibid., 278-80.
39. Ibid., 286.

those who are attracted by his writings and thus dig deeper learn that Sider's Anabaptist upbringing deeply influenced his core theological convictions.

A Complicated Kindness – Miriam Toews (2004)

Canadian writer Miriam Toews' breakout fiction novel *A Complicated Kindness* was first published by Knopf Canada and later by Counterpoint, an imprint of Perseus Books. It won the *Governor General's Award for English Fiction* in 2004, was nominated for the *Giller Prize*, and spent over a year on the Canadian bestseller list. The imaginary Canadian town of East Village, in which the novel is set, is generally considered to be a fictionalized version of Toews' hometown Steinbeck, Manitoba, where she was raised within the Mennonite community. Although critically acclaimed, it is difficult to know how many copies have been sold. On March 10, 2011 Amazon Books ranked it 177,095th in book sales out of more than 800,000 books in inventory. For comparison, on the same day Amazon ranked *Mennonite in a Little Black Dress* 747th, and *The Politics of Jesus* 75,226th.

The story is told by Nomi Nickel, a rebellious sixteen-year-old, who describes her family and the Mennonite community which she finds stifling, in these words: "'We're Mennonites,' Nomi says, 'As far as I know, we are the most embarrassing sub-sect of people to belong to if you're a teenager.'"[40] She describes tourists, and even the Queen of England, coming to their town to see the simple ways of these primitive Mennonite people. Nomi says they were "on display as backward Jesus freaks."[41] The suspense of Nomi's missing mother and sister carries the plot forward. The conservative religious people of East Village live quiet content lives holding tightly to the hope of an eternal glory in the afterlife but utterly lacking in earthly pleasures. Nomi's uncle Hans, also known as "The Mouth," is the town spiritual leader. He rules with an iron fist, excommunicates church members, and insists they be shunned thereafter.

Toews portrays Mennonites as uncharitable Fundamentalist Christians. Her sometimes funny descriptions are often bitter but always insightful, "When I was a kid I stood in the fields pretending I was a Scarecrow. It was a sin to pretend we were something other than what we were but I always enjoyed standing very still in fields. And often, when sin is used

---

40. Toews, *A Complicated Kindness*, 5.
41. Ibid., 11.

in the name of farming, Mennonites turn the other way. Farming is very important to us. I mean very important."[42]

Canadians seem to be more aware and appreciative of their Mennonite neighbors than U.S. citizens are. Although not flattering to Mennonites, the next book to be examined may raise their profile with American readers.

Mennonite in a Little Black Dress (2009) and *Does This Church Make Me Look Fat?* (2012) – Rhoda Janzen

Rhoda Janzen was raised in a Mennonite Brethren home but, when she wrote *Mennonite in a Little Black Dress*, no longer identified herself with the Mennonite faith. She has written a well-reviewed and very popular, self-deprecating memoir with the word Mennonite in the title. It was for a time in the top spot on the prestigious *New York Times* Bestseller list, and remained on the list for nearly a year with more than forty thousand copies in print from five press runs.

Kate Christensen, writing for *The New York Times Book Review*, says, "I loved this book, and Rhoda Janzen. She is a terrific, pithy, beautiful writer, a reliable, sympathetic narrator and a fantastic good sport." *People* magazine gave it four stars calling it "Hilarious and touching" while *Entertainment Weekly* commented "A hilarious collection of musings on Janzen's childhood, marriage, and eccentric family . . . Janzen mines Mennonite culture for comic effect, but she does so with love."[43]

Although Janzen clearly identifies her family's denomination as Mennonite Brethren (MB) and her home church as the Butler MB Church, throughout the book she refers to her family and others from their faith tradition simply as Mennonite. The hyperbolic memoir catalogues her failed marriage of fifteen years and her return to her family of origin in California. Much the way Garrison Keillor spins a satiric tale about Minnesota Lutherans, Janzen's humor pokes fun at Mennonites using her bitingly sharp wit, but always with a loving appreciation for her past.

Mennonite readers are sure to wince at some of the sexual language, as well as the Mennonite stereotypes which Janzen reinforces, yet at least one reviewer gave her memoir a "G" rating, meaning she thought it was acceptable for general audiences. Like most humor writers, Janzen exaggerates for comic

---

42. Ibid., 39.
43. Janzen, *Mennonite in a Little Black Dress*, back cover.

effect when she says "Mennonites marry their cousins" or Mennonites have jettisoned "sex inside of marriage" along with "sex outside of marriage."[44]

Readers can learn much about Mennonites from this book, although Janzen primarily uses Mennonite as a cultural rather than theological term, referring primarily to unusual foods and practices of her German Russian Mennonite ancestors who emigrated from Ukraine. It is not until page 108 that she mentions Mennonites are pacifists. Referring tongue in cheek to her ancestry she says, "As a people, we are pale as pork chops, flavored by centuries of inbreeding and shame."[45] She makes some distinction about various Mennonite groups, once referring to the "Old Order Mennonites" noting women in this group invariably wear head coverings and long modest dresses. *Mennonite in a Little Black Dress* includes an appendix titled "A Mennonite History Primer" but even it is filled with hyperbole.

Janzen's second book, *Does This Church Make Me Look Fat?*, published by Grand Central in 2012, picks up where *Mennonite in a Little Black Dress* left off. Jantzen recounts a turbulent year which brought her into the Pentecostal church, a second marriage, stepmotherhood, and a bout with cancer.

However, unlike in her first book, which was highly critical of organized religion, in her second Janzen becomes a virtual ambassador of faith. She tells her readers far more about the Mennonite religion in which she grew up than about her husband's Pentecostal Church, which she recently joined. Even so, she says she continues to identify both culturally and theologically with Mennonites, rather than Pentecostals.[46]

In many parts of her memoir Janzen contrasts Mennonite faith practices with those of her newly adopted Pentecostal church. She describes Mennonites as "sober and buttoned up" in contrast to Pentecostals who "inhabit [the] moment fully" and act spontaneously.[47] She explains, the differences are most apparent with regard to the person of the Holy Spirit, which Pentecostals fully embrace with an emphasis on the gifts of the Holy Spirit, while Mennonites deemphasize divine gifts focusing rather on the fruits or character traits gained through the work of the Holy Spirit.[48]

Janzen expounds extensively on Mennonite faith and practice explaining their love for a cappella singing, German heritage, controversies

---

44. Ibid., 239.
45. Ibid., 114.
46. Janzen, *Does This Church Make Me Look Fat?*, 6.
47. Ibid., 20.
48. Ibid., 22.

PART II—HOW MENNONITES HAVE USED MEDIA

over the ordination of women, embrace of martyrdom, reluctance to cut women's hair, production of sausage and meats, embodiment of the Fruits of the Spirit, embrace of simple living, rejection of a prosperity gospel, passive-aggressive behavior, pacifist beliefs and practices, migration from Ukraine, rebaptism, and approach to evangelism.[49]

The public is likely to learn more about Mennonites from Janzen's books than from many other sources.

Hiking Through – Paul Stutzman (Synergy Books, 2010/Revell 2012)

In *Hiking Through: Finding Peace and Freedom on the Appalachian Trail*, Paul Stutzman, a self-proclaimed Conservative Mennonite from Berlin, Ohio has written a popular account of his journey as a through hiker[50] on the Appalachian Trail. Synergy Books, a small publisher in Austin, Texas, first published it in 2011. In 2012 it was picked up by Revell, a division of Baker Books, and reprinted. Stutzman's strong Christian faith is foundational to his writing. In chapter 4, "The Narrow Way," Stutzman explains he was born into an Amish family insulated from the outside world. His readers learn about the Amish and Mennonite communities as Stutzman describes his family's move from the Amish church to a Conservative Mennonite church whose beliefs and practices mirror the Amish except Mennonites drove cars rather than horse drawn buggies. Even so, Mennonite church leaders considered a two-tone car with chrome bumpers to be too worldly and of course, the car's radio was forbidden. Stutzman didn't own a television until he married a 'liberal Mennonite' girl. Subsequently he also began attending movies and Cleveland Indian baseball games. Thus the reader comes away with the impression Mennonites are similar to the Amish except less strict culturally. Stutzman does not reveal much about Mennonite beliefs except to place them squarely in the Christian faith. The strongest message in the book is Stutzman's devotion to his wife and his high regard for the institution of marriage.[51]

49. Ibid., 33, 64, 117, 22, 38, 60 and 210, 171, 86, 91 and 203, 01, 09 and 14, 16-20, 31-32, 35.

50. A "through hiker" is a person who attempts to hike the entire 2100 miles of the AT in one season. In a typical season, less that 20 percent of those who begin this arduous journey complete it.

51. Stutzman, *Hiking Through*, 31-42.

BOOKS

Hiking Through ranks among the leaders in a small group of books about the nearly two thousand one-hundred mile long Appalachian Trail. The trail holds a mystique among many who have hiked portions of it or are simply enamored with it. In 1998, travel writer Bill Bryson's hilarious book *A Walk in the Woods: Rediscovering America on the Appalachian Trail* caught the eye of critics and readers of all stripes becoming a runaway *New York Times* bestseller. A film version is reportedly in the works to be released in August, 2015. Originally published in hardcover by Harper Collins, it has since been reprinted in paperback form by Anchor Books.[52]

A third book, *AWOL on the Appalachian Trail* by David Miller, was first produced by Wing Span Publishing in 2006 and was reissued by Mariner Books in 2011. Like *A Walk in the Woods* and *Hiking Through*, it is a personal account of the writer's adventures as a through hiker on the Appalachian Trail.

Vince Ackermann, an avid reader and a section hiker[53] who has completed more than 2/3rds of the trail, has read all three of these books and thinks they are the most popular books about personal journeys on the AT, as the Appalachian Trail is known among those who trek it. Thus, Stutzman has been effective in reaching a popular audience, at least in this niche segment. Those who read *Hiking Through* cannot miss Stutzman's strong Christian faith which began in an Amish home and continues to be nourished in a Mennonite community.

David and Goliath – Malcolm Gladwell (2013)

Malcolm Gladwell is one of the most prolific and insightful writers of the twenty-first century. *The Tipping Point* (2000) and *Blink* (2005) were international bestsellers with more than four and a half million copies sold. In 2005 *Time* magazine named him one of the one-hundred most influential people. All four of his previous books have been on *The New York Times* bestseller list including: *The Tipping Point*, *Blink*, *Outliers*, and *What the Dog Saw*.[54]

---

52. Wikipedia, "A Walk in the Woods," online, 2.

53. A "section hiker" is a person who hikes the AT in smaller segments or sections over a number of years. Some complete the entire trail but, like through hikers, most do not. A section hiker who completes the entire trail is eligible to receive a certificate from the Appalachian Trail Club, just as successful through hikers do.

54. Wikipedia, "Malcolm Gladwell," online, introduction.

Like his previous works, *David and Goliath* is a provocative, nonfiction book which challenges assumptions and draws unlikely conclusions. The book's subtitle: *Underdogs, Misfits, and the Art of Battling Giants*, points to the text's premise, that even those wielding great power must pay attention lest they be toppled by those without power or position who have little to lose and who don't play by the rules. He debunks the theory that more is always better using the concept of the inverted U graph, while giving numerous examples of those who have suffered great adversity but were not crushed by it. Rather, they emerged with an inner strength which allowed them to challenge assumptions and authority, and achieve great things.

On February 2, 2014 *David and Goliath* was number one in *The Washington Post's* Bestsellers Hardcover nonfiction/general category with indications it had been in the top ten for seventeen weeks.[55]

David and Goliath begins with a retelling of the familiar biblical story of David, the shepherd boy who would become Israel's greatest king, doing battle with Goliath, the mighty champion of Israel's greatest nemesis, the Philistines. Gladwell looks at the encounter with fresh eyes, seeing David not as a weakling, but as a skilled "slinger," using an advanced form of weaponry, thereby catching the myopic giant off guard. It is a fascinating retelling which challenges many of the assumptions made about might and power. The book goes on to defy these assumptions further with numerous examples of misfits and underdogs who used their wits and determination to beat tremendous odds and emerge victorious against superior enemies.

However, the book is not entirely about warriors, underdogs, and surprising victories. Gladwell draws on examples from sports, science, education, and the justice system to demonstrate the power of tenacity, cunning, stubbornness, and the refusal to give up.

Malcolm Gladwell grew up in rural Ontario and has returned to his Mennonite roots.[56] He gives credit, in the book's Acknowledgements to the Gathering Church, a congregation in Kitchener, affiliated with Mennonite Church Eastern Canada, a regional body of Mennonite Church Canada.[57]

Three religious traditions play a prominent role in Gladwell's book *David and Goliath* including: Black Baptists, French Huguenots, and North American Mennonites. Gladwell references Black Baptists in describing the nonviolent, but often deceitful, tactics of the leaders of the Civil Rights

---

55. Nielsen Bookscan, "Washington Bestsellers Hardcover."
56. Bailey, "Renewal of Faith," 20.
57. Gladwell, *David and Goliath*, 277.

movement in the American south. He also briefly describes the Huguenots and a French Huguenot pastor, Andre Trocme, and his refusal to cooperate with the authorities in Nazi occupied France during World War II. Trocme and his cohorts gave shelter to thousands of Jews, primarily school aged children, at great personal risk. Among these renowned people of faith, Gladwell inserts the Mennonites in chapter eight, titled "Wilma Derksen." There one finds the story of the Derksens, a Mennonite couple living in Winnipeg, Manitoba whose daughter Candace was kidnaped on her way home from school. Her body was found seven weeks later. There was evidence she had been tortured and raped before she was murdered, yet it was decades before her assailant was discovered and charged.

The Derksens, drawing upon their pacifist Mennonite beliefs and religious traditions, refused to become embittered, or seek revenge. Rather, they offered forgiveness, tentatively at first but ultimately in full, to their daughter's murderer. Quoting Wilma Derksen, Gladwell writes, "The whole Mennonite philosophy is that we forgive and move on. To the Mennonites, forgiveness is a religious imperative: Forgive those who trespass against you. But it is also a very practical strategy based on the belief that there are profound limits to what the formal mechanisms of retribution can accomplish. The Mennonites believe in the inverted U-shaped curve."[58]

Gladwell does not expound on the religious practices of the Black Baptist churches involved in the civil rights movement. Nor does he say much about the Huguenots, except to say they are a persecuted Protestant minority which has lived in Catholic France for centuries. However, Gladwell goes to great lengths to explain Mennonite faith, perhaps because he assumes their faith and practices would not be well known by his readers, or perhaps, because of a desire to share his own religious convictions. Gladwell calls them pacifists and outliers, while pointing to their persecution during the Russian Revolution under Stalin, and their emigration to North America. He notes Mennonite heroes are not warriors or prophets but men and women like Dirk Willems who, in the sixteenth century, was imprisoned for his beliefs. Gladwell describes the familiar story of Willems' winter escape. When the guard, who was chasing Willems, fell through the ice covering the water in the prison moat, Willems stopped, returned, and came to aid his pursuer. For his act of compassion Willems was rearrested and subsequently burned at the stake.[59]

58. Ibid., 255.
59. Ibid., 254-55.

Gladwell contrasts Derksens' actions after the murder of their daughter to those of Mike Reynolds after his daughter's death at the hands of a thief. Motivated by a desire for justice and revenge, Reynolds used his influence to crack down on crime by getting California's "Three Strikes" criminal sentencing law passed through a ballot initiative. Gladwell argues that although California saw a marked decrease in crime, that trend began before the Three Strikes law was passed. The same decrease occurred across the United States, even in areas without a "Three Strikes" law. While Gladwell asks who was right, Wilma Derksen or Mike Reynolds? he cautions that is the wrong question, noting both acted with sincerity and good intentions. The difference was in their perception of power. Reynolds thought there are no limits to power and the more criminals who are locked up the better off society will be. The Derksens resisted every instinct they had to strike back and seek revenge. Rather they relied on their faith to forgive and move on with their lives. They would not let themselves become victims too.[60]

In telling this story Gladwell introduces his readers to the depth of the Mennonite faith, giving them not just a glimpse, but a satisfying taste of its richness.

60. Ibid., 253.

CHAPTER 11

The Internet

Mennonite Church USA and its Agencies' Web Presence

As technology has evolved, Mennonites have used different forms of media for their outreach, moving from tracts and books, to radio and television. And yet, Mennonites have very little presence on television, with the exception of a few Mennonite congregations, notably Calvary Community Church in Hampton, Virginia. Calvary formerly broadcasted its morning worship service on a local cable channel but discontinued this practice around 2008. The latest media frontier is the Internet.

Third Way Media established an official Mennonite presence on the Internet in the mid to late 1990s with the launch of Third Way Café, a web site designed to promote Mennonite faith and values and steer inquirers to local Mennonite churches. The web site invites and personally answers individual questions about Mennonite faith and practices. In 2011, Third Way Café averaged forty-one thousand page views per month with nine-thousand two-hundred absolute unique visitors in the same period.[1]

The Mennonite Church USA, the largest Mennonite group in North America, has a significant but not particularly large presence on the Internet. According to journalist Anna Groff, "Mennonite organizations have joined the Internet revolution in ways that are changing business-as-usual."[2] The following table appeared in an article Groff wrote about this phenomenon for *The Mennonite*.

1. M. Davis, "From Holy Kiss to Quilt Designs, People Are Curious," 7.
2. Groff, "Thousands of Unique Visitors," 41.

PART II—HOW MENNONITES HAVE USED MEDIA

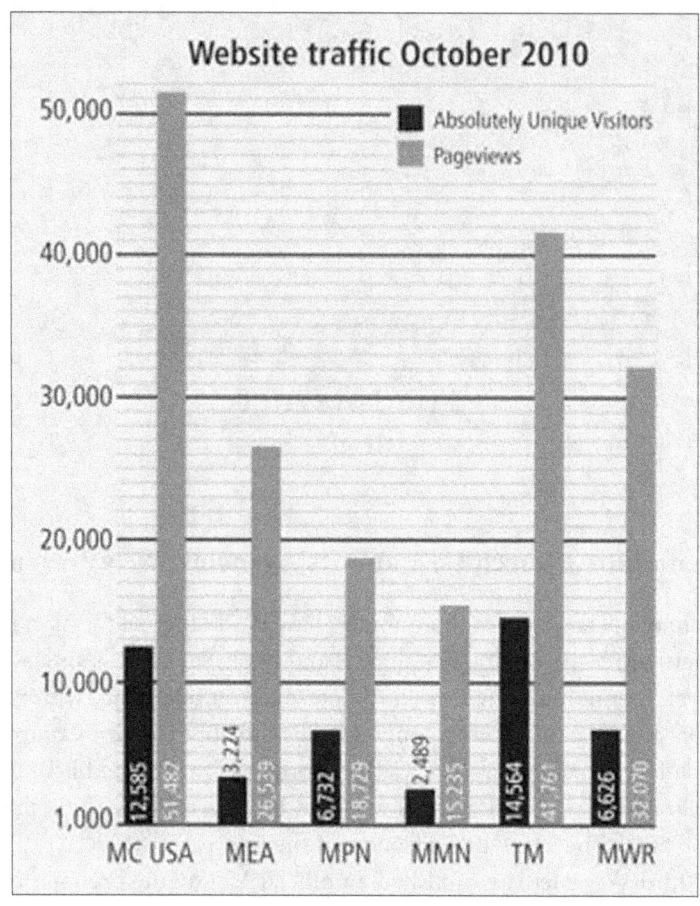

Chart of Web site traffic October, 2010 from *The Mennonite* by Anna Groff.

For the month of October 2010, Mennonite Church USA's (MC USA) web site received the most pageviews (51,482), followed by web sites of *The Mennonite* (TM) and *Mennonite Weekly Review* (MWR), respectively.[3] The other agencies represented in the table are Mennonite Education Agency (MEA), Mennonite Publishing Network (MPN) and Mennonite Mission Network (MMN). The news related sites, e.g., TM and MWR, see more traffic than the agencies due to the nature of their business.

By way of comparison, the Plymouth Brethren church, with about one million adherents worldwide, are a smaller denomination than the Mennonites, who number 1.7 million worldwide. The Plymouth Brethren

3. Ibid., 41.

The Internet

have a very basic, linear web site with ten simple tabs and no search function. When last checked, the site had not been updated in two years.[4] The MC USA web presence alone, which is one of many Mennonite home pages, is far larger and updated on a near daily basis. It far exceeds that of the Plymouth Brethren.

Third Way Media

Third Way Media, formerly Mennonite Media, is an outreach of Mennonite Church USA. Until July, 2011 it was lodged under Mennonite Mission Network then merged with Mennonite Publishing Network under the name MennoMedia. Third Way Media is unique among other denominational media outlets in that its primary focus is not internal but external. Third Way Media is tasked with promoting Mennonite values to the broader public, not promoting the denomination to its own members.

According to Burton Buller, former director of Third Way Media, "Since media is such a strong influence, we want our voice to be a part of it . . . People more and more are getting their spiritual experiences from the media—and if we don't have a presence in that media, we miss out on reaching people who are there . . . . Mennonites have historically been concerned with peace and justice issues and we have something to say on those topics . . . Third Way Café [is] our most successful brand."[5]

In 1998, at a time when only 24 percent of U.S. households were connected to the Internet, Third Way Media launched an internet web site called Third Way Café designed as a welcoming place for those seeking to learn about Mennonites. What began with six topics and about one hundred pages has since grown to more than three thousand pages of Mennonite information, audio files, video clips, essays, reviews, and scriptural reflections. Third Way Café was not the first Mennonite face on the web; Mennolink began as an e-mail list serve in 1992. By 1998 most Mennonite organizations had a presence on the web in a home page.[6]

Third Way Café has two purposes:

---

4. "The Plymouth Brethren." Homepage. Online.
5. Hess, "Faith in Media," 6.
6. M. Davis, "Third Way Cafe Celebrates a Decade."

PART II—HOW MENNONITES HAVE USED MEDIA

1. To inject Anabaptist Christian perspectives into society's marketplace of ideas, providing a prophetic witness at the intersections of faith and contemporary issues.

2. To present content from the bias that following Jesus Christ impacts all of life and that following is often an alternative to current culture.[7]

In 2008 Third Way Café had about eight thousand visitors per month. In the first six months of 2008, people in one hundred and fifty-one countries of the world visited, including forty-four thousand visits from the U.S., seven thousand from Canada, twelve-hundred from the United Kingdom and one thousand from Australia. During October 2010, the same period measured by Anna Groff and plotted in the earlier table, Third Way Café had 41,207 page views and 9,199 unique visitors. Seventy-five percent of those were new visits. These figures are roughly equivalent to those of the denominational news magazine *The Mennonite* during the same period. More recently Melodie Davis noted approximately forty thousand page views and twenty thousand unique visitors to Third Way Café in July, 2013.[8]

Third Way also provides subscriber services which regularly e-mail materials to users who request it. The table below, compiled in January, 2014 lists the service and the number of subscribers.

Subscription Service	*Data as of January, 2014*
What's New	1370
Another Way	1093
Wider View	970
Peace Story	1020
A Sip of Scripture	1082
Media Matters	688
Today's Stress Tip	1188

In May, 2011 the total number of subscriptions to these services exceeded nine thousand, although one person may subscribe to multiple services. Subscription manager Melodie Davis calls them "the dedicated

7. Ibid.
8. M. Davis, "Part 1: When There's News About "Mennonites" That Is Not So Good."

few." By January, 2014, with the addition of a separate MennoMedia blog at Mennobytes.com, only seven subscriptions remained with just over seven-thousand subscribers.

In a separate survey, less than 40 percent of those visiting Third Way Café identify themselves as Mennonite. With nearly a quarter of a million hits annually, Third Way Café is an important source of information for members of the general public who are asking questions about Mennonites and the Amish.

From this data it is clear Mennonites continue to use media in new and evolving ways to both shape identity and as a tool for outreach.

CHAPTER 12

Beyond Anecdotal Evidence to Hard Data

THIS TEXT EXAMINED MANY expressions of spoken, print, and visual media produced by, or referencing, Mennonites. In the process, a strong case has been made which demonstrates Mennonites have stamped a media footprint in excess of their size, particularly with regard to print media. Dozens of examples, spanning centuries, have been used to corroborate the premise that Mennonites have been the subject of popular media and have shaped media for identity and external witness. Some of the evidence was anecdotal. However, by harnessing powerful internet search engines the author has generated hard data which demonstrates the relative size of the Mennonite footprint in print, compared to other denominations.

Anecdotal Evidence of Mennonites' Media Footprint

Although scarce, at least one statement comparing Mennonite demographics and influence to that of other denominations does exist. Franklin Littell, commenting in 1964 on the quality of published materials collected in the Bethel College archives and reprinted in such places as the *Mennonite Quarterly Review* says, "The volume of material made available over the years, in magazine form and in monographs, is truly astonishing when you consider that the American Mennonites number approximately 200,000 souls. The quality of scientific research is not surpassed by that of any church body in the world."[1] Gathering these scholarly materials, which began in

---

1. Littell, *The Origins of Sectarian Protestantism*, 151.

earnest in 1927, was a necessary first step in preparing Mennonites for a future of greater media influence, but these materials were often written in German, or other foreign languages, and were generally not accessible to the general public.

The next major step occurred in 1944 when Harold S. Bender published "The Anabaptist Vision" inspiring a generation of Mennonite scholars. A third and crucial step in the process of Mennonites gaining broader recognition happened thirty years later when acclaimed Mennonite theologian John Howard Yoder published *The Politics of Jesus*, undoubtedly one of the most important expositions of Anabaptist theology ever written. As noted earlier, in 2000 *Christianity Today* named it the fifth most important Christian book of the twentieth Century. Yet, nearly forty years after Yoder, most of the general public has still never heard of the Mennonites, nor do they know what Mennonites believe.

In 1976, just four years after John Howard Yoder rocked the world of Christian ethics, Doris Janzen Longacre, Mennonite Central Committee, and Herald Press published the *More-with-Less Cookbook*. It introduced the general public to a group of Christian disciples known as Mennonites who are great cooks but are also concerned about social justice and world hunger. From there, Mennonites branched out as writers and filmmakers. They also began to appear in films, books, and other media, slowly changing their image, until today some consider this tiny religious group to be "hip."

Hard Data from Published Books

The time line established above, which projects the trajectory of Mennonites' growing print media influence, although intriguing and compelling, is largely speculative. There is now a web based tool which is able to quantify such relationships with regard to print media. In December 2010, Google, in partnership with the Encyclopedia Britannica, Harvard University, and scientists from the Massachusetts Institute of Technology, launched a search engine which allows scholars, or anyone from the general public, to determine the popularity of a particular word, concept, or person by measuring the frequency of its occurrence in a plethora of books written over the last four centuries. The database contains five hundred billion words representing the content of 5.2 million books stripped of their context except for the date of their publication. The database contains works from many languages including English, French, Spanish, German, Chinese,

PART II—HOW MENNONITES HAVE USED MEDIA

and Russian representing about 4 percent of all the books ever written.² Its power allows researchers to trace the evolution of human culture. Similar in concept to the genome map of human DNA, its developers call the database a "culturome."

Tracing the term "Anabaptist" in the culturome reveals a surprising consistency in its frequency of usage from 1800 through 2000 with slight peaks around 1810, 1875, 1910 and its highest usage in 1960 when the term "Anabaptist" maxed out at .00005 percent.³

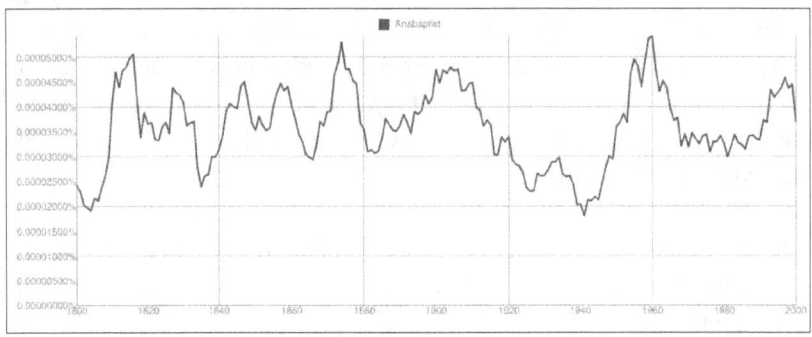

Ngram query "Anabaptist"

Stated another way, the word "Anabaptist" appeared five times for every ten million words searched. The beginning of the run up to the peak roughly corresponds to the publication of Harold Bender's "The Anabaptist Vision" in 1944.

Scientific analysis of the quality of public drinking water often measures trace elements in terms of parts per million (PPM). One PPM corresponds to one milligram per liter. For purposes of comparison, the City of Harrisonburg Public Utilities' 2013 report on the city's drinking water shows two PPM of fluoride, a chemical additive generally considered helpful in maintaining strong teeth. The naturally occurring element copper is present in concentrations of one point three PPM, while lead, a highly toxic carcinogen, can barely be detected at fifteen parts per billion (PPB). One PPB corresponds to one microgram per liter. Thus, the word "Anabaptist" among the words of human culture is similar to a trace element in drinking water with .5 or one-half Words Per Million (WPM).⁴

2. Kapadia, "Google Releases New Books Ngram." News Tonight. Online.
3. Google Books Ngram Viewer.
4. Harrisonburg Public Utilities, "2013 Water Quality Report," online, 2.

Beyond Anecdotal Evidence to Hard Data

A search of the word "Mennonite" showed it barely registered on the scale in 1800, but its use began to increase in 1870, peaking at twenty WPM around 1955, dropping off, then resuming its climb in the early 1970s reaching another peak of seventeen WPM in 1995 before trailing off again[5]

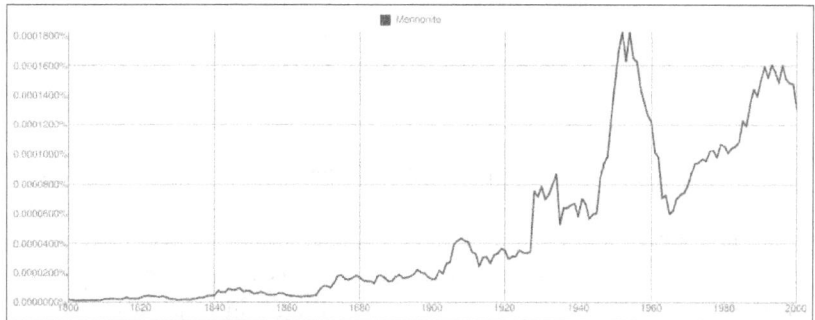

Ngram query "Mennonite"

Again, the run up to the peak in usage of the word "Mennonite" in print began around 1944 when Bender published "The Anabaptist Vision." Another peak started in the early 1970s and continued until approximately 1996. This period of increased public awareness of Mennonites roughly corresponds to John Howard Yoder's publication of *The Politics of Jesus* in 1972 and Doris Janzen Longacre's wildly popular *More-with-Less Cookbook* published in 1976.

The supposition that Mennonites have a print media footprint in excess of their size can be proven scientifically using the "Google Books Ngram Viewer" search tool. Unfortunately, no such tool exists to scientifically quantify such relationships in non-print media. As has already been demonstrated, the word "Mennonite" is more common than "Anabaptist." Similarly the word "Mormon" is in greater common usage than "Latter Day Saints." Comparing "Catholic" and "Jew," the term Catholic is used about five times more frequently in print than "Jew." [6]

---

5. Google Books Ngram Viewer.
6. Ibid.

PART II—HOW MENNONITES HAVE USED MEDIA

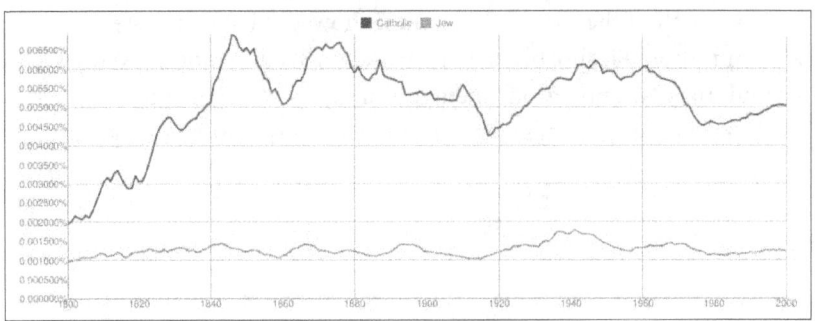

Ngram query "Catholic" and "Jew"

The following graph stacks the terms, "Jew," "Methodist," "Mormon," and "Mennonite." It shows the term "Jew" appears slightly more frequently than "Methodist" except for two brief periods around 1860 and 1910. The word "Mormon" is next in frequency, followed by "Mennonite." The important thing to note is not the exact number of words, or their percentage, but the relationship between the words being compared, noting particularly the periods of peaks and valleys.[7]

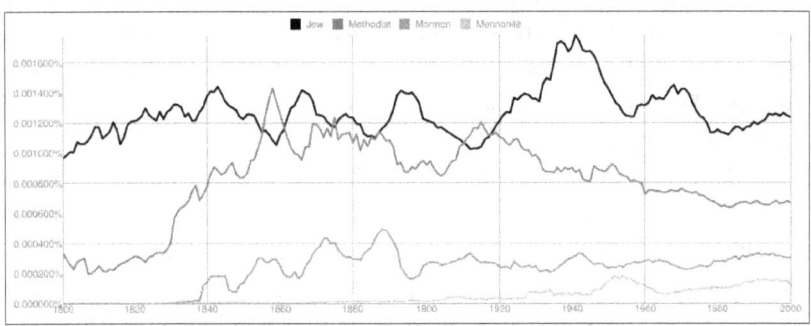

Ngram query "Jew, Methodist, Mormon, Mennonite"

The next graph matches "Mormon" and "Mennonite" and demonstrates the huge increase in popularity of the LDS faith from its beginning in 1830, with John Smith's publication of *The Book of Mormon*, through about 1890. It is interesting to note that in about 1955, when the word "Mennonite" was most in use with twenty WPM, it nearly matches "Mormon," with twenty-five WPM even though Mormons number 1.6 million

7. Ibid.

in the U.S. compared to just 323,000 Mennonites, a group one fifth as big as the LDS denomination.[8]

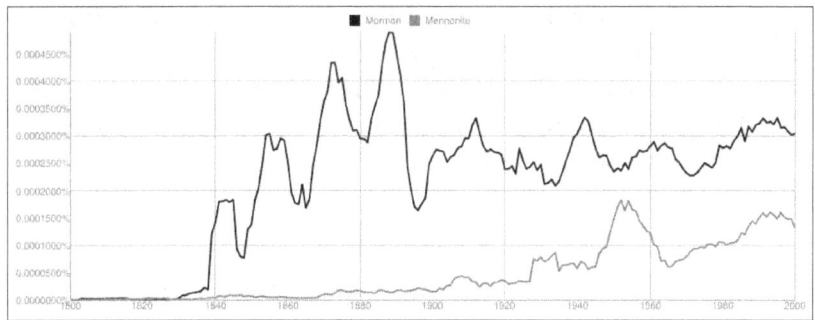

Ngram query "Mormon" and "Mennonite"

Thus it can be scientifically proven that in the latter half of the twentieth century Mennonites have a media footprint in excess of their size, at least in regard to print media. To use a boxing term, Mennonites "punch above their weight."

When compared to "Amish" the word "Mennonite" consistently tracks above and in parallel except for a Mennonite peak, noted previously, which occurred after the publication of "The Anabaptist Vision." The Amish overtook the Mennonites for a brief time, peaking in the period between 1985 and 1992 which corresponds to the release of the blockbuster film *Witness* in 1985.[9]

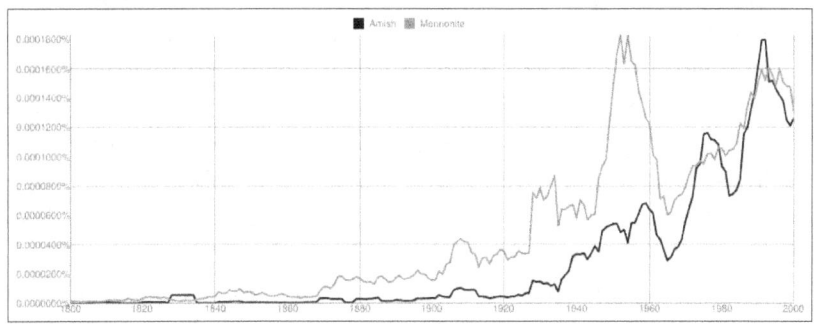

Ngram query "Amish" and "Mennonite"

8. Ibid.
9. Ibid.

PART II—HOW MENNONITES HAVE USED MEDIA

For another measure of comparison, the Plymouth Brethren are a small Christian denomination numbering about one million adherents worldwide, compared to 1.7 Mennonites in eighty countries. Although separatist, the Plymouth Brethren have been highly influential in Evangelical Christian circles. The following Figure, constructed using the Ngram, compares the occurrence of the words "Plymouth Brethren" and "Mennonite." The graph tracking the term "Plymouth Brethren" barely rises above the X-axis or floor of the chart.

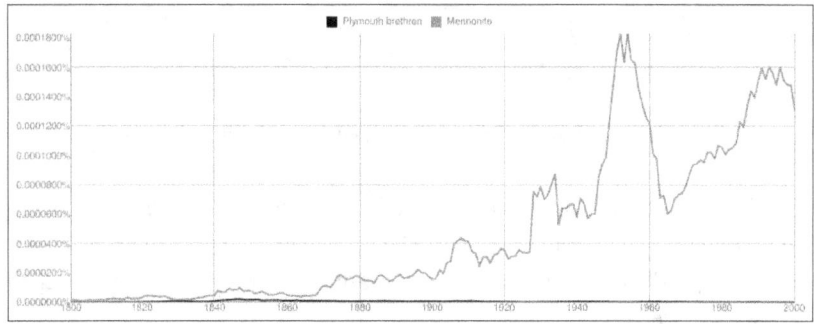

Ngram query "Plymouth Brethren" and "Mennonite"

It clearly shows the word Mennonite is present to a much higher degree in books written between 1800 and 2000 than the words Plymouth Brethren. Part of this disparity can be explained by the fact that after their formation in Dublin, Ireland in the 1820s, the Plymouth Brethren split into two branches in 1848. Notice the small, almost imperceptible, bump in the baseline happened just after 1840. The Ngram for the Plymouth Brethren is otherwise flat. Plymouth Brethren also go by several different names including: Open Brethren, Exclusive Brethren, The Brethren, and even Darbyites. An Ngram search using those names showed a nearly identical flat line except the term "The Brethren" registered slightly higher, but those occurrences were most likely incidental and not related to the Plymouth Brethren religious group.[10]

Based on a limited search, in comparison to Mennonites, Plymouth Brethren have a very small media footprint. Garrison Keillor, who grew up Plymouth Brethren but no longer claims that tradition, is perhaps their best known media personality. In contrast to the many books and plays with Mennonite characters written by non-Mennonites cited in this book, Sir

10. Ibid.

Beyond Anecdotal Evidence to Hard Data

Edmond Gosse's 1907 memoir *Father and Son*, about growing up Plymouth Brethren and Peter Cary's 1988 novel *Oscar and Lucinda*, which is based on Gosse's memoir, appear to be the only two books focused on this religious group. A film adaptation of *Oscar and Lucinda* was released in 1997 and a more recent film, *Son of Rambow* was released in 2008. Neither were major motion pictures.[11] In contrast there are at least six films with Mennonite characters or references.

This is not to say the Plymouth Brethren have not been influential. Influence can be measured in many ways. The most influential Plymouth Brethren members include twentieth century Biblical scholar F. F. Bruce, martyred missionary Jim Elliot, and John Nelson Darby who lived in the 1800s and wrote more than fifty books. Darby is often credited with the development of dispensational and pretribulation theology, both of which have been widely embraced by conservative Evangelicals well beyond Plymouth Brethren circles. This text has focused on a group's presence in popular media, not in scholarly journals, or in the battle of ideas. Although Plymouth Brethren are barely visible in print media, they have been influential, but it is difficult to compare and quantify the relative influence of Mennonites and Plymouth Brethren.

---

11. Ibid.

CHAPTER 13

Conclusion

THIS SURVEY OF MENNONITES and media examined more than three dozen depictions of Mennonites by non-Mennonites in eight different media realms. In addition, it presented nearly twenty examples of Mennonite authors, artists, singers, actors, and businesses, which actively shaped media, at times through denominational channels and at times independently. They did so to witness to their beliefs, reach out to others, and to form a communal identity. Many forms of media portray Mennonites. Mennonites are also actively shaping media. Comparisons to the media presence of other faith traditions were made using anecdotal and quantifiable data such as the Ngram. Anecdotal and hard evidence showed Mennonites "punch above their weight" in the media ring. Mennonites have a media presence, particularly in print, in excess of their size, when compared to many other religious groups.

The question remains, "Why is this relevant?"

First, this text provides touchstones which may be helpful to those within the Mennonite tradition as they seek to be missional and engage society with an Anabaptist vision. Although difficult to quantify, there is a sense among Mennonites that there is a growing hunger for an Anabaptist understanding of the Christian faith. As noted herein, many prominent Christian leaders, such as Brian McLaren, Shane Claiborne, Bill Hybels, and Rick Warren say they have learned from the Anabaptist faith tradition and speak highly of it. Some, such as Anglican Stuart Murray, call themselves neo-Anabaptists. As people seek to learn more about Mennonites and their Anabaptist tradition, it is important that those within the tradition continue to write and engage the arts to communicate their faith and

Conclusion

beliefs. It is important to have an Anabaptist perspective portrayed in the marketplace of ideas through books and other forms of media. This book provides a road map which points toward high and low points along the communications journey across five centuries. The prominent works described herein may help shape future discussions of Anabaptist thought, by setting them in a broader media context.

Second, this books helps the reader understand how the general public perceives Mennonites. It has been said that one of the most difficult things for an individual to do, is to see themselves the way others see them. This book attempts to show those within a particular faith tradition how they are perceived by many North Americans. It has shed light on how Mennonites have been both vilified and admired. Perhaps the most prominent association documented here is the close link in the public's mind between Mennonites and the Amish. That association is understandable since the one group, the Amish, separated from the Mennonites yet continues to embrace many of the same theological convictions and understandings as the Mennonite group they left. That association, and the distinction between the Amish and Mennonites, is further blurred in the public's mind because some Mennonite groups still drive horse and buggies, just like their Amish cousins. The two groups' dress, although distinct for those within the Anabaptist tradition, are largely indistinguishable to those outside the faith. Therefore, any Mennonite group wanting to communicate with the broader public about their faith, beliefs, and practices, must begin with the statement, "We are not Amish." Once that is clear, one can go on to explain the similarities and differences, not only between Mennonites and the Amish, but between those who practice a Mennonite third way, which is neither Protestant nor Catholic, and those in a mainstream or evangelical Christian denomination.

Thirdly, the media survey portrayed here is fascinating, particularly for those who are a part of, or interested in, the Anabaptist tradition. The text undoubtedly delivered some "aha" moments such as when readers learn: Martin Luther called the Anabaptists "schwarmar;" there is a sympathetic Anabaptist character in Voltaire's *Candide*; President Lincoln and General Stonewall Jackson both had something to say about the peaceful Mennonites; Joseph Heller's award winning anti-war novel *Catch-22* is bookended by an Anabaptist Army chaplain; and contemporary best-selling author Malcolm Gladwell is himself a Mennonite.

Lastly, in chronicling Anabaptist appearances in popular literature across the centuries, this text provides a significant piece of scholarship.

PART II—HOW MENNONITES HAVE USED MEDIA

Not since 1929, when Harold S. Bender detailed two centuries of Mennonite literature, has such a project been undertaken.[1] Bender's references were primarily to books, pamphlets, periodicals, and other printed materials, many of them in German, which were written by Mennonites for Mennonites. None of the works cited in Bender's bibliography would have been read widely by the general public and are therefore not included here. In contrast, *Mennonites and Media* describes Mennonite and Anabaptist references in popular media produced by non-Mennonites as well as widely read scholarly works and other media written or produced by Mennonites.

Ideas matter. They shape the way we think and live. They influence our faith and our practice. Up to this point this book has been written in the objective third person voice. Allow me to shift to the more accessible first person voice and conclude with a personal story. My journey illustrates the importance of books and literature, and gives the reader insights into why I wrote this book.

I came to faith as a ten year old boy during Vacation Bible School in my home congregation, First Presbyterian Church, Providence, Rhode Island. At sixteen years of age I came to understand Jesus was more than my Savior and embraced him as Lord. That year I embarked on a life long journey of discipleship.

The military draft ended in 1973 during my senior year in high school. Even though military service was no longer compulsory, I decided to enter the Coast Guard Academy in New London, Connecticut, just fifty-four miles from my Cranston, Rhode Island home. The cadets entering in 1973 were the first all-volunteer academy class since 1940. Cadets receive a full scholarship and monthly stipend. However, they become obligated for military service if they stay on for their junior year. In 1975, as a twenty year old cadet I was wrestling with the decision to stay at the academy and incur a military obligation, or transfer to a civilian college. I was trying to reconcile my Christian faith with the obligations of military service. During that time I read with rapt attention a booklet published by the Officers Christian Fellowship titled "May a Christian Serve in the Military?" penned by General William Harrison.[2] Harrison's essay, and the counsel of senior officers, convinced me that military service was consistent with my Christian faith. So, I stayed at the academy and embarked on a military career.

1. Bender, *Two Centuries of American Mennonite Literature*.
2. Harrison, "May a Christian Serve in the Military?"

Conclusion

As a newlywed in 1980, my wife Cindy, who graduated from Houghton College in New York and embraced an intense form of Christian community during her senior year in college, owned a copy of the *More-with-Less Cookbook*. Therefore, I had a Mennonite cookbook in my kitchen although at the time I had never actually met a Mennonite. Using it, and other resources, Cindy and I strove to live healthily and simply so others could simply live.

Meanwhile, my questions about serving in the military did not end after graduation from the academy. As a young officer I read an Intervarsity book published in 1981 called *War: Four Christian Views* in which four authors describe and support their view on war including: the crusade or preventative war, the just war, nonresistance, and Christian pacifism—a position defended by Myron S. Augsburger then president of Eastern Mennonite College.[3] By then, in 1981, I had met a Mennonite family in New Orleans, Franklin and Retha Baer. After spending two terms of service with Mennonite Central Committee in Zaire, Franklin was pursuing a doctorate at Tulane School of Public Health while Retha worked at Tulane hospital. I was stationed at Coast Guard Vessel Traffic Service New Orleans which operated somewhat like an air traffic control center but for ships on the congested Mississippi River. The Baers and I attended the same inner city congregation, the Irish Channel Christian Fellowship, led by Reverend Bill Brown, a Presbyterian minister striving for racial reconciliation.

In 1989, I divorced, remarrying five years later, this time to a woman who grew up in the Mennonite faith tradition. We met in an adult Sunday school class at Washington Community Fellowship, a church begun by Myron Augsburger. However, I continued to consider myself to be Presbyterian, the denomination of my youth. Sometime between 1991 and 1997, I reread the Intervarsity book about war and realized Myron Augsburger, whom I then knew personally, had written the section supporting Christian pacifism.

In the spring of 1997, after several months of intensive study, I embraced the *Confession of Faith in a Mennonite Perspective*, published by Herald Press in 1995 in preparation for the merger of the Mennonite Church and the General Conference Mennonite Church.[4] I would not have become Mennonite if the earlier 1963 *Mennonite Confession of Faith*, with its narrow requirements that women wear a prayer covering and men's hair

---

3. Clouse, *War: Four Christian Views*.

4. Mennonite Church and General Conference Mennonite Church, *Confession of Faith in a Mennonite Perspective*.

be kept short, had still been in use.[5] At that point, in 1997, I retired from the Coast Guard, which had made it clear my services were no longer needed. I am a now first generation Mennonite and have embarked on a second career in service to Mennonite Church USA.

There were other factors which led to my change of heart including a personal tragedy,[6] a fresh reading of scripture, and a new understanding of early church history. I particularly remember the impact the 1982 British film *Gandhi*, starring Ben Kingsley in the titular role, had on my life. The film, which won eight Academy Awards, made pacifism appealing. Yet, at the time I couldn't reconcile my own muscular Christianity with Gandhi's pacifist Hindu faith. Later, when I discovered the Mennonites, I found a Christian tradition which drew me in. All this is to say, my personal story illustrates the concept that the ideas which shape and reshape our lives are often expressed in books and film. Media matters.

If Mennonite Church USA, and those in other denominations, are serious about being missional, it is important for pastors and church leaders to become like the Apostle Paul, who knew Greek culture and was able to stand before the men of Athens in the Areopagus and use lines of their own poetry to argue theology, or, like the men of Issachar who understood the times and came to assist David at Hebron and make him king. The church, whether locally or in mission around the world, cannot reach a people whose culture it does not understand. I hope this book has demonstrated Mennonites' place in popular North America media and in so doing has given the Mennonites who have read it a place to connect with those in the broader culture and vice versa.

Anabaptist ideas continue to attract people who embrace Christ's way of peace in their journey of discipleship. Not all who embrace neo-Anabaptism will become Mennonite, but all will have been influenced by the witness of Mennonites and Anabaptists who modeled discipleship and peace in their lives and writings.

The world needs the fresh, alternative perspective offered by Mennonites. That is one of the reasons I enjoy working for MennoMedia. Primarily through books, but also through DVDs and on the web, MennoMedia's products not only shape the Mennonite Church in the US and Canada,

---

5. Mennonite Church, "Mennonite Confession of Faith."

6. The story of my personal tragedy is captured in chapter seventeen of *Fifty Shades of Grace* which includes fifty different authors telling about God's grace in their lives. M. Davis, *Fifty Shades of Grace*.

Conclusion

they influence those seeking a deeper, more holistic faith. MennoMedia is projecting Anabaptist thought into the marketplace of ideas. I hope this book has illustrated ways in which that has already happened and in the process allowed you to engage those ideas. I encourage you to continue reading and producing media which challenges and enlightens from a distinctly Anabaptist Christian perspective, thereby building up disciples who are extending Christ's peaceable kingdom.

Bibliography

Alvarez, Alex. "Cue Outrage: Indiana College Bans National Anthem for Being 'Too Violent.'" *Mediaite*. August 26, 2011. http://www.mediaite.com/online/cue-outrage-indiana-college-bans-national-anthem-for-being-too-violent/.
"Amish 'Reality' Shows Keep Coming." *Mennonite World Review*, November 26, 2012.
Amstutz, Laura. "Seminary Offers Class on Communication for People in Ministry." *EMU*. November 19, 2010. http://emu.edu/now/news/tag/julie-gochenour/.
Associated Press. "Landis Kept 'Believing.'" *Daily News Record*, July 24, 2006.
Bailey, Sarah Pulliam. "Renewal of Faith." *Mennonite World Review*, October 28, 2013.
Belford, Barbara. *Oscar Wilde: A Certain Genius*. New York: Random House, 2002.
Bender, Harold S. *The Anabaptist Vision*. Scottdale, PA: Herald, 1944.
———. *Two Centuries of American Mennonite Literature: A Bibliography of Mennonitica Americana 1727–1928*. Vol. 1. Studies in Anabaptist and Mennonite History. Goshen, IN: Mennonite Historical Society, 1929.
Biesecker-Mast, Gerald. *Separation and the Sword in Anabaptist Persuasion: Radical Confessional Rhetoric from Schleitheim to Dordrecht*. Vol. 6. C. Henry Smith Series. Scottdale, PA: Herald, 2006.
Blauser, Brian. "The Steel Wheels on Mountain Stage." *NPR*. January 11, 2012. http://www.npr.org/2011/04/15/135376992/the-steel-wheels-on-mountain-stage.
Blaustein, Claire Marie. "Steel Wheels: Americana, Made-by-Hand." *NPR*. May 10, 2012. http://www.npr.org/2012/05/10/152380141/the-steel-wheels-americana-made-by-hand.
Blosser, Glendon, et al. *Minutes of the Virginia Mennonite Conference, (Proceedings from 1951-1966)*. Vol. 2. Harrisonburg, VA: Virginia Mennonite Conference, 1967.
"Books of the Century: Leaders and Thinkers Weigh in on Classics That Have Shaped Contemporary Religious Thought." *Christianity Today*. April 24, 2000. http://www.christianitytoday.com/ct/2000/april24/5.92.html.
Buller, Burton. *"Does Techno-Faith Have a Future?" And Other Media Musings*. Mission Insight 9. Elkhart, IN: Mennonite Board of Missions, 2000.
———. *Waging Peace: Muslim and Christian Alternatives*. Harrisonburg, VA: Third Way Media, 2011.
Burke, James Lee. *Bitterroot*. New York: Simon & Schuster, 2001.
———. *Heaven's Prisoners*. 1st ed. New York: H. Holt, 1988.

Bibliography

———. *Jesus out to Sea: Stories*. New York: Simon & Schuster, 2007.
Byler, J. Daryl. "Earmarks of a Bestseller: After 25 Years More-with-Less Cookbook is Still Changing Eating Habits and Lives." *A Common Place*, November 2000.
Callen, Barry L. *Radical Christianity: The Believers Church Tradition in Christianity's History and Future*. Nappanee, IN: Evangel, 1999.
"Capturing the Camera-Shy Mennonites." *MSNBC Web*. March 29, 2011. http://www.nbcnews.com/video/nightly-news/41606485#41606485.
Carrera, Raul V. *The Radicals*. Worcester, PA: Vision Video, 1990. Film.
Cassidy, Suzanne. "Meet the Major Legal Players in the Conestoga Wood Specialties Supreme Court Case." *Lancaster Online*. March 25, 2014. http://lancasteronline.com/news/local/meet-the-major-legal-players-in-the-conestoga-wood-specialties/article_302bc8e2-b379-11e3-b669-0014bcf6878.html.
Castello, Piazza. "The Medals Plaza." *MacLean's*. February 24, 2006.
Chismar, Janet. "Speed Skater Cindy Klassen Races for God." *Billy Graham Evangelistic Association*. February 24, 2010. http://billygraham.org/story/speed-skater-cindy-klassen-races-for-god/.
"Choice Books Sells 5 Million Books Again." *Mennonite Weekly Review*, February 7, 2011.
Clouse, Robert G., ed. *War: Four Christian Views*. Downers Grove, IL: InterVarsity, 1981.
Davis, Charles. *Hazel's People*. Worcester, PA: Vision Video, 1980.
Davis, Melodie. "ABC-TV Ends Successful Run of *Waging Peace*." *Links@MennoMedia*. February 2012. http://www.findinghopeinrecovery.com/?Page=6967.
———. *Fierce Goodbye: Living in the Shadow of Suicide*. Harrisonburg, VA: Mennonite Media, 2004. Film.
———. "From Holy Kiss to Quilt Designs, People Are Curious." *Mennonite Weekly Review*, February 12, 2011.
———. *Journey Toward Forgiveness: From Rage to Reconciliation*. Harrisonburg, VA: Mennonite Media, 2001. Film.
———. "Part 1: When There's News About 'Mennonites' That Is Not So Good." *MennoMedia*. August 2, 2013. http://mennobytes.com/part-1-when-theres-news-about-mennonites-that-is-not-so-good/.
———. "Third Way Cafe Celebrates a Decade." *The Mennonite*. September 11, 2008. http://www.themennonite.org/public_press_releases/Third_Way_Caf_celebrates_a_decade.
———. "What's New at Third Way Media, Third Way Café Accessed Frequently After Tragic News." *Third Way Media*. May 25, 2010. http://www.thirdway.com/Subscriptions/?Page=5508|May+25%2C+2010.
———., ed. *Fifty Shades of Grace: Stories of Inspiration and Promise*. Harrisonburg, VA: Herald, 2013.
De Zengotita, Thomas. *Mediated: How the Media Shapes Your World and the Way You Live in It*. New York: Bloomsbury, 2005.
Durnbaugh, Donald F. *The Believers' Church: The History and Character of Radical Protestantism*. Scottdale, PA: Herald, 1985.
Dyck, Cornelius J. *An Introduction to Mennonite History: A Popular History of the Anabaptists and the Mennonites*. Scottdale, PA: Herald, 1981.
English, Chelsea. "Martin, Helen Reimensnyder." *Penn State University Libraries*. 2007. http://pabook.libraries.psu.edu/palitmap/bios/Martin__Helen_Reimensnyder.html.

Bibliography

Evans, Elizabeth. "Denver Mennonites Move toward Lesbian Ordination." *The Christian Century*. February 5, 2014. http://www.christiancentury.org/article/2014-02/denver-mennonites-take-first-step-toward-gay-ordination.

Falsani, Cathleen. "Evangelical, Fundamentalist, Born Again Aren't the Same." *Mennonite Weekly Review*, November 7, 2011.

Fitzhenry, Robert I. *Barnes & Noble Book of Quotations*. New York: Barnes & Noble, 1987.

Franzen, Jonathan. *The Corrections*. New York: Farrar, Straus, and Giroux, 2001.

Frykholm, Amy. "Health-Care Option." *The Christian Century*. September 22, 2009. http://www.christiancentury.org/article/2009-09/health-care-option.

———. "Mennonite Health-Care Plan Sets January Launch." *The Christian Century*. November 17, 2009. http://www.christiancentury.org/article/2009-11/mennonite-health-care-plan-sets-january-launch.

George, Timothy. *Theology of the Reformers*. Nashville: Broadman, 1988.

Gladwell, Malcolm. *David and Goliath: Underdogs, Misfits, and the Art of Battling Giants*. New York: Little, Brown, 2013.

Good, Sheldon C. "Ohio Amish Consider Renegade Bergholz Clan a Cult." *Mennonite World Review*. December 12, 2011. http://www.mennoworld.org/archived/2011/12/12/ohio-amish-consider-renegade-clan-cult/.

Groff, Anna. "Thousands of Unique Visitors." *The Mennonite*. January 1, 2011. http://www.themennonite.org/issues/14-01/articles/Thousands_of_unique_visitors.

Hal Erickson, Rovi. "The Silence at Bethany (1998)." *NYTimes: Movies*. http://www.nytimes.com/movies/movie/119779/The-Silence-at-Bethany/overview.

Hanks, Maxine, and Jean Kinney Williams. *Mormon Faith in America*. Faith in America. New York: Facts On File, 2003.

Harrison, William K. *May a Christian Serve in the Military?* Denver: Officers' Christian Fellowship, 1975.

Hauerwas, Stanley. "When the Politics of Jesus Makes a Difference." *The Christian Century* October 13, 1993. http://www.religion-online.org/showarticle.asp?title=109.

Heller, Joseph. *Catch-22*. New York: Simon and Schuster, 1961.

Hess, Melanie. "Faith in Media." *Beyond Ourselves*. 3 (2009) 4.

Hipps, Shane. *The Hidden Power of Electronic Culture: How Media Shapes Faith, the Gospel, and Church*. El Cajon, CA: Youth Specialties, 2006.

Holsopple, Jerry. *Beyond the News: Sexual Abuse*. Harrisonburg, VA: Mennonite Media. 1993. Film.

Homan, Gerlof D. *American Mennonites & the Great War, 1914–1918*. Edited by Theron F. Schlabach. Vol. 34. Studies in Anabaptist and Mennonite History. Scottdale, PA: Herald, 1994.

Hostetler, John Andrew. *God Uses Ink: The Heritage and Mission of the Mennonite Publishing House after Fifty Years*. Scottdale, PA: Herald, 1958.

Janzen, Rhoda. *Does This Church Make Me Look Fat?* New York: Grand Central, 2012.

———. *Mennonite in a Little Black Dress: A Memoir of Going Home*. 1st ed. New York: Henry Holt, 2009.

Kanagy, Conrad L. *Road Signs for the Journey: A Profile of Mennonite Church USA*. Scottdale, PA: Herald, 2007.

"Kansas M.B. Elected to US Senate." *Mennonite Weekly Review*. November 15, 2010. http://www.mennoworld.org/archived/2010/11/15/kansas-mb-elected-us-senate/.

Bibliography

Kapadia, Amar. "Google Releases New Books Ngram Viewer for Tracking Uses of Words." *News Tonight.* December 18, 2010. http://newstonight.net/content/google-releases-new-books-ngram-viewer-tracking-uses-words.

Kauffman, J. Howard, and Leo Driedger. *The Mennonite Mosaic: Identity and Modernization.* Scottdale, PA: Herald, 1991.

Kaufman, Sarah. "Break Away: Early on, Floyd Landis Learned the Last Shall Be First. Then Came the Tour De France." *The Washington Post,* July 2, 2006.

Kautsky, Karl. *Communism in Central Europe in the Time of the Reformation.* New York: A. M. Kelley, 1966.

Keener, Joyce, et al. *The Silence at Bethany.* New York: Playhouse, 1987. TV Film.

Kenneson, Philip D. *Beyond Sectarianism: Re-Imagining Church and World.* Christian Mission and Modern Culture. Harrisonburg, VA: Trinity, 1999.

King, Marshall V. "Ted and Lee-on the Hunt for Humor and Authenticity." *Festival Quarterly* 22:2 (1995) 2.

King, Sidney, et al. *Pearl Diver.* Thousand Oaks, CA: Monterey, 2008. Film.

Knox, Ronald Arbuthnott. *Enthusiasm: A Chapter in the History of Religion, with Special Reference to the 17th and 18th Centuries.* New York: Oxford University Press, 1950.

Kraybill, Donald B. "Elizabethtown College: Professors' Profile." http://users.etown.edu/k/kraybilld/.

———. *The Riddle of Amish Culture.* Baltimore, MD: Johns Hopkins University Press, 1989.

Kreider, Alan, and James R. Krabill. *Tongue Screws and Testimony.* Elkhart, IN: Mennonite Mission Network, 2008.

Kren, Emil, and Daniel Marx. "The Mennonite Minister Cornelis Claesz. Anslo in Conversation with his Wife, Aaltje." *Web Gallery of Art.* http://www.wga.hu/frames-e.html?/html/r/rembrand/23portra/65portra.html.

Lefever, Alon. "Mennonite Media Resources Business Plan." *MennoMedia.* (2010): 27.

Leggiere, Phil. "Pa. State Troopers Raid Mennonite Farm from Raw Milk Sales." April 27, 2008. http://mondoglobo.wftk.org/blog/qa/2008/04/pa-state-troopers-raid-mennoni.html.

Littell, Franklin H. *The Origins of Sectarian Protestantism: A Study of the Anabaptist View of the Church.* New York: Macmillan, 1964.

"*Living More With Less*: Like a Cookbook for Life." *MennoMedia.* December 11, 2010. http://www.heraldpress.com/titles/livingmorewithless/.

Lofton, Bonnie Price. "Those Famous Mennonite Harmonies: Do They Have a Future?" *Crossroads: Eastern Mennonite University.* 91:2 (2010) 11.

Loller, Travis. "Mennonite Family Among 11 Killed in Ky. Crash." *Fox News.* March 27, 2010. http://www.foxnews.com/us/2010/03/27/mennonite-family-killed-ky-crash.

Longacre, Doris Janzen. *More-with-Less Cookbook.* Scottdale, PA: Herald, 1976.

Longenecker, Stephen L. *Shenandoah Religion: Outsiders and the Mainstream, 1716–1865.* Waco, TX: Baylor University Press, 2002.

Maclean, Alison. *Jesus' Son.* Universal City, CA: Lions Gate, 1999. Film.

MacNelly, Gary Bookins and Susie MacNelly. "Shoe." *King Features.* June 29, 2013. http://www.shoecomics.com/.

Mancuso, Gail. "And One to Grow On." *Modern Family.* 21 minutes. New York: ABC, 2014. TV Episode.

Marrapodi, Eric. "My Faith: 2011 Year in Review." *CNN.* December 26, 2011. http://religion.blogs.cnn.com/2011/12/26/my-faith-2011-year-in-review/?iref=allsearch.

Bibliography

Martell, Nevin. "Sweet Memories and the Storied Pie That Inspired Them." *The Washington Post*, November 24, 2013.

Martin, Helen Reimensnyder. "Tillie: A Mennonite Maid." *Project Gutenberg*. 1904. http://www.gutenberg.org/ebooks/4760.

McCracken, Brett. *Hipster Christianity: When Church and Cool Collide*. Grand Rapids: Baker, 2010.

McFarland, Colleen. "Calvary Hour." *Mennonite Church USA Archives*. https://mla.bethelks.edu/archon/?p=creators/creator&id=275.

Mekeel, Tim. "Intercourse-Based Good Enterprises Closes to Pursue Bankruptcy Liquidation." *Lancaster Online*. December 10, 2013. http://lancasteronline.com/news/intercourse-based-good-enterprises-closes-to-pursue-bankruptcy-liquidation/article_b3a081ab-48ab-5817-9d97-8d6ace19397a.html?mode=jqm.

Melanchthon, Philipp. "The Augsburg Confession of Faith." *The Book of Concord: The Confessions of the Lutheran Church*. http://bookofconcord.org/augsburgconfession.php#article17.2.

Mennonite General Conference. *Mennonite Confession of Faith*. Scottdale, PA: Herald, 1963.

———. *Confession of Faith in a Mennonite Perspective: Summary Statement, Unison Readings*. Scottdale, PA: Herald, 1995.

Mennonite Church USA Executive Board. "Priorities Adopted by Mennonite Church USA to Guide Our Work Together as a Denomination (Pittsburgh, 2011)." http://resources.mennoniteusa.org/about/our-priorities/.

Mennonite Mission Network. "Protestant Props—French Magazine Honors Mennonite." *Beyond Ourselves* 9:1 (2010) 5.

Mennonite World Conference. "Shared Convictions of Global Anabaptists." *Mennonite World Conference*. March 15, 2006. http://www.mwc-cmm.org/article/shared-convictions.

Meyer, Jeff. "The Silence at Bethany (1988) T.V." *IMDB*. http://www.imdb.com/reviews/03/0328.html.

Michener, James A. *Centennial*. New York: Random House, 1974.

———. *The Novel*. New York: Random House, 1991.

Morgan, Angela. "Esther Augsburger Shares Her Faith, Convictions and Ideas through Art." *JMU Monty*. http://www.jmu.edu/monty/ArtOfSharing.shtml.

Murray, Stuart. *The Naked Anabaptist: The Bare Essentials of a Radical Faith*. Scottdale, PA: Herald, 2010.

Nafziger, Tim. "The Groenings, the Simpsons and the Mennonites." *The Mennonite*. August 16, 2007. http://www.themennonite.org/bloggers/timjn/posts/The_Groenings_The_Simpsons_and_The_Mennonites.

Nation, Mark Thiessen. *John Howard Yoder: Mennonite Patience, Evangelical Witness, Catholic Convictions*. Grand Rapids: Eerdmans, 2006.

———. "The Politics of Yoder Regarding *The Politics of Jesus*: Recovering the Implicit in Yoder's Holistic Theology for Pacifism." In *Radical Ecumenicity: Pursuing Unity and Continuity after John Howard Yoder*, edited by John C. Nugent, 37–56. Abilene, TX: Abilene Christian University Press, 2010.

Niebuhr, H. Richard. *Christ and Culture*. New York: Harper, 1951.

Nielsen Bookscan. "Washington Bestsellers Hardcover." *Washington Post*, February 19, 2014.

Bibliography

O'brien, Kathleen. "Obamacare Religious Exemption Hard to Get." *Washington Post*, April 28, 2014.

Oppenheimer, Mark. "A Theologian's Influence, and Stained Past, Live On." *The New York Times*. October 11, 2013. http://www.nytimes.com/2013/10/12/us/john-howard-yoders-dark-past-and-influence-lives-on-for-mennonites.html?pagewanted=all.

Osborne, Millard E. *Along the Road: A Collection of True Stories of Personal and Family Life*. Harrisonburg, VA: self-published, 2010.

"Over the Rhine: A Whole Life in a Song." *NPR Music*. February 8, 2011. http://www.npr.org/2011/02/08/133595205/over-the-rhine-a-whole-life-in-a-song.

Panaritis, Maria. "Lancaster County Man Glen D. Lapp among Afghan Ambush Victims." *Philadelphia Inquirer*, August 9, 2010.

Pellman, Hubert R. *Mennonite Broadcasts: The First 25 Years*. Harrisonburg, VA: Mennonite Broadcasts, 1979.

Peralta, Eyder. "Goshen College Bans National Anthem at Sporting Events." *NPR*. June 7, 2011. http://www.npr.org/blogs/thetwo-way/2011/06/08/137031395/goshen-college-bans-national-anthem-at-sporting-events.

"The Plymouth Brethren Movement." *Plymouth Brethren*. June 8, 2014. http://www.plymouthbrethren.com/index.htm.

Preheim, Rich. "Conflicts of Conscience: Faith Versus the State." *Mennonite World Review*. April 2, 2012. http://www.mennoworld.org/archived/2012/4/2/conflicts-conscience-faith-versus-state/.

Ranck, Dawn J., and Phyllis Pellman Good. *Fix-It and Forget-It Cookbook: Feasting with Your Slow Cooker*. Edited by Phyllis Pellman Good. Intercourse, PA: Good, 2000.

Rembrandt, Harmensz van Rijn. "The Mennonite Preacher Cornelis Claesz Anslo and His Wife Aeltje Gerritsdr Schouten." Oil on canvas. Gemaeldegalerie. Berlin, Germany: Art Resource, 1641.

Reygadas, Carlos. *Silent Light*. Mexico: Palisades Tartan, 2009. Film.

Rhodes, Robert. "Cyclist Wins World's Top Race: Family, Town Celebrate Tour De France Victory." *Mennonite Weekly Review*, July 31, 2006.

———. "Landis' Mother Sees God's Purpose in Victory." *Mennonite Weekly Review*. July 31, 2006.

Rich, Tracey R. "Judaism 101." 2011. http://www.jewfaq.org/whoisjew.htm#Who.

Ritzel, Rebecca. "A Grievous Tragedy, Insightfully Staged." *The Washington Post*. May 11, 2014.

Robbins, Liz. "Crash Devastates a Kentucky Family." *The New York Times*. March 27, 2010. http://www.nytimes.com/2010/03/27/us/27kentucky.html.

Rosenberg, Susan, and Warren Rohrer. *Warren Rohrer: Paintings 1972–93*. Philadelphia: Philadelphia Museum of Art, 2002.

Roth, John D., ed. *Engaging Anabaptism: Conversations with a Radical Tradition*. Scottdale, PA: Herald, 2001.

Russell, Mark. "Google Database Tracks Popularity of 500b Words." *Newser*. December 17, 2010. http://www.newser.com/story/107766/google-database-tracks-popularity-of-500b-words.html.

Ruth, John L. "Memorial Observance for E. Warren Rohrer, 1927–1955." *Festival Quarterly* 22:1 (1995) 3.

Sayles, John. *Matewan*. Santa Monica, CA: Artisan, 1999. Film.

Schlabach, Theron F. *Peace, Faith, Nation: Mennonites and Amish in Nineteenth-Century America*. The Mennonite Experience in America. Scottdale, PA: Herald, 1988.

Bibliography

Schloneger, Mark. "My Faith: Why I Don't Sing the 'Star Spangled Banner.'" *CNN*. June 26, 2011. http://religion.blogs.cnn.com/2011/06/26/my-faith-why-i-dont-sing-the-star-spangled-banner/.

Schmidt, Henry J. *Conversion, Doorway to Discipleship*. Hillsboro, KS: Board of Christian Literature of the General Conference of Mennonite Brethren Churches, 1980.

———. "Kansan Leads Race for Senate." *Mennonite Weekly Review*. October 18, 2010. http://www.mennoworld.org/archived/2010/10/18/kansan-leads-race-senate/.

———. "Mosaic: A Patchwork of Anabaptist News and Ideas." *Mennonite World Review* 90:15 (2012) 24.

———. "Lincoln and Cos." *Mennonite Weekly Review*, December 21, 2009.

Sider, Ronald J. *Rich Christians in an Age of Hunger*. Dallas, TX: Word, 1997.

Snyder, C. Arnold. *Anabaptist History and Theology: An Introduction*. Kitchener, ON: Pandora, 1995.

Spaulding, Dan. "Garrison Keillor Tips His Hat to the Mennonite Crowd for a Great Show." *Elkhart Truth*. October 26, 2013. http://blogs.etruth.com/truthiness/2013/10/26/garrison-keillor-raves-about-goshen-show-mennonites/.

Stames, Todd. "National Anthem Banned at Mennonite College's Sporting Events, Sparking Controversy." *Fox News*. June 7, 2011. http://www.foxnews.com/us/2011/06/07/national-anthem-banned-at-mennonite-colleges-sporting-events-sparking-outcry/.

"Statistical Data" *The Virginia Conference of the United Methodist Church*. http://www.vaumc.org/page.aspx?pid=4228.

"The Steel Wheels on Mountain Stage." *Texas Tech University Public Broadcasting System*. June 19, 2014. http://kttz.org/post/steel-wheels-mountain-stage.

Steiner, Sue Clemmer. "Self in Mennonite Garb." *Canadian Mennonite* 16:9 (2012) 1.

Stutzman, Paul. *Hiking Through*. Austin, TX: Synergy, 2010.

Sundberg, Kerry, and Charles Hadlock. "Quietly Assisting Katrina Victims in Cajun Country." *NBC News*. March 29, 2011. http://www.nbcnews.com/video/nightly-news/42329784.

Swartz, David R. *Moral Minority: The Evangelical Left in an Age of Conservativism*. Philadelphia: University of Pennsylvania Press, 2012.

Swartz, Ted. *Laughter Is Sacred Space: The Not-So-Typical Journey of a Mennonite Actor*. Harrisonburg, VA: Herald, 2012.

Taylor, Steven J. "Did the Conscientious Objectors Make a Difference?" In *Acts of Conscience: World War II, Mental Institutions, and Religious Objectors*. Critical Disability. Syracuse, NY: Syracuse University Press, 2009.

Toews, Miriam. *A Complicated Kindness: A Novel*. New York: Counterpoint, 2004.

Toews, Paul. *Mennonites in American Society, 1930–1970: Modernity and the Persistence of Religious Community*. The Mennonite Experience in America. Scottdale, PA: Herald, 1996.

Tooley, Mark. "Mennonite Takeover?" *The American Spectator*, October 10, 2010. http://spectator.org/archives/2010/10/04/Mennonite-takeover.

Townsend, Bob. "Over the Rhine, Comfortable 'Under the Radar.'" *The Washington Post*, September 8, 2013.

Umble, Diane Zimmerman, and David Weaver-Zercher, eds. *The Amish and the Media*. Young Center Books in Anabaptist & Pietist Studies. Baltimore, MD: Johns Hopkins University Press, 2008.

Visser, Piet. "Aspects of Social Criticism and Cultural Assimilation: The Mennonite Image in Literature and Self-Criticism of Literary Mennonites." In *From Martyr

Bibliography

to Muppy (Mennonite Urban Professionals): A Historical Introduction to Cultural Assimilation Processes of a Religious Minority in the Netherlands, the Mennonites, edited by Alastair Hamilton, S. Voolstra and Piet Visser, Amsterdam, Netherlands: Amsterdam University Press, 1994.

Voltaire, and Haskell M. Block. *Candide: And Other Writings.* 1st Modern Library ed. New York: Random House, 1956.

"Watchman Gospel Signs: Effective Tools for Burdened Watchmen." *New Creation Designs.* http://www.watchmangospelsigns.com/.

"Water Quality Report." *Harrisonburg Public Utilities Department.* April 18, 2014. http://www.harrisonburgva.gov/water-quality.

Weaver, Alain Epp., ed. *A Table of Sharing: Mennonite Central Committee and the Expanding Network of Mennonite Identity.* Telford: Cascadia, 2011.

Weber, Max. *The Protestant Ethic and the Spirit of Capitalism.* New York: Scribner, 1958.

———. *The Sociology of Religion.* Boston: Beacon, 1963.

Weingarten, Gene and Dan. "Barney & Clyde." *The Washington Post*, August 20, 2010.

Weir, Peter. *Witness.* Hollywood: Paramount, 1985. Film.

Wiebe, Rudy Henry. *The Blue Mountains of China.* Toronto, ON: McClelland and Stewart, 1970.

Wilde, Oscar. *The Importance of Being Earnest; A Trivial Comedy for Serious People.* London: L. Smithers, 1899.

Wilson, Sheldon, et al. *KAW.* New York: Sony, 2007.

Yasso, Bart. "Running with the Amish." *Runner's World* 14 (2012) 94–101.

Yates, Peter S. "Silence Is Golden." *Daily News-Record*, March 27, 2014.

Yoder, John Howard. *The Politics of Jesus: Vicit Agnus Noster.* 2nd ed. Grand Rapids: Eerdmans, 1994.

———. "The Problem in How H. Richard Niebuhr Reasoned." In *Authentic Transformation: A New Vision of Christ and Culture*, edited by Glen Stassen et al. Nashville: Abingdon, 1995.

Yoder, Joseph W. *Rosanna of the Amish.* Scottdale, PA: Herald, 1940.

Young, Robin. "Indiana's Goshen College Stops Playing the National Anthem." *Here and Now.* June 13, 2011. http://hereandnow.wbur.org/2011/06/13/national-anthem-goshen.

Index

Note: Page numbers followed by an f, p, or t indicate figures, photographs, or tables respectively.

A

a cappella singing
    at Goshen College, 8–9
    in *Kaw*, 56
    Mennonites known for, 79
    origins of, 100–102
    represented in *Hazel's People*, 123
    in *The Silence at Bethany*, 51
ABC-TV, 119, 120, 121
abortifacient drugs, 38–39
abortion, 38–39
Abrams, Dan, 65
Ackermann, Vince, 141
adult baptism
    Hubmaier's tract defending, 90
    Mennonite practice of, xxii, xxiii, 46
    Protestant adoption of, 71
    Wilde's reference to, 42–45
    Yasso's mention of, 28
Affordable Care Act (2009), 25, 26, 38–39
Against the Terrible Errors of the Anabaptists (Agricola), 4
Agricola, Franz, 3–4
AKIMBO (theater company), 112
Alliance Defending Freedom, 39
Along the Road (Osborne), 83–84

American Mennonites, xxvi, 76
American Playhouse series (PBS), 50–52
The American Spectator, 26–27, 73t, 75
Amish
    athletes, 28–29
    beliefs and practices of, 7, 13, 28, 71, 127
    Bergholz Clan attacks on, 114
    dress and lifestyle of, 28, 81, 159
    films depicting life of, 47–48, 73t, 126–127
    hymn book of, 93
    link to Mennonites, xxiv, 48, 59, 60, 115, 127, 159
    media demonstrating difference between Mennonites and, 13, 18, 28, 123, 127, 129, 140
    moviegoing forbidden by, 83
    Nickel Mines schoolhouse shooting, 28, 35, 113–114
    origins of, xxiii, xxiv
    "the quiet in the land" label, 94
    reference to in *Shoe* comic strip, 33
    settlements of, xxvi
    television portrayals of, 59, 65–67, 76, 114–115
    use of technology, 85

Index

Yankovic's portrayal of, 6–7
The Amish & the Media (Umble and Weaver-Zercher), xvii, xix, 66
Amish in the City (TV program), 65, 66
Amish Mafia (TV program), 65, 66, 76
Amish Paradise (Yankovic's song), 6–7, 73t, 74
The Amish (PBS documentary), 115
The Amish Project (Dickey's play), 114
The Amish Shunned (PBS documentary), 115
Amish (term), 155f–156f
Amman, Jacob, xxiv
Anabaptist Mennonite Biblical Seminary, 35–36
Anabaptist (term), 152f
"The Anabaptist Vision" (Bender), 93, 131, 151, 152
Anabaptists and Anabaptism
    Amish, xxiii
    beliefs of, 17–18, 30
    books portraying, xvi, 14–17, 72, 75, 159
    books written by, 91–94, 101–102
    Catholic criticism of, 45
    circulation of writings of, 77
    condemnation and persecution of by State Churches, xxii, 3–5, 74, 81
    Dutch Anabaptists, xxiv
    films about, 117–118
    identity formation, 91–94
    Knox's depiction of, 14
    literary portrayals of, xvi–xvii
    membership, xxvii
    Münster debacle, xxiii, 14, 74, 75
    origins of, xxi–xxiii, 17, 90
    pacifism of. *See* pacifism
    rejection of icons and devotional art, 45, 107
    renaissance of scholarly studies, 78
    size of group, xx–xxi
    split from Catholicism, 33
    suffering for one's faith, 37
    tracts of, 77–78, 90
    Voltaire's portrayal of, 41–42
    See also Amish; Mennonites
Andrews, Julie, 84
Anglicans, 5, 74
Another Way, 148t
Anslo, Cornelis Claesz, 46p, 72, 73t, 75
apocalyptic literature, 132
Arkin, Alan, 17
Armadillo Shorts (Swartz and Eshleman's play), 112
art
    of Esther Augsburger, 109–111
    Dutch paintings by Mennonites, xxiv
    Mennonite rejection of, 45, 107
    Rembrandt's painting of Mennonite couple, 45–47, 46p, 72
    of Warren Rohrer, 107–109, 108p
    Sistine Chapel, 45
asceticism, 82–85
Ask Third Way Café: 50 Quirky and Common Questions About Mennonites (Hertzler), 71
assimilation, 79, 91
Associated Press, 30–31
athletes
    Klassen, 60–61, 72, 75, 78
    Landis, xxviii, 30–31, 73t, 75, 78
Augsburger Confession (1530), 4–5
Augsburger, David, xviii
Augsburger, Esther, 109–111
Augsburger, Michael, 111
Augsburger, Myron, 109, 117–118, 161
Augustine, Saint, xxxi
aural media
    church leaders' proclamations, 3–5
    contemporary music, 104–106
    dissident communities use of, 89
    music, 6–7, 73t, 82, 100–102
    radio, 7–10, 64, 74, 82, 102–103
    U.S. political leaders' views, 5–6
The Ausbund (hymn book), 94
AWOL on the Appalachian Trail (Miller), 141

B

Baer, Franklin, 161
Baer, Retha, 161
Baldinucci, 46

Index

Baldwin, Alex, 21
baptism
    in LDS church, xxvii
    See also adult baptism; infant baptism
Baptists, xxi
Barnes & Noble Book of Quotations, 42
Barney & Clyde (Weingarten's comic strip), 32f–33, 72
BBC, 114
Beck, Glen, 78
Beckel, Graham, 123
"Bedlam, 1946. Most U.S. Mental Hospitals are a Shame and a Disgrace" (*Life*), 23–24
Believers' Church, xxiii, xxvii, 18, 118
Bemis, Andru, 104
Bender, Harold S., 78, 93, 131, 151, 152, 160
Bender, Madeline, 104
Bennetch, Dennis, 63, 95–96
Bergholz Clan of Ohio, 114
Berks County, Pennsylvania, xxvi
Bernstein, Leonard, 40
Berquist, Karin, 104–105
Berry, Malinda Elizabeth, 134, 135
Beshear, Steve, 35
Bethel College archives, 150–151
Beyond the News— Sexual Abuse (1993 film), 121–122
Beyond the News series, 121–122
Bible, 46, 94. *See also* Scripture references
Big Bear (1998 miniseries), 130
Big Love (film), 71
birth control, 38–39
Bitterroot (Burke), 21–22
Black Baptists, 142–143
Black, Jack, 53
The Blasphemy of Jan van Leyden (Simons), xxiii
Blaurock, George, xxii
Blaustein, Claire Marie, 106
Blink (Gladwell), 141
Block, Melissa, 104
Blough, Neal, 24
The Blue Mountains of China (Wiebe), 129–130

Bluffton College
    baseball team tragedy, 31
    a cappella choir, 102
Book of Common Prayer (Anglican Church), 5, 45
The Book of Mormon (play), 71
The Book of Mormon (Smith), 154f
Bookins, Gary, 33
bookrack evangelism, 98–99
books
    about hiking the Appalachian Trail, 140–141
    bookrack evangelism program, 98–99
    Mennonite attitudes toward, 82
    published by Mennonite authors, 82
    references Jews, Catholics, Mormons, 70f
books by Anabaptists
    The Ausbund (hymn book), 93, 94
    Dordrecht Confession, 93, 94
    Martyrs' Mirror (van Braght), 37, 51, 91–92, 94
books by Mennonites
    From Anabaptist Seed, 128
    Blink (Gladwell), 141
    Choosing Against War (Roth), 128
    A Complicated Kindness (Toews), 122, 137–138
    David and Goliath (Gladwell), xvi–xvii, 141–144
    Does This Church Make Me Look Fat? (Janzen), 139–140
    Fix-It and Forget-It (Good Books), xvi–xvii, 127, 128
    Flickering Pixels: How Technology Shapes Your Faith (Hipps), 86
    Happy as the Grass Was Green (Merle Good), 122–124
    Harmonia Sacra (Mennonite Hymnal by Funk), 101–102
    The Hidden Power of Electronic Culture (Hipps), 86
    Hiking Through: Finding Peace and Freedom on the Appalachian Trail (Stutzman), 140–141
    Know Your Bible (Kent), 99

Index

Laughter is Sacred Space; the Not-So-Typical Journey of a Mennonite Actor (Swartz), 113
"The Little Book" series, 128
Living More with Less (Longacre), 82, 135, 136
The Mayo Clinic Diet (Good Books), 128
Me and My Dad (Ritchie), 128
Mennonite in a Little Black Dress (Janzen), 137, 138–139
Mirror of Baptism (Funk), 93
Mirror of the Martyrs, An Introduction to Russian Mennonites, A Culture of Peace, 128
More-with-Less Cookbook (Longacre), xvi–xvii, 79, 82, 128, 133–135, 136, 151, 153, 161
A Muslim and Christian in Dialogue (Shenk), 120
Outliers (Gladwell), 141
Pilgrim Aflame (Augsburger), 117
The Politics of Jesus (John Howard Yoder), 35, 79, 131–133, 134, 135, 137, 151, 153
Real People (Denlinger), 99
Rich Christians in an Age of Hunger (Sider), 135–137
Rosanna of the Amish (Yoder), 13–14, 126–127
Sailing Acts (Stutzman), 128–129
School Management (Dock), 93, 94
A Sower Went Forth (Palmer), 97
A Table of Sharing (Berry), 134, 135
The Tipping Point (Gladwell), xvi–xvii, 141
The Upside-Down Kingdom (Kraybill), 114, 136
What the Dog Saw (Gladwell), 141
by Rudy Wiebe, 129–131
books mentioning Mennonites
Bitterroot (Burke), 21–22
Burke's writings, 72, 75
Catch-22 (Heller), xvi, 14–17, 72, 75, 159
Centennial (Michener), xvi–xvii, 18–19, 73t, 75
Communism in Central Europe in the Time of the Reformation (Kautsky), 17–18, 73t, 74–75
Enthusiasm: A Chapter in the History of Religion (Knox), 14, 73t
Heaven's Prisoner (Burke), xxvi–xxvii, 20–21
Hipster Christianity (McCracken), 104
Jesus Out to Sea (Burke), 22–23
The Novel (Michener), 19
Rosanna of the Amish (Joseph W. Yoder), 13–14, 126–127
Tillie: A Mennonite Maid (Martin), 12–14, 72, 73t, 126
Two For Texas (Burke), 20
Booth, Kristin, 57
Bovine Spongiform Encephalopathy (BSE), xxix, 57
Boyd, Greg, 26, 27
Braght, Thieleman van, 37, 51, 91–92, 94
Breaking Amish (TV program), 65, 66, 67, 76
Brenneman, James, 9, 10, 64
Bright, Bill, 39
Bristol, Matt, 66
British Broadcasting Company (BBC), 114
Brown, Anthony, 104
Brown, Bill, 161
Brown family, 71
Brown, Jim L., 118
Brown, Kody, 71
Brubaker, Eric, 105–106
Bruce, F. F., 157
Brunk, George R. II, 97
Bryson, Bill, 141
Buckwald, Art, 14
Buller, Burton, 85–86, 119–122, 147
Burke, James Lee
Bitterroot, 21–22
Heaven's Prisoners, xvi–xvii, 20–21
Jesus Out to Sea, 22–23
references to Mennonites, 74, 75
success of, 19–20
Two For Texas, 20
"The Village," 72

176

Index

Burkholder, Owen, 19
buttons, 49
Byler, J. Daryl, 133, 134–135
Byler, J. Ron, 118

C

Cable News Network (CNN), 10, 63–65, 114
Caliborne, Shane, 27
Callen, Barry, 82
Calvary Community Church, 145
The Calvary Hour (Mennonite radio program), 102–103
Campolo, Tony, 27
Can I Buy and Enemy? (Swartz's play), 113
Canada, 130
Candide (Voltaire), xvi, 40–42, 72, 159
Carell, Steven, 59–60
Caring Enough to Confront (David Augsburger), xviii
Carpenter, Cindy, 161
Carpenter, Steven P., 160–163
Carrera, Raul V., 117
cars
  Amish and Mennonite resistance to, xx, xxiv
  Mennonites' use of, 28, 48, 57, 140
  perception from, xx
Carter, Jimmy, 110
Carter, Rosalynn, 120
Cary, Peter, 157
Cascadia Publishing House/Pandora Press, xviii
Castillo, Piazza, 61
Catch-22 (film), 17
Catch-22 (Heller), xvi, 14–17, 72, 75, 159
Catherine II (tsarina of Russia), xxiv, xxv
Catholic Church
  Anabaptists split from, 33
  art of, 45
  condemnation and persecution of Anabaptists, xxii, 3–4, 74
  Münster debacle, xxiii, 75
  sale of indulgences, 32–33
  scandals and coverups, 36
Catholics
  in *Jesus' Son*, 54
  number of, xxi
  references to in literature, 69–70f, 153–154f
CBC, 130
Centennial (Michener), xvi–xvii, 18–19, 73t, 75
Centennial (TV miniseries), 19, 72
Chasez, Scott, 104n10
Chicago Sun Times, 14
Choice Books, 98–99, 103
Choosing Against War (Roth), 128
Christ and Culture (Niebuhr), xxx
"Christ in a Communication Culture" (seminary course), 88
Christendom, 89
Christensen, Kate, 138
Christian Artists Conference, 111
The Christian Century, 25–26, 29, 72, 73t, 75, 131
The *Christian Confession of Faith of the Harmless Christians, in the Netherlands known by the name Mennonists*, 93, 94
Christianity Today, 131, 135, 151
Christopher Award, 50–51
Chronicle of Higher Education, 9, 64
church discipline, xxii, 13
church leaders' proclamations, 3–5, 74, 77
Church of England, 5, 74
Civilian Public Service, 23
Cizik, Richard, 119
Claiborne, Shane, 26, 135, 158
CNN (Cable News Network), 10, 63–65, 114
Coal Wars (1920-1921), 48
Collins, Judy, 121
Common Place Magazine, 133
common-purse communities, xxi
communal practices
  aid to John Howard Yoder's victims, 36
  aid to one another, xxi, 17, 25–26, 34–35

177

Index

condemnation for, 5, 45
The Corinthian Plan (TCP), 25–26, 39, 75
   as Mennonite value, 38, 74
   role of the Ordnung, 85
   in *The Silence at Bethany*, 51
   Yasso on, 28
   See also mutual aid
communion, xxiv
Communism in Central Europe in the Time of the Reformation (Kautsky), 17–18, 73t
A Complicated Kindness (Toews), 122, 137–138
Conestoga Wood Specialties court case, 38–39
Confession of Faith in a Mennonite Perspective, xxix, 161
Conscientious Objection (US Military History Institute), 5–6
conscientious objectors. *See also* pacifism
conscientious objectors (COs)
   in Civilian Public Service, 23
   Lapp, 33–34
   Life article on, 23–24, 72, 74, 75
   Lincoln and Jackson's attitude toward, 3, 5–6, 72, 74, 159
   in *Matewan*, 48–50
Consetoga Wood v. Kathleen Sebelius, 38
Constantine, 89
Constantinian shift, 89
contemporary music, 104–106
contraceptives, 38–39
Coolio, 6
Cooper, Chris, 48
The Corinthian Plan (TCP), 25–26, 39, 75
Cornelius, Carl A., 78
The Corrections (Franzen), 11
COs (conscientious objectors). *See* conscientious objectors (COs)
Covey, Stephen, 78
Creation Chronicles (Swartz and Eshleman's play), 112
Croegaert, Jim, 104
The Cross and the Switchblade (1970 film), 84

Crudup, Billy, 53, 54
The Crusaders for Christ (Mennonite radio program), 103
culture
   media representation of Mennonites' culture, xxxi–xxxii, 72–73
   Mennonite avoidance of, xxx, 31
   portrayal of Mennonites' in films, 72
   See also isolation from society
culturome, 151–157

D

Dahlgren, Tom, 51
Daily News-Record (Harrisonburg, Virginia), 31
Daniels, Greg, 59
Darby, John Nelson, 157
David and Goliath (Gladwell), xvi–xvii, 141–144
Davis, Melodie, 35, 66–67, 148–149
De Sanctis, Ingrid, 112
Dellenbach, John, 110
Dench, Judi, 44
Denlinger, A. Martha, 99
Derstine, Clayton F., 83
Derstine, D. Gerald, 104
Derstine, Norman, 103
Detweiler, Bill, 102–103
Detweiler, Bob, 102–103
Detweiler, Lindford, 104–105
Detweiler, William G., 102
Devil's Playground (Walker's documentary film), 65
Dickel, Brian, 105–106
Dickey, Jessica, 114
discipleship, 82–85
Discovery Channel, 119
A Discovery of Strangers (Wiebe), 129
Disney productions, 116–117
Dobson, James, 39
Dock, Christopher, 93
Does This Church Make Me Look Fat? (Janzen), 139–140
Dordrecht Confession, 93
Dorian Gray (Wilde), 44

Index

Doubt (2008 film), 70
DoveTale (Swartz and De Sanctis's play), 112
drama
    The Amish Project (Dickey's play), 114
    The Book of Mormon, 71
    Candide (Voltaire), xvi, 40, 41–42, 72, 159
    Fiddler on the Roof, 70
    The Importance of Being Earnest (Wilde), 42–45
    Mennonite attitudes toward, 83
    plays and acts of Swartz and Eshelman, 112–113
    The Preacher and the Shrink (Good), 129
    references to Jews, Catholics, Mormons, 70f
Drescher, John, xviii
dress
    of Amish, 28, 81, 159
    books depicting, 129
    films depicting, 123
    of Mennonites, 13, 31, 34, 49–50, 53–54, 57, 62–63, 72, 74, 81, 123, 139, 159
Driedger, Leo, 79, 84–85, 130

E

Eastern Mennonite Seminary, 88
Ebert, Roger, 55
ecclesiological aspect of identity, xxxi–xxxii, 71–73
Edipus (Voltaire), 40
education, 12–13, 18
Ein Spiegel der Taufe (Funk), 93, 94
electronic media, 86–88. *See also* Internet
Elkhart Truth (newspaper), 8
Elliot, Jim, 157
entertainment, 82–83
Entertainment Weekly, 138
Enthusiasm: A Chapter in the History of Religion (Knox), 14, 73t
Episcopal Church, 5, 29
Erickson, Hal, 52

eschatological doctrine, 4–5, 132
Esh family tragedy (2010), 34–35, 73t
Esh, John, 35
Esh, Sadie, 35
Eshleman, Lee, 112
Evangelical Left, 26–27
evangelical (term), xv
evangelicals, xv–xvi, 136
Evangelicals for Social Action, 136
evangelism, xv–xvi, xxv, xxvii, 86–88. *See also* holistic Christian witness; missions; outreach
excommunication, 13
eyewitnesses, xix

F

Father and Son (Gosse), 157
Ferguson, Jesse Tyler, 67
Fibonacci sequence, 109
Fiddler on the Roof (play), 70
Fierce Goodbye (2004 film), 120–121
films
    about Plymouth Brethren, 157
    Big Love, 71
    The Cross and the Switchblade, 84
    Gandhi (1982 film), 162
    The Hiding Place, 84
    Mennonite attitudes toward, 83–85
    The Sound of Music, 84
films by/about Mennonites
    Beyond the News— Sexual Abuse, 121–122
    Fierce Goodbye, 120–121
    Hazel's People, 84, 122–124, 127
    Journey Toward Forgiveness, 121
    Menno's Reins, 122n10, 123
    Miracle in Lane Two, 116–117
    Pearl Diver, 124–125
    The Radicals, 117–118
    Shadow Voices— Finding Hope in Mental Illness, 120
    Waging Peace: Muslim and Christian Alternatives, 119–120, 122

Index

films mentioning Mennonites/ Anabaptists
   Catch-22, 17
   The Importance of Being Earnest, 44–45
   Jesus' Son, 52–54, 72, 74, 75
   Kaw, 56–58, 71, 72, 73t, 74, 75
   Matewan, 48–50, 72, 75
   number of, 157
   references Jews, Catholics, Mormons, 70f
   The Silence at Bethany, 50–52, 73t, 123
   Stellet Licht/Silent Light, 54–56, 72t, 74, 75
   Witness, 47–48, 52, 56, 73t, 155
First and Vital Candle (Wiebe), 129, 130
First Mennonite Church, Denver, 29
Firth, Colin, 44
Fish Eyes (Swartz and Eshleman's play), 112
Fix-It and Forget-It (Good Books), xvi–xvii, 127, 128
Flannery, Sean Patrick, 56
Flickering Pixels: How Technology Shapes Your Faith (Hipps), 86
Floradale Mennonite Church, 119
Ford, Harrison, xvi, 47
forgiveness
   books on, 132, 143–144
   for Esh family tragedy, 35
   Mennonite films on, 120–121, 124–125
   for Nickel Mines schoolhouse shooting, 28, 35, 113
Fox News, 35, 65
Fox News Radio, 10
Franzen, Jonathan, 11
French revolution (1789-1799), xxv
Friendship Evangelism (McPhee), xviii
From Anabaptist Seed (Good Books), 128
Frykholm, Amy, 25
Fundamentalist Christians, xv
Funk, Henry, 93
Funk, Joseph S., 101
Futurama (cartoon series), 59

G

Gandhi (1982 film), 162
Gangsta's Paradise (Coolio's song), 6
Gelassenheit, 85
General Conference Mennonite Church (GC), xxviii, 29
Germantown, Pennsylvania, xxvi
Germany, xxi, xxiii
Gish, Peggy, 120
Gladwell, Malcolm
   Blink, 141
   David and Goliath, xvi–xvii, 141–144
   Mennonite affiliation, 159
   Outliers, 141
   The Tipping Point, xvi–xvii, 141
   What the Dog Saw, 141
Gnadenau Krimmer Mennonite Brethren Church, 58
Gochenour, Julie, 88
Goldmine Pickers, 104
Good Books, xviii, 127–129
Good, Merle, 84, 122–124, 127, 129
Good, Phyllis Pellman, 127
Good, Theda, 29
Google Books Ngram Viewer, 153
Goshen College
   national anthem controversy, 9–10, 63–65
   singing at, 8–9
Gospel Herald (Mennonite periodical), xviii, 83
Gospel Sign Ministry, 95–97
Gosse, Edmond, 157
Gottschalk, Jacob, 92
Graber, Barbara, 112, 122
Graham, Billy, xv, 84, 86, 110
Great Directors (Ismailos's film), 50
Grebel, Conrad, xxi–xxii
greed, 32–33
Green, David, 38–39
Groening, Abraham, 58
Groening, Abram Abraham, 58
Groening, Homer, 58
Groening, Matt, 58–59
Groff, Anna, 145–146, 148

Index

Guns into Plowshares (Augsburger's sculpture), 110, 111p
Gutenberg, Johannes, 90

H

Haas, Lukas, 47
Hackman, Joe, 65
Hahn family, 38–39
hair length, xxix
Hallmark Channel, 120, 121
Hannah's Child (Hauerwas), 36
Happy as the Grass Was Green (Merle Good), 122–124, 127
Harder, Keith, 29
Harmonia Sacra (Mennonite Hymnal by Funk), 101–102
Harrison, William, 160
Hatch, Orin, 78
Hatcher, Teri, 21
Hatfield, Mark O., 110
Hauerwas, Stanley, 26, 36–37, 131, 133
Hazel's People (1973 film), 84, 122–124, 127
head covering, xxix, 13, 28, 34, 139
Health Access Initiative (2003), 25–26
health insurance, 25–26, 38–39, 75
Heart to Heart (Mennonite radio program), 103
Heaven's Prisoner (Burke), xvi–xvii, 20–21
Heaven's Prisoner (film), 21
Hedder, Jon, 78
Heggen, Carolyn Holderread, 121–122
Heller, Joseph, xvi, 14–17, 72, 75, 159
Hell's Playground (Derstine), 83
Henry, Buck, 17
Herald Press
    best sellers, 92, 126, 133
    Confession of Faith in a Mennonite Perspective, 161
    focus of, xviii
    on forbidden activities, 83
    Living More with Less, 135
    Mennonite Community Cookbook, 37
    See also *More-with-Less Cookbook* (Longacre)
Hertzler, Jodi Nisley, 71
Hertzler, Roger, 97–98
Heusinkveld, David, 135
Hibbs, Ben, 101–102
The Hidden Power of Electronic Culture (Hipps), 86
The Hiding Place (1975 film), 84
High, Sabrina, 66
Hiking Through: Finding Peace and Freedom on the Appalachian Trail (Stutzman), 140–141
Hingle, Pat, 123
Hipps, Shane, 86–88, 102
Hipster Christianity (McCracken), 27, 104
hipster (term), 27, 75
Hobby Lobby, 38–39
Hofer, Joseph J., 49–50
Hofer, Michael, 49–50
holistic Christian witness, xv. See also missions; outreach
Holland, xxiv
Holsopple, Jerry, 112, 119–122
holy kiss, 51
Holy Roman Empire, 89
Hone, Frank, 13
Hopper, Dennis, 53
Horsch, John, 78
Horst, Irvin B., 108
Hostetler, D. Michael, 118
Hostetler, Rosanna M. Y., 13–14, 126
Hubmaier, Balthasar, xxii, 77, 90
Huguenots, 143
humility
    of Klassen, 61, 74
    of Mennonite workers in Louisiana, 62–63
    as precept of Mennonite life, xxvi
    Yasso on, 28
Humor and Faith: A Holy Accident (Swartz workshop), 112
Hunter, Holly, 53
Hybels, Bill, 119, 158
Hybels, Lynne, 119
Hymnal: A Worship Book, 104

Index

I

icons, 45, 107
immigration policies, 130
The Importance of Being Earnest (2002 film), 44–45
The Importance of Being Earnest (Wilde), 42–45
infant baptism, xxiii, 4, 42, 43–44
insurance, 46. *See also* The Corinthian Plan (TCP); Obamacare (2009)
inter-marriage, xxiv, xxv–xxvi
interest on loans, 46
Interfaith Broadcasting Commission, 121
Internet
    "Capturing the Camera-Shy Mennonites" video, 63
    Goshen College national anthem controversy on, 9, 10
    Keillor's comments posted on, 8
    Klassen's web site, 61
    Mennofolk's web site, 104
    Mennonite attitudes toward, 85–87
    Mennonite Church USA's presence, 145–147
    Plymouth Brethren church's website, 146–147
    Schloneger's blog and interview on, 10, 64–65
    Third Way Café, 35, 66, 145, 147–149
Ismailos, Angel, 50
isolation from society
    in America, xxvi
    of Amish and Old Order Mennonites, 113
    emergence from, 85–86
    films depicting, 123
    in *Kaw*, 57–58
    necessity and practice of, xxii, 79, 81–85, 98
    prosperity associated with, 17–18
    publics' view of, 71
    in Russia, xxv–xxvi

J

Jackson, Stonewall, 3, 6, 74, 159
Jamison, Kay Redfield, 121
Janzen, Rhoda
    Does This Church Make Me Look Fat? 139–140
    Mennonite in a Little Black Dress, 138–139
Jehovah's Witnesses, 53, 54
Jennings, Ken, 78
Jesus and the Victory of God (Wright), 132
Jesus Out to Sea (Burke), 22–23
Jesus, Rock Ages (Derstine's song), 104
Jesus' Son (1999 film), 52–54, 72t, 74, 75
Jews
    inherited Jewishness, xxvii
    number of, xxi
    references to in literature, 69–70f, 153f–154
John the Baptist, xxxii
Johnson, Denis, 52
Jones, James Earl, 50
Journey Toward Forgiveness (2001 film), 121
Julius II (pope), 45

K

Kanagy, Conrad, 85
Kathleen Sebelius v. Hobby Lobby, 38
Katrina victims, aid to, 61–63
Kauffman, Allan, 8
Kauffman, J. Howard, 79, 84–85
Kauffman, Joel, 116–118
Kauffman, Richard A., 29
Kautsky, Karl, 17–18, 73t, 74–75
Kaw (2007 film), 56–58, 71, 72, 73t, 75
Keener, Joyce, 50
Keillor, Garrison, 7–9, 156
Keller, Father James, 51
Keller, Ludwig, 78
Kenneson, Philip D., xxxi–xxxii, 71
Kent, Paul, 99
Key, Francis Scott, 9–10, 64
King, Sidney, 124–125

Index

Kingsley, Ben, 162
Klassen, Cindy, 60–61, 72, 75, 78
Know Your Bible (Kent), 99
Knox, Ronald, 14, 73t
Koonz, Gayle Gerber, 134
Kraybill, Donald, xi–xii, 66, 85, 113–115, 136
Kreider, James L., 96
Kreider, Robert, 92–93
Kroetsch, Robert, 130
Kropf, Heather, 104

L

La Vie (French Catholic magazine), 24, 72
Lancaster County, Pennsylvania, xxvi
Lancaster Intelligencer (newspaper), 66
Lancaster, Pennsylvania, xxvi
Landis, Arlene, xxviii, 31, 94, 95p
Landis, Charity, 31, 95p
Landis, Floyd, xxviii, 30–31, 73t, 75, 78
Landis, Paul, xxviii, 31, 94, 95p
language barrier, xxv–xxvi, xxvi
Lapp, Glen D., 33–34, 73t
Lapp, Jay, 105–106
Latter-Day Saints (LDS)
    media footprint, 153–154f, 155f
    media stars, 78
    membership, xxvii
    Mormon Tabernacle Choir, 78, 100
    number of, xxi, 155
    references to in media, 69, 70–71, 153, 153f–155f
Laughter is Sacred Space; the Not-So-Typical Journey of a Mennonite Actor (Swartz), 113
LDS. *See* Latter-Day Saints (LDS)
leadership development, xv
Learning Channel, 119
Leary, Denis, 53
Lederach, Paul, 128
Leggiere, Phil, xxix
Lenard, Mark, 117–118
lesbian pastor, 29
Lewis, Beverly, 127

Leyden, Jan van, xxiii, 14, 74
Life, 23–24, 72, 74, 75
Life-Line Books, 98
Lincoln, Abraham, 3, 5–6, 72, 74, 159
literature, xvi–xvii. *See also* books; books by Mennonites; books mentioning Mennonites
Littell, Franklin, 74, 150
The Little Book of Conflict Transformation (Lederach), 128
The Little Book of Restorative Justice (Zehr), 128
"The Little Book" series, 128
Live at Jacob's Ladder (Swartz and Medema's play), 112
lived faith
    aid to Yoder's victims, 36–37
    of conscientious objectors, 33–34, 49–50
    relationship to media, 82–85
    of Willems, 41, 91, 92p, 124, 125, 143
Living More with Less (Longacre), 82, 135, 136
Lombardi, Leigh, 117
Longacre, Doris Janzen
    Living More with Less, 82, 135, 136
    More-with-Less Cookbook, xvi–xvii, 79, 82, 128, 133–135, 136, 151, 153, 161
Longenecker, Stephen L., 30
Love Essence (Augsburger's sculpture), 110p
love for enemies. *See* forgiveness; pacifism
Luther, Martin, 4, 90, 159
Lutheran World Federation, 26
Lutherans, 3, 4–5, 74
Luyken, Jan, 91, 107

M

MacLean, Alison, 53
MacLean (Canadian news magazine), 61
MacNelly, Susie, 33
Mad Cow Disease, xxix, 57

Index

magazines
    The American Spectator, 26–27, 73t, 75
    The Christian Century's, 25–26, 29, 72, 73t, 75, 131
    Christianity Today, 131, 135, 151
    Common Place Magazine, 133
    Entertainment Weekly, 138
    La Vie's, 24, 72
    Life, 23–24, 72, 74, 75
    MacLean, 61
    The Mennonite, 145–146, 148
    Mennonite attitudes toward, 82
    The Mennonite Quarterly Review, 78
    New Republic's review of *Catch 22*, 14
    People, 138
    Pollstar, 106
    Runner's World, 28–29, 72
    Time, 141
Magisterial Reformation, xxii
Maisel, Albert Q., 23–24
Manifesto of 1763, xxv
Mantz, Felix, xxi–xxii
Marpeck, Pilgrim, 77
Marrapodi, Eric, 65
Marrowbone Christian Brotherhood, 34–35
Marshall, Christopher, 79
Martin, Burt, 123
Martin, Helen R., 11–14
Martin, J. D., 104
Marty, Martin, 119
martyrdom
    of early Anabaptist leaders, xxi, xxii–xxiii, 74, 90
    of Jim Elliot, 157
    in Holy Roman Empire, 89
    in *Martyrs' Mirror*, 37, 51, 91–92, 94
    Mennonite willingness, 64
    of Sattler, 117–118
    of Willems, 41, 91, 92p, 124, 125, 143
Martyrs' Mirror (van Braght), 37, 51, 91–92, 94
Matewan (1987 film), 48–50, 72, 75
Matewan, battle of, 48
Matthys, Jan, 14

"May a Christian Serve in the Military?" (Harrison), 160
The Mayo Clinic Diet (Good Books), 128
MBI (Mennonite Broadcasts, Inc.), 98, 103
McCracken, Brett, 27, 104
McGillis, Kelly, xvi, 47
McGonegal, Rosanna, 126
McLaren, Brian, 113, 158
McLuhan, Marshall, xx
McPhee, Arthur, xviii
MDS (Mennonite Disaster Service), 62
Me and My Dad (Ritchie), 128
MEA (Mennonite Education Agency), 146t
Medema, Ken, 112
media
    defined, xix
    Internet, 10, 63, 64–65, 66, 86, 145–147
    lived faith related to, 82–85
    Mennonite attitudes toward, 85–88
    Mennonite distinctions attracting, xxxi, 71, 74
    Mennonite engagement with, xv–xvi, 85–88, 158
    nature of, xv
    portrayal of different religious groups, 70–71
    representation of events, xix–xx
    See also art; aural media; books; drama; films; Internet; magazines; music; newspapers; singing; television
Media Matters, 148t
Mediaite (Abrams Media's blog), 65
mediation, xix
medical care, 48
men of Issachar, vi, 162
The Menace of the Movies (Herald Press), 83
Mennobytes, 149
Mennofolk, 104
Mennolink, 147
MennoMedia, 84, 98, 103, 147, 162–163
Mennonite Broadcasts, Inc. (MBI), 98, 103

Index

Mennonite Central Committee (MCC), 23, 24, 34, 136
Mennonite Church (MC), xxviii, 29
Mennonite Church USA
    Christian Century's praise of Corinthian Plan, 25–26
    film production by, 84
    formation of, xxviii–xxix, 29
    licensing and ordination, 29
    outreach of, 147–149
    priorities of, xv
    "the quiet in the land" label, 94
    response to John Howard Yoder's victims, 36
    size of group, xx–xxi
    web presence, 145–147
    See also Third Way Café (TWC); Third Way Media
Mennonite Community Cookbook (Herald Press), 37
Mennonite Confession of Faith, 161
Mennonite Disaster Service (MDS), 62
Mennonite Economic Development Association (MEDA), 136
Mennonite Education Agency (MEA), 146t
The Mennonite Hour (radio program), 103
Mennonite in a Little Black Dress (Janzen), 137, 138–139
Mennonite Media, 98, 103, 119–122
Mennonite Mental Health Service, 24
Mennonite Mission Network (MMN), 84, 85, 146t, 147
Mennonite Publishing House, 78
Mennonite Publishing Network (MPN), 84, 103, 146t, 147
The Mennonite Quarterly Review (MQR), 78
The Mennonite (TM), xviii, 145–146, 148
Mennonite tracts, 89–90
Mennonite Weekly Review (MWR), xviii, 63, 146t
Mennonite World Review. *See Mennonite Weekly Review* (MWR)
Mennonites
    Amish associated with, 60
    art and, 45–47
    art of, 107–111
    assimilation of, 79
    athletes, xxviii, 28–31, 60–61, 72, 73t, 75, 78
    aural media references to, 3–10
    beliefs and practices of, xxxi, 4–5, 9, 18, 27, 28, 30, 32–33, 39, 46, 79, 82–85, 127, 139–140. *See also* adult baptism; communal practices; pacifism
    books portraying, 11–23
    books written by, 79, 82, 91–94, 101–102
    as contemporary musicians, 104–106
    drama portraying, 40–45
    dress of, 13, 31, 34, 49–50, 53–54, 57, 62–63, 72, 74, 81, 123, 139, 159
    in Dutch Netherlands, xxiv
    in early years in America, xxvi
    engagement with pop culture, xv–xvi
    faith of, 34–35, 56, 64
    fight against injustices, 16, 23–24
    films depicting life of, 12–14
    films mentioning, 47–58
    forgiveness of, 28, 35
    as hip, 6–7, 27, 75, 151
    Internet presence, 35, 66, 145–149
    Janzen's comparison to Pentecostals, 138
    link to Amish, xxiv, 6–7, 8, 48, 59, 115, 127, 159
    literary references to, xvi–xvii
    magazine articles on, 23–29
    media demonstrating difference between Amish and, 13, 18, 28, 123, 127, 129, 140
    media footprint, xvii, 150–157
    migration to America, xxvi, 76
    migration to Russia, xxiv–xxvi
    in the Netherlands, xxiv, 45, 91
    newspaper references to, 30–39
    number of, 146, 155
    origins of, xxi–xxiii
    pacifism of. *See* pacifism
    as a peculiar people, 81–82
    performers, 112–113

Index

priorities of, 27
property signs, 94–98, 95p, 97p
prosperity of, 17–18
"the quiet in the land" label, xxiv–xxvi, 94
references to in media, 69, 153f–156f
religious identity of, xxvii–xxix
Rembrandt as, 45–47
in Russia, 82
as a sect, xxix–xxxii, 71–74
significance of media presence, 158–163
singing of, 8–9, 51, 53–54, 56, 79, 100–102, 123
size of group, xx–xxi
suffering for one's faith, 37
Swiss Brethren, xxi–xxiii
television commentator, 113–115
television program of, 145
television representations of, 58–68
tension between orthodoxy and orthopraxy, 82–85
theology of media, 81–88
tracts of, 89–90
use of media, 77–79
use of radio broadcasts, 102–103
view of abortion, 38–39
visual media on, 40–68
writings of early leaders, 74, 77
See also Anabaptists and Anabaptism; conscientious objectors (COs); isolation from society; pacifism
Menno's Reins (1976 film), 122n10, 123
mental hospitals, 23–24, 75
The Merchant of Venice (Shakespeare), 70
Methodists, xx–xxi, 154f
Meyer, Jeff, 51–52
Michelangelo, 45
Michener, James A.
 background of, 18
 Centennial, xvi–xvii, 18–19, 73t, 75
 The Novel, 19
 The Source, 70
 South Pacific, 18
military service, xxii, xxiii, xxiv–xxv, xxvi, 9, 15, 64. *See also* conscientious objectors (COs)

Miller, David, 141
minister selection, 51
Miracle in Lane Two (Kauffman and Donald C. Yoder's film), 116–117
Mirror of Baptism (Funk), 93, 94
Mirror of the Martyrs, An Introduction to Russian Mennonites, A Culture of Peace (Good Books), 128
The Mirror of the Martyrs (display of copper plates), 92–93
The Mission (1986 film), 70
missional (term), 27
missions
 bookrack evangelism program, 98–99
 a cappella singing, 102
 forbidden in Russia, xxv
 Internet presence, 145–149, 146t
 in LDS church, xxvii
 of Mennonite Church USA, xv–xvi
 Mennonite use of media for, 85–88
 property signs, 94–98, 95p, 97p
 radio broadcasts, 102–103
 role of media in, 86–88, 162
 See also holistic Christian witness
MMN (Mennonite Mission Network), 146t, 147
Modern Family (TV program), 67–68, 73t, 76
Modern Library, 15
modesty, 28
money, 32–33
Moral Minority (Swartz), 135
Moran, Jerry, xxviii
Moravian Hutterites, xxi
More-with-Less Cookbook (Longacre)
 contents of, 82, 128, 134–135
 influence of, 79, 151, 153, 161
 popularity of, xvi–xvii, 133–134
 references to, 136
Mormons. *See* Latter-Day Saints (LDS)
morning-after pills, 38–39
Morton, D. Holmes, 114
Morton, Samantha, 53
Moses, Mark, 51
Mountain Meadow Massacre, 70
Mountain States Mennonite Conference, 29

186

Index

movies. *See* films
MPN (Mennonite Publishing Network), 84, 103, 146t, 147
Münster debacle (1535), xxiii, 14, 74, 75
Murray, Stuart, 27, 158
music
    Amish Paradise (Yankovic's song), 6–7, 73t, 74
    contemporary music, 104–106
    Mennonite attitudes toward recordings, 82
    power of, 100
    See also a cappella singing; singing
musical instrument ban, 101
A Muslim and Christian in Dialogue (Shenk), 120
mutual aid
    aid to Katrina victims, 61–63
    aid to needy, xxi, 41, 49, 132
    aid to one another, xxi, 17, 25–26, 39
    books on, 135–137
    medical aid in Afghanistan, 33–34
    Mennonite practice of, 134
    mental hospital work, 23–24, 75
    See also theater
MWR (*Mennonite Weekly Review*). *See* Mennonite Weekly Review (MWR)
My Lovely Enemy (Wiebe), 130
Myth of a Christian Nation (Boyd), 27

N

Nafziger, Tim, 58, 59
Nation, Mark Thiessen, 132, 133
national anthem controversy, 9–10, 63–65, 74
National Council of Churches, 120, 121
National Mental Health Act (1946), 24
National Public Radio
    on Goshen College national anthem controversy, 9–10, 64, 74
    interview with Kraybill, 114
    interview with Over the Rhine, 104
    Steel Wheels appearance on, 106

"The Nation's Pulse" (Tooley), 26–27
NBC, 121
NBC Nightly News with Brian Williams, 61–63, 72, 74, 76
neo-Anabaptist movement, 26–27
Netherlands, xxiv, 45, 91
Neufeld, Chuck, 104
New Mennonites, 13
New Republic, 14
The New York Times
    article on John Howard Yoder, 35–37
    on Esh family tragedy, 34–35
    response to Schloneger's article, 65
The New York Times Book Review, 138
newspapers
    articles on challenges to Obamacare, 38–39
    articles on Landis, xxviii, 30–31, 73t
    Barney & Clyde comic strip, 32f–33, 72
    Chicago Sun Times, 14
    Chronicle of Higher Education, 9, 64
    Daily News-Record (Virginia), 31
    interview with Kraybill, 114
    Lancaster Intelligencer, 66
    Mennonite attitudes toward, 82
    Mennonite Weekly (*World Review*), 63
    The New York Times, 34–35, 65, 72
    The Philadelphia Inquirer, 33–34, 73t, 108
    reports on Bluffton College baseball team tragedy, 31
    reports referring to Mennonite businesses, xxix
    The Rockingham Register, 30, 72, 75
    The Washington Post, xxviii, 14, 26, 32–33, 37–38, 69–70, 72, 75, 105
Ngram, 69–70, 151, 152f–156f
Nichols, Mike, 17
Nickel Mines schoolhouse shooting, 28, 35, 113–114
Niebuhr, H. Richard, xxx, xxxi
Nolt, Steven, 114
nonconformity, 81–85
nonresistance, xxiii, 91–92. *See also* pacifism
North, Wayne, 19

Index

"Nothing You Can't Lose" (Steel Wheels' song), 105
The Novel (Michener), 19

O

oaths of allegiance, xxii, xxiii, 9, 64
Obamacare (2009), 25, 26, 38–39
O'brien, Kathleen, 26, 39
Oecolampadius, 90
Of This Earth: a Mennonite Boyhood in the Boreal Forrest (Wiebe), 129
The Office (TV program), 59–60, 73t
Ohio (Over the Rhine album), 104
Old Order Amish, xxiv, 28
Old Order Mennonites
　beliefs of, xxiv
　isolation from society, 71
　media shyness, xx
　moviegoing forbidden by, 83
Oldham, Will, 49
Oliansky, Joel, 50
On the Christian Baptism of Believers (Hubmaier), 90
O'Neill, Ed, 67
opera, 83
Oppenheimer, Mark, 36
Ordnung, 85
orthodoxy, 82
orthopraxy, 82
Osborne, Millard, 83–84
Oscar and Lucinda (1997 film), 157
Oscar and Lucinda (Cary), 157
Osmond, Donny, 78
Osmond, Marie, 78
Outliers (Gladwell), 141
outreach
　bookrack evangelism program, 98–99
　a cappella singing, 102
　Internet presence, 145–149
　in LDS church, xxvii
　of Mennonite Church USA, xv–xvi
　property signs, 94–98, 95p, 97p
　radio broadcasts, 102–103
　role of media in, 86–88, 162

See also holistic Christian witness; missions
Over the Rhine, 104–105
Oyer, John, 92–93

P

pacifism
　of Amish in films, 47
　of Anabaptists, xxii, xxiii, xxiv–xxv, xxvi, 18, 39, 74, 91
　Augsburger on, 161
　books on, 131
　Burke's portrayal of, 20–23, 74
　during Civil War, 30
　confiscation of Mennonite tracts on, 78
　discussed on NPR, 64
　films on, 162
　of Lapp, 33–34
　Lincoln and Jackson's attitude toward, 5–6
　in *Matewan*, 48–50, 74
　Mennonite books on, 129, 143
　Mennonite films depicting, 123, 124–125
　of Mennonites, 46
　New York Times association with Mennonites, 36
　religious identity and, xxvii
　in *The Silence at Bethany*, 51
　Swartz's play about, 113
　in *Tilly, A Mennonite Maid*, 13
　Tooley's concerns about, 26–27
　Voltaire's reference to, 42
　Weingarten's mention of, 32
　Willems's example of, 41, 91, 92p, 124, 125, 143
　during World War I, 58, 78
　during World War II, 23–24
　John Howard Yoder's book on, 35
　See also conscientious objectors (COs); nonresistance; peacemaking
Page, Geraldine, 123
Palmer, Martha Shenk, 97

Index

Palmer, Ralph, 97
Pankratz, Maria, 55
Parker, Oliver, 44
Parker, Trey, 71
Parsons, Talcott, xxix
pastors
    Corinthian Plan for, 25–26, 39, 75
    ordination of homosexual woman, 29
Paul (apostle), xv, xxxii, 162
PBS, 50–52, 115, 119
peace churches, 52
Peace of Augsburg (1555), 3
Peace of Westphalia (1648), 3
Peace Shall Destroy Many (Wiebe), 129
Peace Story, 148t
peacemaking, 119–120, 122, 128. *See also* pacifism
Pearl Diver (2004 film), 124–125
Peasants' Revolt (1524), xxi, xxii, 17
Pennsylvania Dutch, 12, 37–38
Pennsylvania Dutch language, xxvi, 12, 59–60
Pentecostals, 139
People magazine, 138
Perkins, Anthony, 17
Perkins, John, 121
persecution
    of Anabaptists by Catholics and Protestants, xxi, xxii–xxiii, 26, 44, 81
    of believers by Holy Roman Empire, 89
    of conscientious objectors, 49
    of Mennonites in America, 58
    response to, 5
The Philadelphia Inquirer, 33–34, 73t, 108
Phillips, Kyra, 64–65
photographs, 57, 83, 113
Pietist groups, xxvi
Pilgrim Aflame (Augsburger), 117
Plato, 100
pledge of allegiance, 9, 64, 65
Plymouth Brethren, 146–147, 156f–157
political leaders
    confiscation and burning of Anabaptist tracts, 77–78
    defense of Anabaptists, 3, 5–6, 72, 74

The Politics of Jesus (John Howard Yoder)
    Amazon's rank for, 137
    influence of, 35, 79, 134, 135, 151
    public awareness peak due to, 153
    theology in, 131–133
Pollstar (magazine), 106
popular culture, xv. *See also* isolation from society
poverty, 134–137
A Prairie Home Companion (Keillor's radio program), 7–8, 9
prayer covering, xxix, 13, 31, 34, 139
The Preacher and the Shrink (Merle Good's play), 129
priesthood of all believers, xxii, xxiii
print media
    Anabaptist tracts, 89–90
    books, 11–23, 74–75, 91–94, 126–144, 151
    magazines, 23–29, 75, 78
    nature of, 87
    newspapers, 30–39, 75
    property signs, 94–98, 95p, 97p
    tracts, 77–78, 89–90
    use of term "Anabaptist," 152f
    use of term "Mennonite," 153f–156f
printers, 77
printing press, 90
The Problem in How H. Richard Niebuhr Reasoned (John Howard Yoder), xxxi
property signs, 94–98, 95p, 97p
proselytizing. *See* evangelism; missions; outreach
Protestant Republic of the Seven United Netherland, xxiv
Protestants, xxii
Prussia, xxiv–xxvi, 94
Prussian Mennonites, xxiv–xxvi
Public Broadcasting Service (PBS), 50–52, 115, 119
public service. *See* mutual aid

Q

"the quiet in the land" label, xxiv–xxvi, 94

Index

R

Radical Reformation, xxii, xxiii, 22, 45
The Radicals (1990 docudrama), 117–118
radio
    adaptation of *First and Vital Candle* for, 130
    Fox News Radio, 10
    Mennonite attitudes toward, 82
    Mennonite programs, 102–103
    National Public Radio, 7–9, 9–10, 64, 74, 104, 106, 114
    A Prairie Home Companion, 7–9
Rain in the Valley (Steel Wheels' song), 106
Ralston, John, 57
Real People (Denlinger), 99
rebaptism, xxii, xxiii, 42–45
Red Wing (Steel Wheels' album), 106
Reed, Rex, 124
Reformed Churches, 3, 107
Reist, Hans, xxiv
Religion News Service (RNS), 26, 29, 39
Religious Freedom Restoration Act (1993), 38
religious identity, xxvii–xxix
religious practices
    media representation of Mennonites' practices, xxxi–xxxii, 72–73
    of Mennonites, 79
Rembrandt, 45, 46p, 72, 73t, 75
Republic (Plato), 100
Reuel, Jonathan, 104
Reunion Vocal Band, 104
Reyes, Dwight, 62
Reygadas, Carlos, 54–56
Rich Christians in an Age of Hunger (Sider), 135–137
Ries, Rachel, 104
Ritchie, Alison, 128
Ritzel, Rebecca, 114
The Rockingham Register, 30, 72, 75
Rogge, Jacques, 60
Rohrer, Warren, 107–109
Romney, Mitt, 78
Rosanna of the Amish (Joseph W. Yoder), 13–14, 126–127
Rosenberg, Susan, 109
Roth, John D., 128
Rudy Wiebe: Collected Stories 1955-2010 (Wiebe), 130
Runner's World, 28–29, 72
Russia
    four-part singing in, 101
    Mennonite migration from, 129–130
    Mennonite migration to, xxiv–xxvi
    Mennonites' prosperity in, 18, 82
Ruth, John L., 109

S

sacerdotal idea, 46
Sailing Acts (Stutzman), 128–129
Samuel (prophet), xxxii
Sanders, Kerry, 62
Sattler, Margaretha, 118
Sattler, Michael, xxii, 77, 117–118
Sayles, John, 48, 50
Schindler's List (1993 film), 70, 117
Schleitheim Articles (Sattler), xxii, xxiii, 117
Schloneger, Mark, 10, 64–65
School Management (Dock), 93, 94
Schouten, Aeltje Gerrhsdr, 46p, 72, 73t, 75
Schrag, Paul, xxviii, 63
Schulornung (Dock), 93
Scotti Brothers, 6
Scripture references
    1 Chronicles 12:32, vi
    Psalm 130: 7, 96
    Isaiah 55: 7, 96
    Matthew 5: 39, 91
    Matthew 6: 24, 33
    Acts 2:44, xxi
    Acts 17: 16-34, xv
    Ephesians 4: 32, 96
    I Thessalonians 5: 16-18, 61
    James 4: 7, 94
    1 Peter 2: 9, 81
Sebelius, Kathleen, 38
section hiker, 141n53
sects

Index

aspects of identity, xxxi–xxxii, 71–74
defined, xxix–xxx, xxxi
self-denial, 82–85
Sensenig, Rev. David, 31
September 11 terrorist attacks, 121
September Dawn (2007 film), 70
Sermon on the Mount, 33, 46–47, 91
Seven Things Children Need (Drescher), xviii
Shadow Voices— Finding Hope in Mental Illness (2005 film), 120
Shakespeare, William, 42, 70
shaped notes musical system, 101
Shapiro, 104
Sharp, John E., 117, 118
Sheen, Martin, 17
Shenandoah Religion (Longenecker), 30
Shenk, David, 120
Shenk, Gerald, 112–113
Shoe (Bookins and Mac Nelly's comic strip), 33
shoofly pie, 37–38
shunning, xxiv, 13
Sider, Ron, 27, 135–137
The Silence at Bethany (1988 film), 50–52, 73t, 123
Silent Light (2007 film), 54–56, 72t, 74, 75
Simons, Menno
  break with Catholic Church, xxiii
  on mutual aid, 134
  pacifism adopted by, 74
  wood block portrait of, 108p
  works of, xxiii–xxiv, 77
Simons, Peter, xxiii
Simply in Season (World Community cookbook), 82
The Simpsons (TV program), 58–59, 73t, 75
Sine, Tom, xviii
singing
  in *Kaw*, 56
  Keillor at Goshen College and, 8–9
  Mennonite a cappella singing, 51, 79, 100–102
  of Mennonite woman in *Jesus' Son*, 53–54
represented in *Hazel's People*, 123
in *The Silence at Bethany*, 51
A Sip of Scripture, 148t
Sister Wives (TV program), 71
Sisters and Brothers Productions, 118
Sistine Chapel, 45
slavery, 30, 46
Smith, Duncan, 26
Smith, Joseph, 154
Smucker, Jim, 28
social justice, 74
sociological aspect of identity, xxxi–xxxii, 71–73
The Sociology of Religion (Weber), xxix
Son of Rambow (2008 film), 157
Sondheim, Stephen, 40
The Sound of Music (1965 film), 84
The Source (Michener), 70
South Pacific (Michener), 18
Sower, Christopher, 93
A Sower Went Forth (Palmer), 97
Spaulding, Dan, 8
spiritual conversion, 51
Stames, Todd, 10
Star Spangled Banner (Key's song), 9–10, 64
State Churches, xxii, xxiii, 3–5, 18, 89
Steel Wheels, 104, 105–106
The Steel Wheels: Lay Down, Lay Low (album), 106
Steinmann, Kai, 35
Stellet Licht (2007 film), 54–56, 72t, 74, 75
Stoltzfus, Levi King, 66
Stone, Matt, 71
Stonestreet, Eric, 67
Strathairn, David, 50
Stutzman, Linford, 128
Stutzman, Paul, 140–141
suicide, 120–121
Sundberg, Scott, 62
Supreme Court case, 38–39
Swartz, David, 135
Swartz, Ted, 112–113
Swiss Anabaptist movement, xxi–xxiii
Swiss Brethren, xxi–xxiii

Index

T

A Table of Sharing (Berry), 134, 135
Taylor, Rod, 56
TCP (The Corinthian Plan), 25–26
technology, 85
Ted & Lee Theater Works, 112
television
    The Amish (PBS documentary), 115
    Amish reality shows, 65–67, 76
    The Amish Shunned (PBS documentary), 115
    BBC, 114
    Big Bear (1998 miniseries), 130
    CBS broadcasts on Klassen, 61
    Centennial miniseries, 19, 72
    CNN, 10, 63–65, 114
    coverage of Klassen, 60–61
    Fierce Goodbye on, 120–121
    Fox News, 35, 65
    Journey Toward Forgiveness on, 121
    Mennonite attitudes toward, 82–83, 85–87
    Mennonite Family Life spots, 103
    Mennonite films aired on, 119
    Mennonite presence on, 145
    Mennonites' reluctance to use, 79
    Modern Family, 67–68, 73t, 75, 76
    NBC Nightly News with Brian Williams, 61–63, 72, 74, 76
    The Office, 59–60, 73t
    portrayal of Klassen, 60–61, 72, 75
    Shadow Voices— Finding Hope in Mental Illness on, 120
    The Simpsons, 58–59, 73t, 75
    Sister Wives, 71
    Waging Peace: Muslim and Christian Alternatives on, 119–120
The Temptation of Big Bear (Wiebe), 129–30
Ten Boom, Corrie, 84
theater
    Mennonite attitudes toward, 83
    The Preacher and the Shrink (Good), 129
    See also drama

theological aspect of identity, xxxi–xxxii, 71–73
Third Way Café (TWC), 35, 66–67, 145, 147–149
Third Way Media
    Internet presence, 35, 66–67, 84, 145, 147–149, 148t
    mission of, 84, 85, 98, 103, 120
Thirty-Nine Articles of Religion (Anglican Church), 5
Thomas, Rachel, 123
"Three Strikes" criminal sentencing law, 144
through hiker, 140n50
Tiessen, Hildi Froese, 79, 130
Tillie, A Mennonite Maid (Martin), 12–14, 73t, 126
Time, 141
The Tipping Point (Gladwell), xvi–xvii, 141
TM (*The Mennonite*), 145–146, 148
Today's Stress Tip, 148t
Toews, Miriam
    A Complicated Kindness, 122, 137–138
    role in *Silent Light*, 55–56
Tooley, Mark, 26–27
Towes, Miriam, xvi
Townsend, Bob, 105
tracts, 77–78, 89–90
Trappe, George, xxv
Trocme, Andre, 143
Truthiness (Spaulding's blog), 8
Turner, Ted, 95
20 Most Asked Questions About the Amish (Good and Good), 129
Two For Texas (Burke), 20
Tyrell, R. Emmett, Jr., 26

U

Umble, Diane Zimmerman, xvii, xix, 66
The Upside-Down Kingdom (Kraybill), 114, 136
U.S. political leaders, 5–6

Index

V

Vermahnung (Marpeck), 77
"The Village" (Burke), 22-23
Virginia Mennonite Conference, 83, 103
visual media
    art, 45-47, 75, 107-111
    drama, 40-45, 112-113
    effect on church and culture, 86-88
    films, 47-58, 116-125
    television, 58-68, 113-115
Voight, Jon, 17
Voltaire
    background of, 40, 41, 74
    Candide, xvi, 40, 41-42, 72, 159
    Edipus, 40
voting, xxvi, 9, 64

W

Waging Peace: Muslim and Christian Alternatives (2011 film), 119-120, 122
Wagler, Trent, 105-106
A Walk in the Woods: Rediscovering America on the Appalachian Trail (Bryson), 141
Walker, Lucy, 65
Wall, Cornelio, 55-56
Wallis, Jim, xviii, 26, 27
Wangerin, Walter, Jr., 121
War: Four Christian Views, 161
Warren, Rick, 158
The Washington Post
    article on Landis, xxviii, 30
    article on shoofly pie, 37-38, 72
    article on The Corinthian Plan, 26
    Barney & Clyde comic strip, 32-33
    feature on Over the Rhine, 105
    review of *Catch-22*, 14
    Shoe comic, June 29, 2013, 33
Watchman Gospel Signs, 97-98
Weaver, Patty, 133-134
Weaver, Todd, 28
Weaver-Zercher, David L., xvii, xix, 66
Weber, Max, xxix
Weingarten, Dan, 32-33
Weingarten, Gene, 32-33
Weir, Peter, 47, 56
Weisser, Norbert, 117
Welch, Bud, 121
Wexler, Haskell, 50
What the Dog Saw (Gladwell), 141
What Would Lloyd Do? (Swartz's play), 112
What's New, 148t
"Why I Don't Sing the National Anthem" (Schloneger), 10, 64
Wider View, 148t
Wiebe, Rudy
    Big Bear (1998 miniseries), 130
    The Blue Mountains of China, 129-130
    A Discovery of Strangers, 129
    First and Vital Candle, 129, 130
    My Lovely Enemy, 130
    Peace Shall Destroy Many, 129
    popularity of works of, xvi
    Rudy Wiebe: Collected Stories 1955-2010, 130
    The Temptation of Big Bear, 129, 130
    Of This Earth: a Mennonite Boyhood in the Boreal Forrest, 129
Wiggam, Margaret, 58
Wilde, Oscar
    Dorian Gray, 44
    The Importance of Being Earnest, 42-45
Wilder, Susan, 51
Wilkerson, David, 84
Willems, Dirk, 41, 91, 92p, 124, 125, 143
William B. Eerdmans Publishing House, 129, 130, 131
Williams, Brian, 61-63
Williams, David, 35
Wilson, Rainn, 60
Witherspoon, Reese, 44
Witness (1985 film), xvi-xvii, xxvi-xxvii, 47-48, 52, 56, 73t, 155
work ethic, xxiv, 28, 63
World War I, 78
worldly entertainment, 83, 103
Wright, N. T., 27, 132

Index

Y

Yankovic, Weird Al, 6–7, 74
Yasso, Bart, 28–29
year of Jubilee, 132
Yoder, Archibold, 78
Yoder, Brad, 104
Yoder, Donald C., 116
Yoder, Elizabeth, 126
Yoder, John Howard
    influence of, 27
    New York Times article on abuses by, 35–37
    The Politics of Jesus, 35, 79, 131–133, 134, 135, 137, 151, 153
    The Problem in How H. Richard Niebuhr Reasoned (John Howard Yoder), xxx–xxxi
Yoder, Joseph W., 13–14, 126–127
Yoder, Justin, 116
Yoder, Terry, 28
Yoder, Walter E., 101
Young, Robin, 10, 64

Z

Zehr, Howard, 128
Zengotita, Thomas de, 100
Zimmerman, Jolin, 66
Zwingli, Ulrich, xxii, 90

www.ingramcontent.com/pod-product-compliance
Lightning Source LLC
Chambersburg PA
CBHW070315230426
43663CB00011B/2133